T0398295

Beethoven Studies 4

Did you know that Beethoven contemplated, however fleetingly, writing more than forty symphonies and that for the *Missa solemnis* he sought stimulus from a Latin–German dictionary? And what about the underappreciated sociable side of Beethoven's music to set alongside the familiar one of the heroic? *Beethoven Studies 4* is a collection of ten chapters that approach the composer and his music from an appealing range of critical standpoints: aesthetic, analytical, biographical, historical and performance. Alongside essays that offer new information on Beethoven's compositional practice and broaden understanding of the music's contemporary and posthumous appeal, there are essays on his interaction with specific environments, Bonn and post-Napoleonic Austria, and vocal and piano performance practice. The volume will appeal to cultural historians and practitioners as well as Beethoven enthusiasts.

KEITH CHAPIN is Senior Lecturer in the School of Music at Cardiff University. He has served as co-editor of *Eighteenth-Century Music* and associate editor of *Nineteenth-Century Music*, as well as on the editorial boards of *Acta musicologica* and the *Revue de musicologie*. He co-edited *Musical Meaning and Human Values* with Lawrence Kramer and *Speaking of Music: Addressing the Sonorous* with Andrew Clark.

DAVID WYN JONES is Professor of Music at Cardiff University. He has published widely on Beethoven, including *The Life of Beethoven* and *The Symphony in Beethoven's Vienna* with Cambridge University Press. In 2013–15 he was awarded a Leverhulme Major Research Fellowship, and he is currently a member of the Advisory Committee for a major research project in the Institute of Musicology, University of Vienna.

Beethoven Studies 4

Edited by
KEITH CHAPIN
Cardiff University

DAVID WYN JONES
Cardiff University

CAMBRIDGE
UNIVERSITY PRESS

University Printing House, Cambridge CB2 8BS, United Kingdom

One Liberty Plaza, 20th Floor, New York, NY 10006, USA

477 Williamstown Road, Port Melbourne, VIC 3207, Australia

314–321, 3rd Floor, Plot 3, Splendor Forum, Jasola District Centre,
New Delhi – 110025, India

79 Anson Road, #06–04/06, Singapore 079906

Cambridge University Press is part of the University of Cambridge.

It furthers the University's mission by disseminating knowledge in the pursuit of
education, learning, and research at the highest international levels of excellence.

www.cambridge.org
Information on this title: www.cambridge.org/9781108428521
DOI: 10.1017/9781108552813

First published 2020

A catalogue record for this publication is available from the British Library.

Library of Congress Cataloging-in-Publication Data
Names: Chapin, Keith Moore, editor. | Wyn Jones, David, editor.
Title: Beethoven studies 4 / Keith Chapin, David Wyn Jones.
Description: [1.] | New York : Cambridge University Press, 2020. | Series: Cambridge composer
    studies | Includes bibliographical references and index.
Identifiers: LCCN 2019045616 (print) | LCCN 2019045617 (ebook) | ISBN 9781108428521
    (hardback) | ISBN 9781108449939 (paperback) | ISBN 9781108552813 (epub)
Subjects: LCSH: Beethoven, Ludwig van, 1770-1827–Criticism and interpretation.
Classification: LCC ML410.B42 B428 2020 (print) | LCC ML410.B42 (ebook) | DDC 780.92–dc23
LC record available at https://lccn.loc.gov/2019045616
LC ebook record available at https://lccn.loc.gov/2019045617

ISBN 978-1-108-42852-1 Hardback

Contents

Figures

Tables

Appendices

Music Examples

Contributors

TOM BEGHIN, Research Fellow, Orpheus Institute, Ghent

KEITH CHAPIN, Senior Lecturer, School of Music, Cardiff University

BARRY COOPER, Professor of Music, University of Manchester

KATHERINE HAMBRIDGE, Assistant Professor in Musicology, Durham University

DAVID WYN JONES, Professor of Music, Cardiff University

BIRGIT LODES, Professor of Historical Musicology, University of Vienna

GIORGIO SANGUINETTI, Associate Professor of Music Theory, University of Rome Tor Vergata

MICHAEL SPITZER, Professor of Music, University of Liverpool

W. DEAN SUTCLIFFE, Professor, School of Music, University of Auckland

JOHN D. WILSON, Postdoctoral Fellow, Institute for Musicology, University of Vienna

Preface

This volume shares the aim of its progenitors in presenting 'a broad selection of current work on Beethoven' with a range of 'biographical, critical, and analytical contributions'.[1] However, it would be to court understatement to say that much has happened in the world of scholarship in the four decades since the publication of *Beethoven Studies* (1973/1974), *Beethoven Studies 2* (1977) and *Beethoven Studies 3* (1982).[2] Contributors to the last volume were linked by an interest in 'sources for Beethoven's life and for his creative activity',[3] and such issues rightly remain central. At the same time, scholars have done much to recontextualize Beethoven, often shining a light on traditions that were important to Beethoven but to which Beethoven himself was relatively peripheral. Thus, while this volume focuses on Beethoven – as is right and proper for the series – it acknowledges that Beethoven's position within the field has changed dramatically in the last four decades. The existence of many other composer studies volumes testifies to this fact, not to mention the wide range of literature that looks away from composition towards other aspects of musical production and reception.

The volume represents a cross-section of scholarly work on Beethoven, a vibrant field that no single volume could cover comprehensively. It includes scholars from six different countries and a variety of scholarly traditions. The ten essays are thus diverse by design. At the same time, certain themes and correspondences emerge. It is worth reviewing both this diversity and these commonalities as a way to take stock of Beethoven scholarship generally. As it does so, this preface gives a brief introduction (with the author's name in full) to each chapter in the collection as well as noting connections (with the author's surname alone) to the threads that weave across the volume.

---

[1] Alan Tyson, 'Preface', *Beethoven Studies 3*, ed. Alan Tyson (Cambridge, 1982), p. vii.
[2] Alan Tyson (ed.), *Beethoven Studies* (New York, 1973; London, 1974); Alan Tyson (ed.), *Beethoven Studies 2* (Oxford, 1977); Alan Tyson (ed.), *Beethoven Studies 3* (Cambridge, 1982).
[3] Tyson, 'Preface', *Beethoven Studies 3*, p. vii.

The types of sources featured here indicate one way that the discipline has developed. Sketches and scores remain important. Barry Cooper, for example, offers a comprehensive survey and thematic catalogue of Beethoven's sketches for symphonies, some unfinished, others barely begun. Despite the relative lack of support for the symphony during the composer's lifetime, Beethoven made over thirty starts in the genre between ca. 1788 and 1826. Cooper's survey alerts us to nodal points in Beethoven's production of symphonies.

The prominence of scores amongst types of sources is not surprising, as it is Beethoven's music that continues to attract attention. Almost all the essays in this collection link their considerations to specific pieces, often offering new ways to hear and interpret them. It is worth noting, however, that while written or notated primary sources remain central, their spectrum is broader than ever, from partimenti (Sanguinetti) to library catalogues (Wilson), and from journals (Jones) to dictionaries and handwritten notes (Lodes), to name only some of the source types on show. Yet scholars also look beyond the written record to the material culture from the past – Beethoven's pianos and hearing aids (Beghin), for instance.

These sources are used to illuminate diverse types of contexts for Beethoven's musical production – geographical, compositional, critical, to name a few. John Wilson considers the musical library within whose compass the young Beethoven worked at the archducal court of Elector Maximilian Franz in Bonn, thereby situating his work in a particular locale with its distinctive connections to broader traditions. The library was one of the largest in Europe, and also one that saw considerable growth during the 1770s and 1780s. Some seeds of Beethoven's approaches to church, chamber and theatre music can be gleaned from a glimpse at the transformations that the library underwent, but also a vision of the high standards of the models around him.

Both Giorgio Sanguinetti and W. Dean Sutcliffe examine Beethoven's ties to eighteenth-century compositional contexts. Sanguinetti shows how Beethoven drew upon his education in partimenti at different points in his career. While Beethoven's education in these melodic-cum-harmonic (and generally contrapuntal) 'tonal prototypes' was typical of his time, he bent them variously over his career. He shaped them to the topics and the genres with which he worked, now using them with respect for tradition, now transforming them almost beyond recognition, now treating them as archaic reminders of past traditions. Sutcliffe, for his part, shows Beethoven's ties to a musical aesthetic of graciousness. Importantly, this aesthetic is a matter of musical discourse, and his analyses enumerate ripostes, understatements, negotiations of assertive and gracious gestures, and other dialogues in which the process of discussion is often more important than firm agreement. Other scholars examine sources for the critical discourse of the time, as communicated for example by the Austrian *Allgemeine musikalische Zeitung* (Jones).

The cumulative result of these diverse materials and matters is that this volume offers varying takes on common themes. With regard to the expressive aspect of Beethoven's music, Sutcliffe's chapter on graciousness finds an interlocutor in Michael Spitzer's on the heroic qualities of Beethoven's music. In a reading of the *Eroica* Symphony that tacks from the history of emotion to the histories of state ritual and military strategy, Spitzer notes that the histrionic heroic gestures composed into the symphony correspond to historically specific forms of the emotion of glory, as displayed in rites of mourning and fighting. Glory differs from vainglory according to the process by which it arises and is expressed, a statement as true for battles as it is for symphonies. Other expressive arenas include the pastoral (Chapin) and the jolts and jogs of the late style (Sanguinetti, Lodes, and Beghin).

Expressive gestures of music link bespeak cultural values, and many of the chapters here look carefully at the values that informed both Beethoven's creative activity and the reception of his music, from graciousness (Sutcliffe) to patriotism (Hambridge, Jones and Spitzer) to sovereignty (Chapin) to gender identity (Hambridge). The path from expressive qualities to cultural values is at times relatively direct, but at others proves exceedingly complex. As Katherine Hambridge shows, Pauline Anna Milder (1785–1838), the soprano who sang Leonore in the first three productions of Beethoven's opera, troubled eighteenth-century dualisms of style and gender. Her voice eschewed the binaries of French and Italian vocal styles and echoed her cross-dressing on the stage. At the very time that Beethoven was at work on what would become an epitome of German opera, Milder's career tracked and facilitated the emergence of a new German style of singing.

Expressive gestures may bespeak cultural values, but they are rooted in physicality. If Hambridge focuses attention on the physical characteristics of a singer, Tom Beghin turns to the physicality of Beethoven himself as a performer. Beghin examines the last three piano sonatas with consideration for the physical experience of Beethoven himself, playing particular pianos and developing a hearing machine to sense their tones. Beghin's research is communicated physically too, through videos of performances using reconstructions of Beethoven's pianos and hearing aids. Far from being ineffable, the sonatas are alive with vibrations, physical surfaces and tactility. Keith Chapin considers Beethoven as a performer of a different type. Beethoven often thematized the nature around him so as to project the attenuation of human control over the world. This is in line with his own creative activity, which expresses not so much a controlling self (as E. T. A. Hoffmann would have it) as lack of control of his own bodily nature. In this, he resembled Schiller and other idealists. Their confident declarations of artistic prowess were in fact performative responses to their hypochondria, a condition recognized as interweaving physiology and psychology.

The late style has always seemed odd, even out of step with its time, yet its oddities are very much reflections of Beethoven's engagement with things of his time. These can range from issues of instrument construction (Beghin) to the high aims that Beethoven was never shy in proclaiming. As David Wyn Jones shows in an examination of the *Allgemeine musikalische Zeitung mit besonderer Rücksicht auf den österreichischen Kaiserstaat*, artists of the time followed a variety of high purposes, including a patriotic museum culture, a collective public ethos and religious sensitivity. Beethoven engaged with the musical styles and genres associated with these goals: respectively, a sophisticated (and often contrapuntal) manufacture, oratorio and church music. Beethoven shared the high aims of his time, even if he developed them in his own particular way. As Birgit Lodes shows, Beethoven pursued these aims in dialogue with his time in another way too. A transcript of the text of the mass Ordinary in Beethoven's hand shows that he attended carefully to Ignatius Aurelius Feßler's translation of the mass Credo (in a book that had been proscribed in Vienna). To elucidate its meaning, Beethoven looked up its every word in a Latin-German dictionary. Beethoven's odd takes on a genre with strong traditions and conventions flow from his careful but often idiosyncratic attention to the meanings and prosody of individual words.

While surveying a variety of themes, *Beethoven Studies 4* tracks Beethoven's career along rough chronological lines. It begins with Beethoven perusing scores in the archducal library in Bonn and ends with him wrestling at the piano in the intimacy of his chambers. It stops at many places along the way. It marks a quarter-millennium since Beethoven's birth, but it reflects the interest of the present in its consideration of political, social and ecological issues, of questions of gender and national identity and of performance alongside composition. And, of course, it marks the music which continues to make its mark.

Abbreviations

1 | From the Chapel to the Theatre to the *Akademiensaal*: Beethoven's Musical Apprenticeship at the Bonn Electoral Court, 1784–1792[*]

JOHN D. WILSON

It is worth remembering, if seldom remembered, that when Beethoven moved to Vienna in November 1792 to study composition with Haydn, he was already a grown man who had amassed nearly a decade of professional experience as a paid court musician. Just as rarely borne in mind is his portfolio of at least forty completed works that show a growing ambition to establish himself not only as a piano virtuoso, but as a serious composer who could competently write for the largest forces that were available to him in Bonn. Symptomatic in both respects is Douglas Johnson's seminal contribution to *Beethoven Studies 3*, which skilfully analyses how Beethoven's publications from 1794–95, especially Opp. 1, 2 and 4, grew out of revisions to earlier compositions. While acknowledging the Bonn origins of these works Johnson chose a title that simultaneously erases them by referring to 1794–95 as 'Decisive Years in Beethoven's *Early* Development' (my emphasis).[1]

If it is hardly customary to characterize the published opuses of any twenty-four-year-old composer as 'early', to do so with one who had been publishing music for twelve years is a curious lapse from the scholar who, after Thayer, has contributed the most to our knowledge of the Bonn works;[2] it is also a symptomatic one. The tendency to undervalue Beethoven's Bonn years has, until very recently, been entrenched in both popular and scholarly narratives of the composer's creative development, one that seldom acknowledges any composition earlier than his Op. 1, except those like the Cantata on the Death of Emperor Joseph II (WoO 87) and the

[*] This article has benefited from two grants from the Austrian Science Fund (Fonds zur Förderung der wissenschaftlichen Forschung) for a research programme at the Institute for Musicology, University of Vienna: 'The Operatic Library of Elector Maximilian Franz' (2013–15) and 'The Sacred Music Library of Elector Maximilian Franz' (2016–18).
[1] Douglas Johnson, '1794–1795: Decisive Years in Beethoven's Early Development', *Beethoven Studies 3*, ed. Alan Tyson (Cambridge, 1982), pp. 1–28.
[2] See especially Douglas Johnson, 'Beethoven's Early Sketches in the Fischhof Miscellany' (PhD thesis, University of California, Berkeley, 1977).

three piano quartets (WoO 36) from which he would later reuse material. True enough, this systematic exclusion of the first third of Beethoven's life has begun to wane, with some recent biographies giving more weight to Beethoven's early works and their context in Bonn's blend of courtly life and powerful aristocratic networks.[3] But still, as Ulrich Konrad has reminded us, there is an instinctive tendency to draw the portrait of Beethoven the courtier in sharp relief against a more broad-stroke background of Bonn as a hotbed of the German Enlightenment, a tendency which, while not counterfactual, inspires a kind of tunnel vision as it pertains to the young musician's intellectual horizons, his perceived career options, and the creative products that were responses to a complex environment that needs to be understood on its own terms.[4] Put another way, Bonn Beethoven is too often viewed retroactively as a harbinger of Vienna Beethoven, particularly Heroic Beethoven, with the composer denied serious consideration as a rational individual operating in a particular set of circumstances.

It is not the intention here to do full justice to Beethoven's early creativity and Bonn's role in the formation of his personality. But, to the detriment of our full understanding of Beethoven's long apprenticeship, the habitual skimming over the Bonn years also devalues the Bonn Electoral Court as a musical centre in its own right. Its cultural life in the 1770s and 1780s is often vastly underestimated in the Beethoven literature. While not always portrayed as a backwater, it is often treated condescendingly, as a respectable if sleepy province, a distant pre-echo of Vienna. Recent research into the primary sources – in particular the remaining portion of the court music library in the Biblioteca Estense Universitaria in Modena and other documents pertaining to the theatre and chapel – has turned this view on its head.[5] In its final decade, between Elector

---

[3] Insightful general treatments of the Bonn period can be found in Konrad Küster, *Beethoven* (Stuttgart, 1994), pp. 13–36; David Wyn Jones, *The Life of Beethoven* (Cambridge, 1998), pp. 1–27; and Barry Cooper, *Beethoven* (Oxford, 2000), pp. 1–43.

[4] Ulrich Konrad, 'Der "Bonner" Beethoven', *Bonner Beethoven-Studien*, 12 (2016), pp. 65–80.

[5] The results of the two research projects based at the University of Vienna, directed by Birgit Lodes and carried out by Elisabeth Reisinger and myself, are to appear in five volumes published by the Beethoven-Haus in the series 'Musik am Bonner kurfürstlichen Hof', under the imprint of Schriften zur Beethoven-Forschung. The following volumes have appeared to date: Birgit Lodes, Elisabeth Reisinger and John D. Wilson (eds.), *Beethoven und andere Hofmusiker seiner Generation. Bericht über den internationalen musikwissenschaftlichen Kongress Bonn, 3. bis 6. Dezember 2015* (Bonn, 2018); Elisabeth Reisinger, Juliane Riepe and John D. Wilson (eds.), *The Operatic Library of Elector Maximilian Franz: Reconstruction, Catalogue, Contexts* (Bonn, 2018); and Elisabeth Reisinger, *Musik machen – förden – sammeln. Erzherzog Maximilian Franz im Wiener und Bonner Musikleben* (Bonn, 2020).

Maximilian Franz's reorganization in 1784 and the French occupation in 1794, the Bonn Hofkapelle, already acclaimed during the reign of his predecessor Maximilian Friedrich, grew in number and quality to rank among the finest in Europe. Like Beethoven, several of the next generation's leading virtuosos, composers and pedagogues – such as Anton Reicha, Ferdinand Ries, and the cousins Bernhard and Andreas Romberg – spent their formative years in this highly charged atmosphere. And this concentration of talent, especially young and emerging talent, was far from fortuitous, rather a result of Maximilian Franz's reputation as a knowledgeable patron and his many years of informed personnel choices. Most of all, the extensive music library that the elector maintained and continually expanded – which formed the core of the repertoire for the chapel, theatre, and *Akademiensaal* concerts – played no small role in their education. This repertoire showed a sharp receptivity to the newest and most challenging works from across Europe, and in this way made the Bonn court a rival to the most rarefied circles of *Kenner* in Vienna or Berlin, while avoiding the insular character that these often assumed. Just as Beethoven's first twenty-two years cannot adequately be summarized as 'Not Yet Beethoven', Electoral Bonn's musical life in its last decade is inaccurately characterized as a 'little Vienna'.

The Unparalleled Music Library of a 'Profound Connoisseur'

An anonymous Bonn musician, most likely Christian Gottlob Neefe, was not merely flattering his new boss when, in August 1784, he praised Maximilian Franz in print as a 'profound connoisseur' and credited his patronage for the town's affinity for music 'continually expanding more and more, its taste becoming more refined every day'.[6] Neefe, or any other resident of Bonn with musical inclinations, would have immediately recognized a serious collector in their midst. In April, the newly arrived elector had brought with him from Vienna a music library that included around 2,350 works in every significant genre: symphonies (c. 380), trios (c. 460), quartets (c. 900), concertos and cassations (close to 100), other chamber music (c. 330), ballets (26) and vocal works large and small (c. 150).[7] While in Bonn, he would continue to collect new works with

---

[6] *Beiträge zur Ausbreitung nützlicher Kenntnisse*, No. 20 (20 August 1784), pp. 161–7, at p. 161.
[7] The quantitative analysis in this paragraph is indebted to Elisabeth Reisinger, for which see *Musik machen*, Appendix E.

an enthusiasm that bordered on mania, until his library reached a height of around 3,500 items, not counting sacred music, which was maintained separately in the chapel. By way of comparison, the Duchess Anna Amalia's music collection in Weimar, one of the most legendary of its day, included close to 3,000 works at the time of her death in 1807.[8] Another equally legendary contemporary collection by a different Anna Amalia, the Princess of Prussia, was even larger: at her death in 1787, it encompassed over 3,800 works in over 600 volumes.[9] The musical holdings of the Imperial Court Library in Vienna, the so-called 'Kaisersammlung', are harder to estimate, but they probably did not approach their present quantity of 3,200 shelf marks until well into the nineteenth century, representing 150 years of accumulation by many generations of Habsburg rulers.[10] Therefore, Maximilian Franz's music library not only ranks among the largest of its kind in the late eighteenth century (that is, before the more voluminous one by his nephew, Archduke Rudolph), but also the most rapidly assembled. His zeal for keeping track of his music collection was such that, before leaving Vienna, he commissioned an extraordinarily detailed 642-page inventory that includes incipits for every instrumental work.[11] New acquisitions after 1784 were similarly entered in the blank spaces, largely in the hand of Franz Anton Ries, who appears to have acted as music librarian in Bonn. This inventory, preserved today in the Biblioteca Estense Universitaria under the shelf mark 'Catalogo Generale 53 I-II' (new shelf mark ε40.4.10, referred to hereafter as 'Cat. Gen. 53') is a rich source for reconstructing the library; when the different layers of handwriting are teased out and cross-referenced with the surviving manuscripts and other sources, it is possible also to document its growth between 1784 and 1794.[12]

But Maximilian's library distinguished itself from its more famous rivals in another respect, as Elisabeth Reisinger has observed. Typically, such music collections served an important representational function, their gilt leather volumes an expression of their collectors' erudition. The elector, on

---

[8] Richard Münnich, 'Aus der Musikaliensammlung der Weimarer Landesbibliothek', *Aus der Geschichte der Landesbibliothek zu Weimar und ihrer Sammlungen*, ed. Hermann Blumenthal (Jena, 1941), pp. 168–84. But, as Münnich notes, many of the rarities often associated with this collection were acquired in the nineteenth century.

[9] Eva Renate Blechschmidt, *Die Amalien-Bibliothek. Musikbibliothek der Prinzessin Anna Amalia von Preußen (1723–1787)* (Berlin, 1965).

[10] Reisinger et al., *The Operatic Library*, pp. 224–5.

[11] For an overview, see Juliane Riepe, 'Eine neue Quelle zum Repertoire der Bonner Hofkapelle', *Archiv für Musikwissenschaft*, 60/2 (2003), pp. 97–114.

[12] Reisinger et al., *The Operatic Library*, pp. 231–50.

the other hand, was far more interested in pieces that he could play himself – he was a skilful viola player as well as an able pianist and singer – or ones that he could have played by the musicians available to him.[13] As the extant sources reveal, he seldom went to the trouble of having his scores and parts bound at all, with the exception of sacred music (see below). This practical bent was paired with the sensibilities of a methodical completist: while still in Vienna, where he had two excellent violinists in his retinue,[14] Maximilian managed to compile an almost encyclopedic compendium of string duos, trios and quartets from Vienna, South Germany, London and Paris. In one especially striking example of this, by 1784 he owned every single commercially available *quatuor concertant* by the prolific Giuseppe Maria Cambini, amounting to 139 works.[15] Virtually every significant composer in the early history of the string quartet is represented in impressive quantities: Johann Baptist Vanhal (forty-two), Anton and Carl Stamitz (thirty-six and twenty-seven), Carlo d'Ordonez (eighteen) and, of course, Joseph Haydn (thirty-three). No less impressive was his collection of Luigi Boccherini's chamber music: forty-two quartets (everything up to Op. 32), thirty quintets, twelve sextets and thirty-five trios in Maximilian's library represent practically the composer's entire catalogue of chamber music published before 1784.[16] In the pre-1784 acquisitions, similar trends are evident in symphonies for strings alone. This is not to say that Maximilian did not sometimes acquire works that he had no means to perform. His ballet scores all date from his time in Vienna, and for some reason his Italian operas include the working score and complete instrumental parts to Pasquale Anfossi's *L'avaro* performed at the Kärntnertortheater in 1776–77 (a rare survival of performance material for Viennese opera from that era).[17] But these were exceptional cases springing from a parallel collecting impulse, the score usually memorializing a momentous family event – the weddings, births and coronations that constituted the milestones of the Habsburg dynasty.[18]

---

[13] Ibid., p. 225.

[14] Dorothea Link, 'Mozart's Appointment to the Viennese Court', *Words about Mozart: Essays in Honour of Stanley Sadie*, ed. Dorothea Link with Judith Nagley (Woodbridge, 2005), pp. 153–78, at p. 161.

[15] As listed in Dieter Lutz Trimpert, *Die Quatuor Concertants von Giuseppe Cambini* (Tutzing, 1967), pp. 243–306.

[16] As listed in Yves Gérard, *Thematic, Bibliographical and Critical Catalogue of the Works of Luigi Boccherini* (London, 1969).

[17] See Reisinger et al., *The Operatic Library*, pp. 359–61.   [18] Ibid., p. 227.

In Bonn, Maximilian also retained a small chamber ensemble (to which Beethoven belonged as a viola player and pianist),[19] and continued to collect new trios, quartets and quintets. But now with an entire Hofkapelle at his disposal, his acquisitions took a different direction. The bulk of his energies was now channelled into works that showcased his new ensemble's strengths, especially German operas, symphonies and piano music. Notably, the last of these, which includes both concertos and sonatas, was the single largest area of growth after 1784.[20] In this endeavour, Maximilian Franz discovered among his court musicians a kindred spirit with whom he promptly entered a symbiotic partnership. Beginning in July 1784, the court horn player and aspiring music dealer Nikolaus Simrock was granted a yearly stipend of forty Reichsthaler to source new music, along with the privilege to use the works he acquired for the court as the basis for copies that he sold to the public. As Simrock acquired new works, he would typically advertise them in the local newspaper, the *Bönnisches Intelligenzblatt*; the same works would inevitably also be entered in the elector's inventory.[21] Often, opera scores would be rearranged locally, set idiomatically for keyboard and their texts translated, the latter two services provided by Neefe. By 1790, due in equal part to Simrock's resourcefulness, the elector's insatiable taste for new works, and the industry of Neefe and others in adapting these works, Bonn constituted a hub for the dissemination of music to other theatres. Among Simrock's clients were German troupes in Mainz, Mannheim, Hamburg and even Berlin.[22]

Many clues throughout 'Cat. Gen. 53', as well as in the surviving manuscripts, suggest that the elector did not reserve the items in his library for his own private amusement, but made them freely available for performances elsewhere at court and even lent them out to individuals. A comment in ink under the listings for sacred music, 'Die KirchenMusik ist dem Capellmeister übergeben', reflects the fact that at some point after his arrival in Bonn, Maximilian transferred the entirety of his somewhat modest collection of such music to Andrea Luchesi for use in the chapel. In the listings of opera, marginal remarks in pencil of 'Reicha' or 'R' next to certain titles indicate that Joseph Reicha, who acted as music director of the theatre from 1789, borrowed several scores; not every work he examined

---

[19] A-Whh, Habs.-Est. FA, 172, Mappe 5.   [20] Reisinger, *Musik machen*, Appendix E.
[21] Reisinger et al., *The Operatic Library*, pp. 162–72.
[22] A survey of all known Simrock opera scores can be found in ibid., pp. 373–80.

was taken up for performance at court.[23] Finally, both Luchesi and the young Beethoven apparently borrowed items of instrumental music, as attested by two small leaves that still remain inserted in the inventory.[24]

The breadth and scope of Maximilian's music library, its focus on the most current repertoire and the openness with which the elector handled it, provided one of the clearest early signs of the direction in which he would take the Hofkapelle. There is every reason to believe that from 1784 musical tastes were, indeed, becoming 'more refined by the day'. This was balanced, however, by the elector's stern sense of economy and an instinctive distaste for the extravagant self-glorification that often characterized musical representation in eighteenth-century courts. Economic prudence ensured that the theatre would remain closed for over four years and many court musicians would either lose their jobs or have their salaries reduced,[25] while the avoidance of musical self-representation seems to have contributed to a creative chill at court during which previously industrious composers, including the young Beethoven, ceased to write anything new at all for several years.[26] But it would be a mistake to view even Maximilian Franz's early reign as times of mere austerity and reduction of means. Rather, closer attention reveals significant developments from the beginning of his rule in all three sectors of the electoral palace where musicians performed, chapel, theatre and concert hall; all three underwent significant reforms that, sooner than has been previously thought, resulted in a rejuvenated musical life, just as Beethoven was coming of age.

Sacred Music at an Ecclesiastical Court

Beethoven's earliest experience as a court musician would have been in the small palace chapel,[27] newly rebuilt after the disastrous fire of 1777. In 1781, he was engaged as an *Accessist*, an unpaid assistant organist to Neefe. As a Protestant from Lower Saxony, Neefe appears not to have filled the role of first organist to anyone's satisfaction, leading to a disastrous personnel

---

[23] Ibid., p. 245.   [24] 'Cat. Gen. 53', fols. 103bis and 103ter.

[25] Ian Woodfield, 'Christian Gottlob Neefe and the Bonn National Theatre, with New Light on the Beethoven Family', *Music & Letters*, 93/3 (August 2012), pp. 289–315.

[26] A new chronology of Beethoven's compositions based on paper studies has revealed that he apparently stopped composing abruptly in 1784 and did not resume until 1787. See John D. Wilson, 'Music Papers in Electoral Bonn', *Bonner Beethoven-Studien*, 13 (in preparation).

[27] To avoid confusion, I use here the English 'chapel' or 'palace chapel' instead of 'Hofkapelle', which in German can take on the meaning of the entire court music establishment.

report in 1784 (see below). This also seems to have meant that Beethoven, who by then had already learned the fundamentals of Catholic service playing under Gilles van dan Eeden, Zensen and Willibald Koch, acted frequently in this capacity when Neefe's workload increased.[28] The longest such spell occurred in 1783 and 1784, when Luchesi travelled to Italy, leaving Neefe in charge.[29] But it can also be assumed that after the theatre was reopened in 1789, Neefe, whose real talents and inclinations had always lain in opera, would have delegated more and more to his assistant.

For all this, Beethoven's often weekly stints in the palace chapel take on a surprisingly marginal role in biographical accounts.[30] This is all the more regrettable because Beethoven and his colleagues encountered a rich and varied repertoire there. This is already clear in the inventory of the palace chapel drawn up during the change in leadership in May 1784 (hereafter 'Inventarium 340'), discovered by Adolf Sandberger in the early 1910s.[31] Although its listings of liturgical music include only genres and names of composers, these alone testify to a wide palette of styles, not only from Vienna, the Rhineland and Munich, but from Bohemia, Bologna, Venice and Rome as well. Admittedly, the continued importance of sacred music in the life of Electoral Bonn could not be thoroughly appreciated until the surviving sources had been studied in depth.[32] There may have been legitimate reasons to believe that, under Maximilian Franz, sacred music withered on the vine under similar attitudes that motivated the anticlerical reforms of his brother, Joseph II. In fact, little is known about how these reforms actually affected sacred music at the imperial court in Vienna, as the sources for this period still await study. For Bonn, however, the musical sources are very well preserved, in both quantity and quality. Of the 410 works in various genres that were inventoried before the court

[28] Alexander Wheelock Thayer, *Ludwig van Beethovens Leben*, rev. ed., vol. 1, ed. Hermann Deiters (Leipzig, 1917), pp. 137, 140. See most recently Julia Ronge, 'Beethovens kirchenmusikalische Ambitionen. Pläne, Ideen und Fragmente', *Kirchenmusikalisches Jahrbuch*, 99 (2015), pp. 59–79.

[29] Theodor Anton Henseler, 'Andrea Luchesi, der letzte Bonner Hofkapellmeister zur Zeit des jungen Beethoven. Ein Beitrag zur Musik- und Theatergeschichte des 18. Jahrhunderts', *Bonner Geschichtsblätter*, 1 (1937), pp. 225–364, at pp. 320–3.

[30] But see the attempt by Jeremiah Walker McGrann to reconstruct the mass repertoire and its influence on Beethoven: 'Beethoven's Mass in C, Opus 86: Genesis and Compositional Background' (PhD thesis, Harvard University, 1991), pp. 559–63.

[31] Adolf Sandberger, 'Die Inventare der Bonner Hofmusik', *Ausgewählte Aufsätze der Musikgeschichte* (Munich, 1924), vol. 2, pp. 109–34, at pp. 114–28.

[32] This and the following paragraphs represent ongoing research by Elisabeth Reisinger, myself, and a consortium of scholars, which will appear as volumes 4 and 5 of 'Musik am Bonner kurfürstlichen Hof'. A database of the musical sources can be accessed at www.univie.ac.at/muwidb/sacredmusiclibrary/.

was evacuated in 1794, at least 352, or 86 per cent of them, made their way to Modena, offering a rare glimpse into a lively practice of sacred music at a sacred court that remained vital up until the end. The bright, beautiful bindings of the performance parts, for which the aged Johann Meuris was paid a small yearly stipend to maintain, reflect the representational importance that sacred music held in Bonn.

Fascinatingly, several of the manuscripts show layers of constant revision, often quite comprehensive. Here, the industrious hand of Kapellmeister Luchesi is vividly in evidence. In full scores of masses and other large concerted works that were frequently compiled from the original sets of parts by Bonn copyists, Luchesi alters details large and small: textures thickened to better support the vocalists, wind parts added, solo and choral voices differentiated, entirely new obbligato violin parts composed and *contrafacta* devised to keep pace with changing liturgical necessities. Since it has been possible to date the paper on which the different layers of local parts were written, correlation of musical sources with administrative ones has allowed for a nuanced chronology of the changes to music in the chapel under Maximilian Franz.

To understand these, it is necessary briefly to sketch the development of the ensemble and the accumulation of its repertoire from the 1750s onwards. Under Elector Clemens August (r. 1723–1761), the repertoire showed a strong influence of the Wittelsbach court in Munich, from which works by Ercole Bernabei and Andrea Bernasconi were acquired, as well as smaller anonymous works for Advent, Christmas, Lent and Easter. Around the same time, copies of several sacred works were purchased from St Vitus Cathedral in Prague as well; these included, notably, Christmas masses and offertories in typical Bohemian pastoral style by composers such as František Brixi and Josef Antonín Sehling.[33] This repertoire was filled out by the Bonn court trumpeter and violinist Johann Ries, who flattered his employer's love for the hunt with a small number of exuberant sacred compositions dedicated to St Hubert (patron saint of hunters) and St Florian (patron saint of Upper Austria), replete with horn calls and trumpet fanfares. After Luchesi was named Kapellmeister in 1774 he reshaped the repertoire after his own Venetian tastes, composing several dozen works in all genres and for all occasions.[34] His concertmaster, Gaetano Mattioli, developed the orchestra to a much higher level and used his contacts with

---

[33] Milada Jonašová, personal communication. For the wide dissemination of Bohemian Advent music, see Mark Germer, 'The Austro-Bohemian Pastorella and the Pastoral Mass to c. 1780' (PhD thesis, University of New York, 1989).

[34] For the most recent overview of Luchesi's sacred works, see Claudia Valder-Knechtges, *Die Kirchenmusik Andrea Luchesis* (Berlin, 1983), esp. pp. 182–263.

the Accademia Filarmonica of Bologna to obtain large-scale concerted masses by the likes of Davide Perez, Antonio Mazzoni, Gabriele Vignali, Pietro Sales and Giovanni Pergolesi. Masses from Vienna and Salzburg, as well as from Mannheim and Oettingen-Wallerstein, also entered the repertoire during the 1770s.

Mattioli may have been behind the acquisition of instrumental music, notably symphonies from Mannheim and Paris, plus a considerable number by Joseph Haydn. Some may also have been copied from the library of Court Councillor Johann Gottfried Mastiaux, who by 1783 had his own large collection of Haydn symphonies.[35] It is likely that the 155 symphonies and overtures listed in Inventarium 340 were intended primarily for use in chapel services, since there was no discernible tradition of court concerts at the time (see below). A fact overlooked by Sandberger and others since him, this list of symphonies and overtures appears as a subsection of 'Music Belonging to the Chapel', between similar lists for liturgical music and oratorios. This brings Bonn in line with other cloisters and churches in German Catholic territories, where movements of symphonies were regularly performed during mass.[36]

Maximilian Franz appears not to have made radical changes right away, apart from handing over his collection of sacred music to Luchesi. A new inventory was begun in 1785, which is now lost, but new acquisitions were numbered consecutively following on from Inventarium 340; the high survival rate of sacred music manuscripts thus allows for a fairly unproblematic reconstruction. The first wave of reforms took hold in 1787.[37] At around this time, it seems the performance of symphonies in services was discontinued. In their place, offertories and motets with full orchestral accompaniment were sung instead. To fill this need, hundreds of works by Georg Reutter the younger were acquired, apparently bought secondhand from cloisters in and around Vienna whose music establishments had been disbanded under Joseph's reforms. These, too, were freely adapted by the Kapellmeister to meet local needs and to show off the ensemble's strengths.

As Joseph had done in Vienna, German congregational singing was introduced in Bonn, while the number of solemn services in Latin requiring full orchestra and choir was somewhat reduced, if far less drastically

---

[35] Christian Gottlob Neefe, 'Nachricht von der churfürstlich-cöllnischen Hofcapelle zu Bonn und andern Tonkünstlern daselbst', *Magazin der Musik*, 1 (1783), pp. 377–96, at p. 392.

[36] Mary Sue Morrow, 'Patrons and Practices', *The Symphonic Repertoire, Vol. 1: The Eighteenth-Century Symphony*, eds. Mary Sue Morrow and Bathia Churgin (Bloomington and Indianapolis, 2012), pp. 75–99, at p. 77.

[37] Anna Sanda, personal communication.

than has often been assumed. Balancing this, the orchestra and choir were enlarged for those occasions when they were needed. Newly copied parts, and new revisions by the Kapellmeister, show that utilizing the full ensemble for every work was a priority. Most important, the new parts show that the full range of the repertoire as it had accumulated over the last three decades remained in use. This must have meant that a great variety of music – old and new, from far and near, and with no particular focus on any one composer or style – was heard in the chapel.

However, under Maximilian Franz new sacred works by local composers were rare. After 1784 Luchesi wrote only a handful of smaller hymns and settings of the Christmas antiphon Alma Redemptoris, and none after 1790. These made use of the full instrumental and vocal resources available, but as a creative figure Luchesi seems to have withdrawn to the sidelines. His withdrawal could have been a personal decision, or due to the feeling that his music was considered old-fashioned within certain intellectual circles.[38] While neither of these can be ruled out, it is perhaps also indicative of a broader trend. Andreas Romberg, who had composed a mass in 1787 while still in Münster, wrote no further liturgical music in Bonn; and although Beethoven went as far as sketching a fugal Tantum ergo in late 1790,[39] by which time he had written two cantatas, no sacred works by him can be associated with the Bonn palace chapel either. The only court musician who composed meaningful quantities of sacred music was the tenor Ferdinand Heller, who was evidently being groomed as Luchesi's successor. His two masses, a requiem and a Te Deum, all of them written between 1787 and 1792, reflect a more personalized approach to the texts, in many ways consistent with the aesthetic of church music promulgated by Ferdinand d'Antoine, and which provide a useful touchstone to Beethoven's much later Mass in C and *Missa solemnis*.[40]

Opera in Bonn: From a 'School of Morals for the People' to a Commercial Venture

For concentrated periods during Beethoven's childhood, teens and early adulthood, the theatre in the east wing of the electoral palace sprang to life. As well as being the location where Beethoven's grandfather and father

[38] Henseler, 'Andrea Luchesi', p. 328.
[39] Ronge, 'Beethovens kirchenmusikalische Ambitionen', pp. 60–1.
[40] See Gustav Fellerer, 'Ferdinand D'Anthoins Ästhetik der Kirchenmusik 1784', *Colloquium Amicorum. Joseph Schmidt-Görg zum 70. Geburtstag*, eds. Siegfried Kross and Hans Schmidt (Bonn, 1967), pp. 82–92.

demonstrated their vocal ability, and later the young Beethoven his assured orchestral viola playing, opera in Bonn provided the court ensemble with its most public-facing venture. Its existence was, at times, precarious, marked by fits and starts, with the stage remaining dark for long periods; also the character of its repertoire changed markedly over time, as did the makeup of its audience. Bonn was not alone in this regard. Indeed, Beethoven's first twenty-two years witnessed fundamental changes in courtly culture and society throughout German-speaking Europe, and court theatres reflected these changes vividly: how they were run, what ideological functions they promoted, who sat in the auditoriums and what they saw and heard.[41]

Under Clemens August, opera in Bonn was an exclusive affair open only to invited guests of the nobility, as reflected in the magnificent series of *Bönnische Ballstücke* painted by François Rousseau around 1754. But, perhaps inspired by a successful commercial venture initiated by Johann van Beethoven in the late 1760s in which operas were performed by a plucky small band for a paying audience on the Bonn Marktplatz, Maximilian Friedrich began to contemplate a different model. With the engagement of Luchesi, Mattioli and their opera troupe in December 1771, the elector issued a theatrical decree stating that all Bonn residents and 'honourable foreigners' ('Ehrbare Fremde') were free to come to the performances.[42] For three successive seasons, from 1772 to 1774, both the Italian virtuosi and German court singers (a rare constellation) performed Italian and French comic operas in their original languages. The repertoire was a mixture of popular works by, among others, André Grétry, Antonio Salieri and Tommaso Traetta, but also featured works by Luchesi.[43] This venture was, however, short-lived. An odd combination of salacious court intrigue and the death of Ludwig van Beethoven the elder led to the dismissal of the troupe in May 1774, while Luchesi and Mattioli stayed on as Kapellmeister and concertmaster respectively.[44]

When the theatre opened again five years later, it again featured a travelling troupe, but of an entirely different sort. Gustav Friedrich Wilhelm Großmann and his players, the remnant of the recently dissolved troupe of Abel Seyler, had developed a strong reputation for naturalistic

---

[41] Of particular merit are Ute Daniel, *Hoftheater. Zur Geschichte des Theaters und der Höfe im 18. und 19. Jahrhundert* (Stuttgart, 1995) and Jörg Krämer, *Deutschsprachiges Musiktheater im späten 18. Jahrhundert. Typologie, Dramaturgie und Anthropologie einer populären Gattung*, 2 vols. (Tübingen, 1998).

[42] D-DGla, Kurköln II, 486.   [43] Reisinger et al., *The Operatic Library*, pp. 20–5.

[44] Ibid., pp. 27–8.

acting of cutting-edge spoken plays, both original works in German and translations from French and English. Großmann had another talent: propaganda. Specifically, he was sensitive to the need after the Seven Years' War for courtly employers to appear more interested in the well-being and education of their subjects, while reducing the appearance of costly spectacle. In a typical Großmann turn of phrase (though published anonymously), a 1779 announcement in a regional theatrical journal declared that Maximilian Friedrich had 'in addition to other improvements in every field of knowledge, raised the art of German Theatre into a school of morals for His people'.[45] The troupe had begun to distinguish itself musically as well, thanks to Neefe's gifts in teaching actors how to sing. Their repertoire from 1779 to 1784 showed an increasing prominence of opéra comique (in German translation) and German operas and Singspiele by Neefe, Johann Hiller and Georg Benda. It was a formula that proved popular, if never quite commercially lucrative for the troupe, since the elector eventually made the performances free to attend. To make ends meet, Großmann spent more of his time on the road with half of his ensemble, leaving the other half in Bonn under the direction of his pregnant and ailing wife Karoline. Their previous standards could not hold. When, in a few short months in early 1784, the deaths of Karoline and of State Minister Kaspar Anton Belderbusch were followed by that of Maximilian Friedrich, the ensemble was in disarray. Maximilian Franz saw no reason to renew their contracts, and the troupe dispersed.[46]

Neefe remained, disheartened by his dwindling relevance at court, and would have to wait a further five years for his fortunes to recover.[47] But in very short order, the new elector started planning the theatre's return. While travelling troupes appeared each spring for short seasons, Maximilian Franz received – having obviously solicited – three detailed proposals for how a German court theatre could both remain financially viable and support the education of audience and artists alike.[48] These three documents, overlooked in Maximilian's estate until their unearthing by Elisabeth Reisinger, are undated but can be assigned through internal evidence to between 1785 and 1787.[49] They also show that, contrary to the previous scholarly view, Maximilian Franz's delay in reopening the theatre cannot

---

[45] 'Kurfürstlich-Kölnisches Hoftheater zu Bonn', in *Litteratur- und Theatre-Zeitung*, 2 (1779), No. 52 (25 December 1779), pp. 817–21, at p. 817.

[46] Reisinger et al., *The Operatic Library*, pp. 47–104.

[47] Woodfield, 'Christian Gottlob Neefe', pp. 294–6.

[48] A-Whh, HA Habsburg-Este, Karton 150, fols. 107–10, 136–41 and 147f.

[49] Reisinger et al., *The Operatic Library*, pp. 114–31.

be ascribed to a lack of interest, but a perceived need to establish a fiscally responsible institution that reflected his high musical expectations and representational necessities.

Finally, by January 1789 the Bonn Court Theatre was reopened. To place the theatre on a firm financial footing, the running of day-to-day operations was placed entirely in the hands of the directors, Joseph Reicha and Anton Steiger, who were authorized to charge admission. To boost ticket revenues, the old Baroque interior was renovated to add three rows of boxes on either side, with all hierarchical class distinctions in the seating assignments abolished.[50] The preceding years had seen an increased investment in the orchestra and vocalists: by the end of the decade, the Hofkapelle's numbers increased from forty to fifty-one musicians.[51] This entailed the addition of oboes and clarinets to the permanent ensemble, staffing of the wind section with specialists in each instrument and a considerable expansion of the string section. Beyond this, twenty-two singers and instrumentalists were hired by the theatre itself, not as members of the Hofkapelle.

By the time Beethoven began playing the viola in the orchestra in 1789, the theatre ensemble had been fully transformed into a full-scale opera company capable of the most challenging new repertoire, as signalled by Neefe in the 1790 *Berliner Annalen des Theatres*: 'The comedic offerings are not what they were under Großmann, who nonetheless is remembered warmly here. The strengths of the local theatre lie in the opera.'[52] This was not mere spin. Not only had the proportion of opera to spoken theatre increased significantly since the Großmann era, but the works chosen tended to be multi-act, full-evening operas, as opposed to the single-act works followed by spoken *Nachspiele* that Großmann had offered.[53] More significant, the orientation of the new repertoire was increasingly toward the most ambitious recent offerings from Vienna stages: to pull off Salieri's *Axur, re d'Ormus*, Dittersdorf's *Das rote Käppchen*, or Mozart's *Le nozze di Figaro* and *Don Giovanni* requires not only a large and highly skilled orchestra, but at least seven or eight strong singers and a chorus. This was beyond the reach of all but the largest German-language court and civic theatres, which is why, besides Bonn, *Don Giovanni* was heard by 1790 only in Mainz, Hamburg and Berlin.[54] More surprisingly, it was this

[50] Ibid., pp. 133–6.   [51] For the full rosters, ibid., pp. 202–4.

[52] 'Auszug eines Briefes aus Bonn, vom 3. März 1790', in *Annalen des Theatres*, 5 (1790), p. 100.

[53] For statistics, see Reisinger et al., *The Operatic Library*, pp. 84–9 and 152–7.

[54] See Cristina Urchueguía, *Allerliebste Ungeheuer. Das deutsche komische Singspiel 1760–1790* (Frankfurt and Basel, 2015), CD-ROM Database, entry 475.

ambitious fare that tended to be repeated the most often on the Bonn stage. *Figaro* was heard four times in the 1790–91 season alone, and *Das rote Käppchen* a total of five times in 1792. These performance statistics back up the content of an often-quoted review that attributed the cool reception of Giuseppe Sarti's *Fra i due litiganti il terzo gode* to a local preference for more complex and richly scored operas:

[Sarti's opera] has made a greater sensation everywhere else but here; perhaps because it came too late to our stage, since we are already too accustomed to Mozartian music. Most Italian compositions now seem as thin as hunger. Nevertheless, Salieri's, Righini's, and other similar work is justifiably well received.[55]

In all, the Bonn Court Theatre's known repertoire between January 1789 and August 1793 added up to eighty-two performances of forty works.[56] A glaring omission from this ambitious programme is, again, work by local court musicians. Although Luchesi and Neefe were both highly regarded composers for the stage, their works were not revived. Both Rombergs composed operas while in Bonn, which likewise never saw the light of day, despite Neefe's high opinion of them.[57] There are several possible reasons for this, the most likely being financial pressure, which led the theatre to mount only works that had proven successful elsewhere. In fact, the only two local works to be staged were apparently composed by members of the nobility. Ferdinand d'Antoine had one occasional work performed, *Der Fürst und sein Volk*. The second was described in the press as a 'karakteristisches Ballet' and attributed to Count Ferdinand von Waldstein but, as later generations discovered, was in fact composed by the twenty-year-old Beethoven, his *Ritterballett* (WoO 1).

The Establishment of a 'Large Public Concert' in Bonn

Of the spaces in the electoral palace in which the young Beethoven performed, by far the least understood, but perhaps the most important during his late teenage years, was that of the *Großer Akademiensaal*, where court concerts were held. Though the topic is touched upon occasionally in the secondary literature, authors have either underestimated its importance

[55] Heinrich Reichard (ed.), *Theatre-Kalender, auf das Jahr 1793* (Gotha, 1792), p. 126.

[56] For the complete revised playing schedule, including guest performances in Münster, see Reisinger et al., *The Operatic Library*, pp. 189–200, also online at www.univie.ac.at/operaticlibrary/db.

[57] Ibid., p. 161.

or, at the other extreme, ascribed to it a much longer tradition than the evidence allows. There are, in fact, many reasons to believe that concerts were a rarity before 1784, but, by Beethoven's final departure, they had become a central pillar of musical life at court. It is also likely that several of his early compositions were first heard in this setting. Many unanswered questions remain and many sources await evaluation. The following should therefore be considered a summary of what is known so far and an indication of what further research might uncover.

The *Großer Akademiensaal*, located directly above the court theatre, certainly existed in the early 1740s, when the east wing of the palace was built, but evidence of concerts there is sparse until the reign of Maximilian Franz. The only documented concert under his predecessor occurred during the two-week festivities surrounding Maximilian Franz's election as co-adjutant in 1780.[58] No programme for this event has survived, nor can it be certain who provided the music. As discussed above, the much smaller collection of instrumental music listed in Inventarium 340 belonged to the chapel, and there was no separate collection of instrumental music at this time held in the *Akademiensaal* or the theatre. This alone would not be a reason to assume that concerts at court were rare, but an often-overlooked comment by Neefe towards the end of his 1783 notice in Cramer's *Magazin der Musik* seems to confirm that concerts were, indeed, not yet common:

Suffice to say, one can certainly gather from all this that a music-loving visitor would never leave Bonn without musical sustenance. Still, it would be desirable that, under the protection of His Electoral Grace, a large public concert be established. Through this, the residence would gain yet another adornment, and the worthy cause of Music would be better promoted.[59]

Neefe appears to have had his wish within a year of Maximilian Franz's accession, but this was at first a Pyrrhic victory. In July 1784, his salary was halved as a consequence of one of the many negative evaluations that were handed down to court musicians.[60] In November, he unsuccessfully petitioned the court for a reinstatement of his full salary, recommending himself as piano accompanist 'in future court concerts'.[61] Thus far, documents detailing the founding of concerts have not been discovered among the court archives, but that desire was evidently a decisive factor in the

---

[58] D-DGla, Kurköln II, 390, fol. 21r.

[59] Neefe, 'Nachricht von der churfürstlich-cöllnischen Hofcapelle', p. 395.

[60] Woodfield, 'Christian Gottlob Neefe', pp. 293–4.   [61] D-DGla, Kurköln II, 3016, fol. 182.

hiring of Joseph Reicha in 1785: he had previously been Kapellmeister at Oettingen-Wallerstein, a court known for its strong tradition of instrumental music. From his first appearance in the Hofkalender of 1786 he is called 'Koncert-Direktor', as opposed to his predecessor Mattioli, who from 1777 had served as 'Instrumentalmusik-Direktor'. Even more tellingly, Reicha's petition for employment in June 1785 originally listed his title as 'Concert-Meister', but this was crossed out and changed to 'Concert-Directeur'.[62] Unusually, an Italian tenor, Lodovico Simonetti, was also later hired, at a high fee, but his discernible duties included neither services in the court chapel nor performances in the opera house; while his contract has not survived, the only possibility is that he was hired purely to sing in concerts.

By 1786 concerts appear to feature with regularity and to have included visiting performers alongside court musicians. In a letter to Großmann from 1 February, Neefe explains an arrangement with the visiting French comedy troupe from Hessen-Kassel, in which 'They are offered free admission to our concerts, and we to their comedies. [Marie Wilhelmine] *Rousselois* has already sung at one of our concerts; today someone is singing whose name I don't know. The elector never goes to the theatre, but is at every concert.'[63] That *Akademien* were occasions when musicians were able to mingle with nobility is clear from a later passage, where Neefe observes with acid irony that 'the French and especially *Rousselois* know how to behave very differently with the local *noblesse* than do our dumb German women and girls'.[64] Sometimes members of the nobility participated as performers and even the elector himself seems to have joined the viola section on occasions. Anton Reicha's colourful reminiscences of these concerts, dictated in old age, include a string-breaking young Beethoven playing a Mozart piano concerto, Reicha improvising a flute cadenza during an unnamed symphony and the following surprising incident:

There was a countess who often used to sing at the concerts given there, in which the prince [sic] himself took part, playing the viola in symphonic pieces. This countess, who had a very fine voice, sang with such feeling that she electrified all those who heard her. On one occasion she sang the sixth scene, in the key of D minor, from Mozart's *Idomeneo* [Electra's rage aria 'Tutte nel cor vi sento'], which made such an impression upon Beethoven and myself that we did nothing

---

[62] D-DGla, Kurköln II, 473, fol. 10r.   [63] D-LEu, Sammlung Kestner, I C II 290, 23.
[64] Ibid.

but dream of it day and night for several weeks in succession. So deeply did it impress me that I have never forgotten it.[65]

Programmes were apparently not made public, or at least not announced in the *Bönnisches Intelligenzblatt*, leading Thayer (who did not know the Neefe correspondence or Reicha's autobiography) to conclude that *Akademien* were not regular events.[66] The one exceptional mention shows that there was a regular procedure in place for local dignitaries and foreign guests to acquire tickets. In advance of the dedication of the new university on 19 November 1786, the lengthy preview of the three-day festivities in the *Intelligenzblatt* announced the following:

> At 5:30 in the evening, there will be a grand concert in the *Großer Akademiensaal*, which is open not only to the high aristocracy and the entire Electoral Council with their wives, but also their adult sons and daughters, clergy, officers, members of the university, as well as all foreigners of distinction … As usual, tickets for the court retinue and foreigners can be obtained from the office of the Electoral Court Forager Ali, whereas academics can obtain theirs from that of the University Counsel, Court Chamberlain Esser.[67]

It is unclear from this wording whether members of the university were regularly granted access to court concerts, or only for this special occasion. Either way, the makeup of the audience seems, at first glance, not to live up to the 'large public concert' that Neefe envisioned in 1783. Nor does it equal the relatively open access to the theatre that Maximilian Friedrich had initiated in 1779, something that was revived ten years later under Steiger and Reicha as a ticket-selling commercial venture. On the other hand, it is not the vestige of exclusivity that Beethoven would later encounter in Vienna, where his symphonies were often first performed in purely aristocratic circles before being given in large public *Akademien*.[68] Rather, the audiences for these court concerts were a mixture of nobility, court officials, guests, travelling musicians and, possibly, the city's leading intellectuals.

No precise data has yet surfaced that would help us estimate how frequently these concerts occurred, and whether they were held throughout

---

[65] 'Notes sur Antoine Reicha', MS autobiography from c. 1824, F-Po, Carton 2073, transcribed with English translation by Gordon Hallman in Millard Laing, 'Anton Reicha's Quintets for Flute, Oboe, Clarinet, Horn, and Bassoon' (PhD thesis, University of Michigan, 1952), pp. 335, 337.

[66] Thayer, *Ludwig van Beethovens Leben*, vol. 1, p. 431.

[67] *Gnädigst-Priviligiertes Bönnisches Intelligenz-Blatt*, No. 46 (14 November 1786), p. 191.

[68] David Wyn Jones, *The Symphony in Beethoven's Vienna* (Cambridge, 2004), pp. 176–180.

the year or during certain seasons only. However, to judge from the size of the collection, in particular the surviving orchestral parts for symphonies now in the Biblioteca Estense Universitaria, they appear to have been mounted in numbers that eclipsed those typically found in Vienna during the same period.[69] Beyond the 330 symphonies he already owned in 1784, Maximilian also appropriated much of the chapel's orchestral music, after its use in services had been curtailed. Between these and the new acquisitions made with the help of Simrock, he eventually expanded his library to include over 650 items of orchestral music.[70] As was customary at other courts, the original set of parts was supplemented by local copies of parts for violins and basso, and occasionally, if it was absent from the original set, a separate, designated bassoon part was derived from the basso. These appear not to have been copied wholesale for every existing symphony, but gradually, as the works were prepared or considered for performance. The existence of local parts, in combination with a consideration of their paper types, potentially offers a clue as to which works were heard in *Akademien* and roughly when.

A full picture must wait until the extant sources have been thoroughly studied, but a preliminary survey of the material seems to reveal a clear preference for works that were brand new, and for ones that were longer and more challenging. For instance, Haydn's ambitious newer symphonies such as Nos. 74–81 and the more substantial among his earlier works (such as the No. 44 in E minor, 'Trauer', and No. 46 in B) were likely all performed or rehearsed, whereas his shorter symphonies from earlier decades and newer works such as the Eight Notturni (Hob. II/25–32) remained untouched. For Mozart, whose symphonies are rather sparingly represented in Maximilian's inventory, most of the surviving ones show signs of performance, including K. 200, K. 297 ('Paris') and K. 551 ('Jupiter'), as well as the three-movement symphony derived from the 'Posthorn' serenade (K. 320). Other symphonies of the 1780s and early 1790s that appear to have been performed include several by Ignaz Pleyel, Adalbert Gyrowetz, Joseph Martin Kraus, Johann F. X. Sterkel and Franz Anton Hoffmeister (including his 'La Primavera'), while decades-old ones by Johann Christian Bach, Leopold Hofmann and Carlo d'Ordonez seem to have remained on the shelf. It remains to be determined, through a more systematic analysis of the over 250 surviving shelf marks, if this observed

[69] As described in ibid., pp. 34–56.

[70] As was customary for the time, orchestral genres such as serenades and overtures were also included under this rubric.

bias toward the new and difficult is truly representative, or if there were occasional performances of older music. One clue that this might have happened has recently been spotted in a surprising location: musical sketches by the young Beethoven. One stray leaf in the Fischhof Miscellany originally served as the first page of a first violin part to Johann Sebastian Bach's cantata, 'Der Herr denket an uns' (BWV 196), written by one of Simrock's copyists.[71] That a sixty-year-old cantata originally intended for Lutheran services was copied and possibly even performed in Bonn raises several mysteries, especially since the fragmentary part includes not only the brief sinfonia (titled 'Ouvertüre'), but also the ensuing four-part chorus, suggesting that it originally belonged to a set of performance parts for the complete work.[72] If a performance in the chapel or any other religious ceremony would have been out of the question, its place in a court concert seems conceivable, if still remarkably inquisitive and open-minded.

Shortly before Palm Sunday on 30 March 1787, an *Akademie* was the occasion at which Haydn's *The Seven Last Words of Christ* (Hob. XX:1a) was first heard in Bonn.[73] The most surprising thing about this perform-ance was its currency: the Viennese premiere, the first outside Spain, had occurred a mere four days earlier.[74] In the Modena copy (Mus.D.167), one of the earliest along with those in Oettingen-Wallerstein, Regensburg and Berlin, each of the parts contains the Latin movement headings in a different hand, apparently added during rehearsal.[75]

As well as symphonies and other orchestral works, *Akademien* also included concertos, single arias and larger ensembles from operas that were otherwise not performed in the court theatre. For local composers, these genres offered them a rare opportunity to present their own com-positions. While in Bonn – or shortly before his arrival in autumn 1790 – Andreas Romberg wrote two violin concertos (Nos. 6 and 7) and later, in 1792, finished a further one (No. 8).[76] The preserved parts of Nos. 7 and 8 are written on familiar Bonn paper, which suggests that they might have been copied out for a performance at court. Also dating from 1792 is a Symphony concertante for violin and cello by Romberg.[77]

---

[71] D-B, Mus.ms.autogr.Beethoven, L. v. 28, fol. 36.

[72] Barry Cooper, 'A Newly Identified Bach Cantata Fragment in a Beethoven Manuscript', *Eighteenth-Century Music*, 14/1 (2017), pp. 111–16.

[73] *Magazin der Musik*, 4 (1787), cols. 1385–6.

[74] Carl Ferdinand Pohl, *Joseph Haydn* (Leipzig, 1882), vol. 2, p. 215.

[75] Hubert Unverricht (ed.), *Joseph Haydn Werke IV*, Kritischer Bericht (Munich, 1963), pp. 12–14.

[76] The score and parts are preserved in D-Hs, ND VI – 3679 ml.   [77] D-Hs, ND VI – 395 df.

Anton Reicha also claimed to have composed several works for the court concerts in Bonn: 'At the age of seventeen [that is in 1787], I had a performance given of a symphony for grand orchestra, along with many Italian scenes composed for an excellent Italian tenor whom the Archduke Maximilian had engaged. These scenes in particular turned out to be a success.'[78] Indeed, several arias and symphonic movements, once considered lost, have recently been discovered in his estate.[79] In any case, he must have been misremembering his age, as the only Italian tenor who fits the bill would have been Simonetti, who arrived in Bonn sometime in 1789.

Beethoven's early concertos and other orchestral works might also have been intended for *Akademien*. Unfortunately all either survive in fragmentary form or have been lost entirely. The sole source for his Piano Concerto in E flat (WoO 4) is a professionally copied piano score[80] written on paper that was used in Bonn between 1787 and 1790, which would be consistent with a performance at a court concert.[81] The earliest version of his Piano Concerto in B flat, Op. 19, and his Oboe Concerto (WoO 206) are both lost. Fragmentary full scores of two further works, both of which appear to have once been complete, may also represent works heard in *Akademien*: the Violin Concerto (WoO 5) and the *Romance cantabile* for flute, bassoon, piano and orchestra (WoO 207). The former is written on the same paper and with the staves drawn by the same unusual eight-stave rastrum – neither of which appears elsewhere in Beethoven's manuscripts – as Romberg's Violin Concerto No. 6, suggesting that it may have been composed with him in mind.[82] The *Romance cantabile*, a slow movement in E minor, may have once belonged to an entire concerto in G major; a fragmentary cello part of a fast movement in this key in Beethoven's hand still exists.[83] Finally, three concert arias composed in Bonn, two for bass, 'Prüfung des Küssens' (WoO 89) and 'Mit Mädeln sich vertragen' (WoO 90), and one for soprano, 'Erste Liebe, Himmelslust' (WoO 92), seem to have been intended for *Akademie* performances between 1790 and 1792, featuring Joseph Lux and Magdalena Willmann respectively.[84]

It may be significant that the surviving copies of Romberg's and Reicha's symphonies lack sets of performance parts, since this genre was largely

---

[78] 'Notes sur Antoine Reicha', p. 299   [79] See especially F-Pn, MS-13107 and L-19671.

[80] D-B, Mus.ms.autogr.Beethoven, L. v. Artaria 125.

[81] Wilson, 'Music Papers in Electoral Bonn'.   [82] Ibid.   [83] D-BNba, HCB BSk 17/65c.

[84] BTW, vol. 2, pp. 220–3 and 226–8.

represented by composers from elsewhere on *Akademie* programmes. Thanks to a long notice by Carl Ludwig Junker, one full programme of a large concert by the Bonn orchestra has survived.[85] This well-known report describes two evenings out of six weeks of daily performances that the core of the ensemble gave in Mergentheim between 11 September and 22 October 1791, encompassing masses, *Tafelmusik*, opera and orchestral music.[86] In Mergentheim the full extent of court music under Maximilian Franz was represented for the first time outside Bonn, and it is possible to understand those offerings as an indication of normal practice back in Bonn. The programme of the concert Junker attended on 12 October is of particular interest:

1 Symphony by Mozart
2 Recitative and Aria (composer unknown), sung by Simonetti
3 Cello Concerto (composer unknown), played by B. Romberg
4 Symphony by Pleyel
5 Aria by Vincenzo Righini, sung by Simonetti
6 Double Concerto for Violin and Cello (composer unknown), played by the Romberg brothers
7 Symphony by Paul Wineberger

This marathon programme is noteworthy for its symmetrical construction, anchored by symphonies and filled out with items that showcased the Hofkapelle's most capable soloists. The three symphonies seem to occupy a privileged status, their composers worthy of mention, while the virtuoso showcases were mostly not. Two of these, Mozart and Pleyel, were not in attendance and their place on the programme therefore seems to signal an appreciation of their reputation as composers of challenging works. Even if both the Rombergs had written the works they played, this apparently was not considered a selling point. The Mergentheim programme as a whole, considered from the elector's point of view, projects an image of his Hofkapelle as first-rate performers of difficult repertoire, but gives little regard to its members as composers.

* * *

---

[85] Carl Ludwig Junker, 'Noch etwas vom Kurköllnischen Orchester' in *Musikalische Korrespondenz der teutschen Filharmonischen Gesellschaft für das Jahr 1791*, No. 47 (23 November 1791), cols. 373–6, continued in No. 48 (30 November 1791), cols. 379–82.
[86] See Adolf Sandberger, 'Zur Reise nach Mergentheim und Aschaffenburg', *Ausgewählte Aufsätze*, vol. 2, pp. 131–4.

Paradoxically, the rich panoply of musical life that Beethoven experienced at Bonn after 1784 also constituted a significant hurdle to his emergence as a composer. Had he been born in Mannheim a decade earlier, he would surely have been encouraged to add his name to the illustrious roster of composer-performers as soon as he showed any inkling of talent and he may well have composed masses, operas and symphonies much earlier than he actually did. But in an environment where not even the Kapellmeister (Luchesi), the opera director (Neefe) or the orchestra director (Reicha) – all of them experienced composers – felt encouraged to provide the court with music, the teenage Beethoven must have quickly felt significant headwinds. Perhaps he felt keenly the pressure that any new work would have to stand up alongside the hundreds of composers in his new employer's library, the long legacy of musical traditions in the chapel, the exciting and complex new masterpieces in the theatre and the cele-brated symphonies in the *Akademiensaal*. That it took him over a decade to stake his claim to these genres is well known, if the reasons are still poorly understood. On the other hand, that Beethoven's music, alone among his peers in the Hofkapelle, made it into his employer's library and was performed in the court theatre (albeit without attribution), and that he alone was sent to Vienna to perfect the craft of composition, suggest that, for whatever reason, he was viewed differently from his colleagues: someone who was worth the investment.

2 | Gracious Beethoven?

W. DEAN SUTCLIFFE

It is no secret that Beethoven inherits many musical essentials from his predecessors, even if that has normally been confined to a handful of well-known composers – principally Haydn and Mozart, with occasional nods to figures like Clementi and C. P. E. Bach. On the other hand, surely no composer's reception has been more consistently marked by claims for newness, by a ready assumption of a fundamental difference from everything that came before. Consequently, the larger critical pattern has involved a push and pull between viewing Beethoven as (late) Classicist and as (early) Romantic. Yet there may be a consensus that, whatever else he may share with earlier generations of composers technically and formally, the expressive climate of Beethoven's works owes little to prior example – that this music 'behaves' in quite new ways. In particular, the composer would appear to part company with what we might call the sociable musical style of the later eighteenth century. This could be defined for present purposes as involving an aesthetic that balances collective and individual claims, leading to a characteristic tone of voice that is wary of making absolute statements, that is often marked by relatively gentle, concessive accents.[1] Such an ethos seems remote from the rugged individualism that is one of the most entrenched aspects of the Beethoven image, with its associated elements of heroic activity, titanic struggle and visionary power.

Yet one should not forget that Beethoven's music is often also charming, funny and understated – among other attributes that one might link with a sociable style. Of course, any Beethoven commentator is likely to acknowledge as much. If few are likely to deny the presence of gentler accents, these do, nevertheless, tend to be collectively swamped by the 'noisier' elements. Indeed, for Nicholas Mathew, the basic 'historical mechanism . . . that has produced and sustained Beethoven's unmistakable musical voice' – those fundamental attributes by which the composer is known well beyond the musicological field – has involved the 'subtraction or suppression of

---

[1] I define the musical sociability of this time at much greater length in my book *Instrumental Music in an Age of Sociability: Haydn, Mozart and Friends* (Cambridge, 2019).

whatever has counted as un-Beethovenian'.[2] For Mathew what has been taken out of the equation are such works or genres as songs, choral works, 'the even-numbered symphonies', 'the more lyrical compositions' and, in particular, works that are patently political in their orientation. Such parts of the output have been treated as 'incidental' to the greater message.[3] However, even if we concede that such subtraction is unlikely ever to be fully reversed, that is not the end of the story, since in my understanding, sociability is not just about a certain tone of voice or certain prevailing affects. More fundamentally, it concerns the management of different musical opinions, as it were, the interaction of different gestures. There is, in other words, a certain inbuilt tension to sociable musical manners. Without the cut and thrust of such interaction, we would be dealing less with a world that was properly social – involving the interplay of strong, potentially conflicting (musical) personalities – and more with a world that was, instead, idyllic. Recognizing this allows us to grasp what I would call the more purely 'technical' side of sociability, within which matters of affect count for less than the ways in which difference is managed. Here the emphasis falls on the various ways in which musical materials are reciprocally organized, and how this takes place on different scales of musical utterance, from the motive to the phrase to the section and beyond.

A further part of a sociable musical orientation involves a more or less explicit courting of the listener, finding various ways to secure the attention of a social 'participant' whose mind might otherwise wander off. But securing attention involves a trade-off between novelty and familiarity of discourse: a certain level of comfort must be established in order for that listener to have a stake in the unfolding of the musical sound. And so formulas and conventions need not be broken in order to render communication more vivid – this being just about the commonly asserted thought when the name of Beethoven comes up for discussion. Conventions only evolve into such because they serve a positive social or communicative purpose; they can be fully artistically effective even when apparently 'unimproved' by some sort of novel treatment.

This assertion offers a point of departure for a survey in which I examine Beethoven's continued participation in a sociable musical culture, which he does with higher levels of commitment than might commonly be allowed. I will make exclusive reference to the solo keyboard sonatas.[4] One justification for this is that the genre does not seem to offer the sort of built-in

[2] Nicholas Mathew, *Political Beethoven* (Cambridge, 2013), p. 3.   [3] Ibid., p. 3.
[4] Commentary on the sonatas is based on the edition by B. A. Wallner (Munich, 1980).

social element that all 'chamber music', and indeed all ensemble music in general, must be conceded to contain. Instead I choose a genre that could be associated with a more individual, private brand of rhetoric, and one that has often formed a strong point of focus for the predominant Beethovenian imagery. To return to the matter of formula, while presenting everyday turns of phrase in their proper place acknowledges the existence of something like a common language – without which there is no basis for communication – to be able to present them in a new light shows a kind of versatility of thought that is a prime sociable virtue. The ability to think on one's feet when the lines of communication become tangled, so to speak, is part of the plan, the difference in the musical sphere being that such *faux pas* are generally deliberately contrived, so as to renew the perception of everyday figures of speech.

This may take the form of a scrambling of formal function, as it does in the finale of the Sonata in E flat Major, Op. 31 No. 3. The movement opens with a six-note melodic closing formula set to a rollicking accompaniment, and this formula – a falling dominant-seventh arpeggio leading to a resolution to the tonic, played four times in registral dialogue – only reappears when the opening theme returns to mark the recapitulation. It is otherwise ignored as other materials receive all the attention. To be more precise, what acts as a marker of formal opening, and sounds plausible enough in that role, will turn out to find greater and more convincing employment as a close. This change of perspective emerges late in the movement, with a more expansive treatment of the figure starting only from bar 280. Initially, we simply hear a near-replica of its two previous appearances, save for its pianistic inversion: now the right hand plays the accompanimental ostinato while the left hand reiterates the formula. This time, though, the material does not give way to other ideas. Instead, it repeats itself ever more insistently, first of all at a supertonic level (from the upbeat to bar 291), followed straight away by a further shift to the subdominant, A flat major. The momentum of this unexpected insistence comes to a crashing halt on a thick *fortissimo* diminished-seventh chord in bar 307. Immediately thereafter our figure returns at its original pitch, unaccompanied, in the left hand. Overlapping with this is a textural answer by the right hand that is also a harmonic answer: the figure has become a straight falling tonic arpeggio. But the right hand immediately follows this in bar 311 by returning to the original shape, dominant-seventh arpeggio resolving to a tonic. With the ostinato-style accompaniment now being kept separate from our figure, the left hand plays a simple dominant-seventh chord in support. It is at this point that our six-note figure, simply and subordinately accompanied, explicitly takes on a closing function. It not only closes off the large paragraph that began with the return of the opening material (bars 280–312), but also sounds like an appropriate way to finish the movement altogether.

Just in case the reversal of formal function of this figure was not clear enough, Beethoven backs up and repeats the approach to this pivotal moment, offering the listener another opportunity to grasp the process. In addition to a further reversal of roles between the hands when our figure re-enters after the thumping *fortissimo* chord, a *poco ritardando* is marked to clinch the matter (bars 319–322). This is more than a straightforward role reversal, though, whereby an opening is recast as an ending. The very fact that the figure has been reiterated so many times of late means that it also behaves like closing material: multiple repetitions of small-scale figures are what characteristically happens at this point of a structure. Such reiterations then continue as the figure receives further intensive treatment in a kind of stretto from the upbeat to bar 323. Beethoven first reverts to the original unadorned version, which is now played by both hands in unison, with the ostinato accompaniment now having been left behind for good. This is followed by a series of chromatic equivocations as the figure is repeated without its anacrusis, a classic kind of liquidation, and the final version we hear resolves to the tonic at bar 328 before giving way to a series of loud closing chords. Thus, having had its natural formal function revealed, the figure now fulfils a post-cadential role, effectively a form of further closing, before it disappears, job done. One might claim, though, that even those final chords – seemingly the most formulaic of closing gestures in their alternation of dominant-seventh and tonic sonorities – themselves represent a compression or distillation of our figure, which after all did no more than compose out the same fundamental progression.

Such a play with the form-functional implications of a familiar-sounding figure, and the way in which it implies a listener who will be rewarded for paying attention, are familiar from the practice of previous generations, most notably in the case of Haydn. What is also characteristic is the understated handling of the change. The actual execution of the moment of reversal (or clarification) in bars 310–312 and 320–322 is decidedly ordinary, quite matter-of-fact, with its soft dynamic and use of middling register hardly crying out for notice; it is, rather, the larger contextual manipulation that makes the point. But renewal can be accomplished more dramatically than this. What is renewed in the scherzo of the Sonata in A Major, Op. 2 No. 2, is not even substantial enough to be called a formula. Instead, it is simply the use of a 'feminine ending' to a phrase.

The perfect symmetry of the opening strain, an eight-bar period, is capped by matching endings to each of its four-bar units: both conclude with a falling step, a restruck suspension–resolution pair on the first two beats of bar 4 being answered by an appoggiatura plus resolution on the first two beats of bar 8. Immediately after the double bar we hear an equivalent eight-bar structure, but with a series of reversals. Each four-bar unit now grows towards a *forte* conclusion, as opposed to the steady *piano* of the original period, and Beethoven swaps the textural disposition – the left hand now takes up the tune while the right hand plays the intervening chords. Most strikingly, though, the original falling-step conclusion to the earlier phrases is overturned. At the point of cadence in bar 12 the right hand effectively resumes melodic leadership, and it does so by now rising a step. This is reinforced not just by the *forte* dynamic but by the more active harmonic progression, V7-I, as opposed to the decorated single chords that we heard at the equivalent points of bars 4 and 8. These reversals turn what was an unmarked, gracious phrase ending into something that has a sharper aural edge, and that impression is augmented as the succeeding four-bar phrase transposes what we have just heard up a further step – an instance of the Monte schema that is often found after the double bar of such a form.[5]

However, the truly defamiliarizing moment has yet to occur. Bar 17 replicates the rising step heard at the ends of the phrases in bars 12 and 16, but this is now heard as an isolated two-note event, surrounded by silence on both sides; together with the increased dynamic of *fortissimo*, this creates a highly assertive gesture. Further, the left hand now joins in by delivering its own rising pair of notes, helping to create a harmonically open-ended progression: i6 to iv in the key of G sharp minor as opposed to the previous V7-I chords. By such means, what should be an unmarked, routine way of delineating a unit of musical grammar, a weak-beat ending to a phrase, becomes an object of attention. This gesture is then just as vividly undercut. Bar 18, after a silence on the first beat of the bar, offers a much more a concessive $V^{6/4-5/3}$-I close in G sharp minor at a dynamic level of *piano*. This close is, once more, entirely formulaic, giving the impression that amidst the *fortissimo* eruption and the surrounding silences a complete phrase has been strangled out of existence.

The rest of the middle section then studiously avoids any recurrence of the 'feminine ending', concentrating instead on the repeated-note pattern

---

[5] For further information on the Monte see Robert O. Gjerdingen, *Music in the Galant Style* (New York, 2007), esp. pp. 89–106.

that had led up to the original phrase endings in bars 4 and 8. This middle section then melts into a longer silence, *pianissimo* and *rallentando*. Thereafter the opening eight-bar period returns exactly as heard before, in all innocence, as if nothing had happened in the interim. However, Beethoven then closes the scherzo by adding an extra four-bar phrase whose final melodic gesture – the rising step g$\sharp^2$ to a^2, chordally thickened and delivered *fortissimo* – revives the challenge that had arisen in the middle of the scherzo.

The point of this interplay between (innocent) routine and (calculated) novelty can hardly be to cast aside the formulaic in favour of more 'authentic' expression, as so much critical reception would have it. Both sides arguably gain by the transaction. Our perception of the standard locution of a falling weak-beat phrase ending is renewed, and the 'strong reading' of the figure that emerges in the middle section can only have its effect because of its reliance on the norm as a frame for comprehension. We are encouraged to listen carefully to even the most seemingly everyday things – which may be renewed in our perception either through outright deformation or simply through contextual manipulation. The latter is often the case with the phenomenon that I call the simplifying cadence, in which a straightforward cadential arrival undercuts a preparation that leads us to expect something more highly flavoured. We have already encountered a specimen in the finale of Op. 31 No. 3: the repetitive build-up that begins at bar 280, followed by that crashing diminished-seventh chord in bar 307, are succeeded by the transformation of the opening figure into a closing cadential one. After such preparation the actual realization of the cadence, as noted above, sounds entirely ordinary, if playfully so.

The same sense of wry understatement may be heard, for example, in the first movement of the Sonata in D Major, Op. 28 ('Pastoral'). The build-up to the essential expositional closure[6] is a very protracted one. The decisive cadence in the dominant could in fact have taken place some twenty-five bars earlier than it does, but Beethoven launches a very large-scale 'one-more-time' repetition of the preceding thirty-two-bar section (which, admittedly, also transposes that section so as to centre it on the dominant key). Thus from bar 126 we hear once more the same series of brilliant flourishes that had earlier been launched at bar 104, once again promising to sweep us towards an affirmative cadence. Beethoven then

---

[6] The term derives from James Hepokoski and Warren Darcy, *Elements of Sonata Theory: Norms, Types, and Deformations in the Late-Eighteenth-Century Sonata* (New York, 2006), where it is first defined in full at pp. 120–4.

adds to the suspense by inserting a loud rising scale in the left hand that had not been heard earlier. But as this drives upwards, it seems to lose confidence, as it were, and what follows in bars 133–35 is the plainest possible cadence, in longer note values and delivered *piano*.

After the same sequence of events has been replicated in the recapitulation, the movement then ends with a similar effect. Following a *pianissimo* return of the opening theme from bar 438, its final two bars are reiterated four times, interspersed with off-beat *sforzando* notes in the right hand that trace a rising tonic arpeggio, and accompanied by a *crescendo*. But just at the point when we might expect this grand build-up to culminate in a forceful final gesture or two, the dynamic level starts to weaken, and we finish instead with the simplest, softest peroration imaginable: short single *pianissimo* chords of V7 followed by I. I have already suggested that there is a wry flavour to such a procedure, a kind of gently comic understatement, though it need not be heard in this way; one could instead hear (and play) this conclusion as poignantly atmospheric. Indeed, it can be both at once, and such ambivalence of tone (in a nutshell, 'are you serious or are you joking?') is characteristic of a sociable orientation, where it is left to the listener to read the signals.[7] But at such a juncture we might also adopt our 'technical' perspective: arguably more fundamental than deciding on one particular affect is to grasp how the reversal represented by the simplifying cadence arises from a continual 'social' interplay of different musical elements, whether this involves texture, articulation, dynamic level or any other parameter.

Such matters come to the fore even more strongly when simplifying cadential manoeuvres are found in slower movements, when they call a halt not to brilliance but rather to some kind of heightened lyricism. Such is the case at the close of the solemn Adagio of the Sonata in C Major, Op. 2 No. 3. From bar 79 an eloquent melodic line in the highest register is temporarily suspended as the phrase pauses on a subdominant chord in bar 80. Quite counterintuitively, the c$\sharp^3$ that resolves the downbeat appoggiatura on d$\sharp^3$ is marked *sforzando*, reversing the unwritten rule that notes of resolution should be performed more softly than their preceding dissonances. In its unnatural use of accentuation, this detail suggests a heightened expressive state; and at the same time, it acts as a form of renewal on the smallest scale of linguistic operation, similar to the

---

[7] For a discussion of this quality in a particular part of Haydn's output see my article 'Expressive Ambivalence in Haydn's Symphonic Slow Movements of the 1770s', *The Journal of Musicology*, 27/1 (2010), pp. 84–133.

treatment of the 'feminine ending' that we traced in the scherzo of Op. 2 No. 2. After the pause, the melodic line moves effortfully upwards, *forte*, followed by a histrionic leap downward, from e³ down to a *sforzando* B, a distance of well over three octaves. Such a leap can trigger several associations. It could signal a Grand Cadence schema, according to which the plunge into registral depths would be followed by a rising line (scale or arpeggio), which is in turn generally succeeded by a trill to mark the point of cadence.[8] Alternatively, this registral disjunction would signal a vocal model, an aria in high style in which histrionic leaps (*cantar di sbalzo*) form part of the expressive apparatus (a section in the slow movement of Op. 2 No. 1, at bars 16–21, features a series of such leaps); in the case of a piano work, these wide intervals can, of course, be exaggerated because of the instrument's wide range.

However, the implications of neither of those models are followed through. Both would suggest a continuation of extrovert expression, whereas in the current case the dynamic marking immediately shrinks to *pianissimo*, all parts now inhabit a low register and the end of the movement is reached with a minimum of fuss. A comparable case occurs at the comparable point of the Largo, con gran espressione of the Sonata in E flat Major, Op. 7. In the final bars of this movement (86 ff.) a different device is employed – a valedictory reharmonization of the opening theme that features chromatic enrichments – but the same sort of signal is sent, one that involves a final expressive heightening before the end is reached. (The close of the Andante of Haydn's Symphony No. 94 in G Major, the 'Surprise', is another example of the device.) Here, though, the affecting transformation of the theme, being conducted in a *pianissimo* whisper, is brutally undercut when the left hand's falling chromatic bass line reaches an F♯ in bar 88³. This note is, out of the blue, played *fortissimo*, the effect enhanced because the left hand has been doubling its line in octaves. The right hand then responds in kind with a *fortissimo* octave of its own. But this hyper-assertive gesture has no sooner arrived than it departs, as the dynamic level is immediately scaled back, a diatonic ii6 chord is reached and after a melodic flourish the phrase finishes with a further example of our phenomenon – a simple, even skeletal, V-I completion of the cadence.

Robert Hatten ties the eruption on F♯ followed by a mollifying F♮ in the bass at bar 89³ to a wider argument about the manipulation of those two

---

[8] For a definition and discussion of this phenomenon see Floyd Grave, 'Freakish Variations on a "Grand Cadence" Prototype in Haydn's String Quartets', *Journal of Musicological Research*, 28/2–3 (2009), pp. 119–45.

pitch classes throughout the movement, but more to the point here is the affective reading that he proposes for this ending. For him, 'the F♮ serves to disperse the tension generated by this sudden irruption and yields or resigns graciously to an embellishing turn figure. That figure then cues the *galant* style for a somewhat tenuously positive ending, one undermined by recent exposure of the tragic tensions lurking beneath an otherwise optimistic surface.'[9] There is much I would agree with here, including, importantly for our purposes, the notion of a gracious yielding after an aggressive gesture. However, his relative weighting of 'positive' and 'tragic' elements is indicative of a wider critical preference whereby the latter always wins out over the former, carries greater expressive weight, as if the more optimistic state of mind represents a sort of false consciousness. The definitive counterblast against such priorities, in the context of reception of Mozart's music, has been written by Wye J. Allanbrook.[10]

In the case of this particular movement, one might ask why the priorities could not be reversed. Why could we not understand the simple, unexaggerated close, and the plain speech that it represents, as the more authentic gesture, and the prior brutal interruption (along with those heard earlier in the movement) as something that is, to name a few possibilities, intransigent, perverse or just over the top? Is there not just as much feeling in the tender, subdued close as in the previous outburst? And that is before one considers the more ironic interpretation that a simplifying cadence frequently allows – an undercutting of what in retrospect can be made to seem to have been trying too hard, aiming for too grand an effect. This need not imply, however that anyone should be forced to take sides, to praise one affect while damning the other; as already suggested, interaction in its own right is foundational to such processes, and one implication of that is tolerance of different types of musical 'personality'. To this one might add, in defence of Hatten's relative weighting of the various elements at play in the final few bars, that the simplifying close seems disproportionately short relative to the gestural weight of the *fortissimo* interruption; it barely has time to register before the movement is over. In this sense, the simplifying cadential close represents an abrupt utterance in its own right. A further ironic perspective offers itself for consideration if one notes that this laconic cadential arrival allows the whole final phrase to complete itself

---

[9] Robert S. Hatten, *Musical Meaning in Beethoven: Markedness, Correlation, and Interpretation* (Bloomington, 1994), p. 61.

[10] Wye J. Allanbrook, 'Mozart's Tunes and the Comedy of Closure', in *On Mozart*, ed. James M. Morris (Cambridge, 1994), pp. 169–86.

within a standard four-bar duration, from the lead-in to bar 87 through to bar 90. In other words, whatever internal dramas it may contain, the phrase is perfectly, pleasingly regular in bringing the movement to a punctual close.

To touch on such possibilities is also to note the positive role that inhibition plays in the behaviour of this music, and the phenomenon of the simplifying cadence may be argued to demonstrate this very plainly. Inhibition is not something readily associated with Beethoven, who is routinely celebrated precisely for the lack of this quality, in implicit or explicit distinction from his predecessors. One feature that might seem to uphold the traditional image would be those 'spells of absentmindedness' that Karol Berger finds to be particularly common in the composer's early piano music.[11] For him they represent a shift from a 'real' to an 'imaginary' world 'into which the mind of [the performing character] escapes', into a world of 'contemplation' rather than 'action'.[12] William Kinderman describes this phenomenon, in the case of the first movement of the Sonata in F Major, Op. 10 No. 2, as involving 'regressive episodes and digressions', as a means of avoiding normal continuity of utterance.[13] Such departures from the straight and narrow might seem to suggest a certain kind of unself-consciousness, a disregard for the niceties of normal communication, but they are, on the other hand, also staged events. After all, this state of reverie does not last; the compositional persona becomes once more self-aware, snaps back to Berger's 'reality', begins once again to operate more efficiently and lucidly. We should not assume that the dream state is somehow truer or more authentic than the normal state that it temporarily denies. Rather, we can understand the larger phenomenon as yet another type of interplay between different musical-expressive typologies. And it also serves the end of increasing listener attention by suspending normal service. It is a characteristically Beethovenian means of 'doing things wrong' that is already a fundamental communicative procedure in the music of the preceding generation, most recognizably so with Haydn.

The same might apply to an even more characteristically Beethovenian procedure – what I call the 'crescendo to nothing'. This typically involves an accumulation of dynamic weight and gestural power followed by a

[11] Karol Berger, 'Beethoven and the Aesthetic State', *Beethoven Forum 7*, eds. Lewis Lockwood, Christopher Reynolds and Elaine R. Sisman (Lincoln, NE, 1999), pp. 17–44, at p. 19.
[12] Ibid., pp. 21 and 35.
[13] William Kinderman, 'Beethoven's High Comic Style in the Piano Sonatas of the 1790s, or Beethoven, Uncle Toby, and the "Muckcart-Driver"', *Beethoven Forum 5*, eds. Christopher Reynolds and James Webster (Lincoln, NE, 1996), pp. 119–38, at p. 131.

sudden withdrawal to *piano*. Miriam Sheer, noting that it is a 'personal mark' of the composer's style, believes that it is used 'to understate harmonic arrival'.[14] Without denying that, I would offer a more behavioural perspective on this fingerprint. In its conjunction of 'big' followed by 'small', it can clearly be allied with the simplifying cadence, and often also occurs at the end of a phrase, but is generally even more abrupt in effect. It undermines entrainment in the musical flow and instead creates a hard perceptual edge, making the listener more conscious of the very act of listening. It also evinces a discursive self-consciousness on the part of the composer, whereby the 'natural' continuation is not allowed to take place. In the last few bars of the minuet from the Sonata in B flat Major, Op. 22, a *crescendo* in conjunction with metrical disruption (hemiolas followed by rhythmic diminution of the movement's main motive) surely demand a clarifying and affirmative close, and this comes to pass rhythmically in the form of two clear-cut crotchet chords in the final bar (30). However, the dynamic marking undermines the sense of rhythmic relief: an abrupt *piano* starting on the downbeat when a continuation at *forte* would have been so much more straightforward. Such effects are so physically as well as aurally counterintuitive that it is no surprise that most performers approach such a *subito piano* marking half-heartedly, but if applied in earnest (which is no easy matter), we may apprehend it as an ironic scaling-back of what could (should) have been an assertive close.

While this particular case represents a relatively local effect, many Beethovenian movements are saturated with the *crescendo* to nothing. Even in as boisterous a work as the 'Waldstein' Sonata, Op. 53, one finds a constant pulling-back from full-throated completion of thoughts by means of sudden *piano* markings. And the discursive implications of such dynamic-gestural incongruity need not be comic or ironic. The Adagio of the Sonata in D Minor, Op. 31 No. 2 ('Tempest'), is another movement that is rich in the device. If I argue that the device is born of the inhibition that forms part of a sociable mindset, that does not mean that what results is an expressive subtraction. The very first example in the movement shows that – bars 6–7, where a *sforzando* (admittedly not a *crescendo*) on a diminished-seventh chord leads at the start of bar 7 to a supertonic 6-3 chord with a double suspension. The normal weighting of such an event would see the moment of suspension, of maximum dissonance, bar 7^1, carry the greatest emphasis, followed by a tailing-off into the moment of

[14] Miriam Sheer, 'A Comparison of Dynamic Practices in Selected Piano Sonatas by Clementi and Beethoven', *Beethoven Forum 5*, pp. 85–101, at pp. 94 and 93.

resolution. Instead, Beethoven marks the downbeat *piano* and, just as counterintuitively, follows that with a *crescendo*. The *piano* marking is itself, in fact, a form of agogic emphasis – it is hard to imagine how one could play this sequence of events in strict time. And it has to be *subito piano*: there are no intervening notes to play with. Later, in bars 24–27, a rising melodic sequence accompanied by a distinctive drum-roll-type motive, together creating a wonderful sonority, are marked with a *crescendo* that lasts for nearly three full bars at Adagio tempo. This builds up dramatic momentum on a large scale, but then the culminating point of the line, which arrives at the start of bar 27, is marked *piano*. Such signs of gestural inhibition carry a positive expressive charge – in this case, they help to make the mood more elevated than it would otherwise be, if all the 'natural' dynamic contours and stress points were to be performed as expected. More broadly in tune with my thesis, such moments renew perception and command attention on the part of the listener. For all that, I cannot quite subscribe to Hatten's assertion that the '*subito* dynamic changes' found throughout this movement show the composer countering the unmarked metric flow so as to create a 'strong sense of subjectivity'.[15] These dynamic changes may indeed be expressively enriching, as I myself have just argued, but a critical narrative that seems to impute an automatically positive value to 'subjectivity', however defined, ignores the extent to which this behavioural trait is rooted in inhibition, in not allowing any one affect or type of material to run away with the musical discourse.

Another way of putting this is to reiterate that musical materials and gestures – whether this means motives, textures or dynamic levels – must notice and negotiate with each other, as it were. It is as if musical utterance itself is imbued with social consciousness. One useful shorthand for this process is to speak of assertive and gracious elements that operate in constant interaction, and a particularly characteristic behavioural schema involves the assertive being answered by the more gracious. Thus the categorical is answered by the more concessive, the strong by the gentle. While what I call the gracious riposte[16] most evidently operates on a relatively local scale, it can encompass much larger stretches of music. At the level of a whole work it could be said to be the underlying basis for the

---

[15] Robert S. Hatten, *Interpreting Musical Gestures, Topics, and Tropes: Mozart, Beethoven, Schubert* (Bloomington, 2004), p. 146.

[16] See my article 'The Shapes of Sociability in the Instrumental Music of the Later Eighteenth Century', *Journal of the Royal Musical Association*, 138/1 (2013), pp. 1–45, at pp. 6–9, for a first definition and discussion of this sociable musical trait.

two movements of the Sonata in C Minor, Op. 111. At the level of a complete movement it is readily apprehensible in the 'In Tempo d'un Menuetto' that opens the Sonata in F Major, Op. 54, and here the contrast not only operates on a very large scale, but the order of events is reversed. A gentle, leisurely opening section that delivers on the promise of a minuet style is succeeded by crassly contrasting material from the end of bar 24.

This opening (A) pointedly minds its periodic manners, being constructed from a series of very clear mini-sentence structures, and each sentence is built on the basis of a dialogue of registers. There is no room for such niceties in what follows (B): a virtual moto perpetuo, with little differentiation between the beats of what is ostensibly still triple time. It sounds like it begins on a downbeat rather than the notated third beat, and then a series of *sforzando* markings on every beat of bars 26 and 27 seems calculated to emphasize the point ever more strongly. And it soon offers explicit metrical dissonance in the shape of hemiolas from bar 30. Its continuous triplet rhythms do not so much contrast with the differentiated dotted values that prevailed in A as obliterate them. Further, this material is marked *sempre forte e staccato*, as opposed to the predominantly soft legato execution of what came before. And its formal function is far from clear: it might be a (rather premature) trio section, or it might be a particularly propulsive transition.

When A eventually returns, it does so in varied-reprise style, making it more intricate and more continuous, as if in mild response to the behaviour exhibited by B. The B section then returns, initially just as before, but its explosion of libidinal energy is quickly curtailed as it turns into a preparation for the return of A. This in turn resumes from where it left off, but the impulse for varied repetition becomes ever stronger, and it moves into yet shorter note values, which soon become a steady stream of sextuplet semiquavers. This seems to prompt A to burst out beyond the anticipated phrase structure. From bar 129, the point of expected cadential close, it continues without a break via a long descending sequence, and we may start to realize that the A material has, in its own terms, become just about as propulsive as B. In particular, the sequence involves hemiola groupings, borrowing from the example of B and quite unlike the more even, balanced sense of phrase rhythm that had always governed A to this point. In tandem with this, the dynamic level goes beyond the customary *piano*: in bar 127, shortly before the sequence begins, a *crescendo* is indicated, and this remains unmodified until a *mezza voce* is marked at bar 135. By that point, a lengthy cadenza that was launched at bar 132 is nearing its end. This is built on the contours of the (instrumental) Grand

Cadence schema, but then finishes in purely vocal fashion with a single-line *Eingang* that slows down to Adagio. This cadenza represents the culmination of a process whereby A has over the course of the movement taken on something of the free-wheeling character of B.

This process continues when from bar 137 A resumes in something akin to its opening form, above a deep pedal in continuous triplets. From bar 144 the rising triadic motion on which the start of every unit of A has been based is now expanded and turned into a rising fanfare, unmistakeably conveying an affect of grandeur. This prompts a climax at bar 148 that is built on repeated diminished-seventh chords over an F pedal, starting *fortissimo* before diminishing in volume to *pianissimo* as the diminished seventh slides into a dominant seventh, and as triplet rhythms give way to duple ones. The thick thrashed-out *fortissimo* chords suggest a counterpart to the only similar gesture heard earlier, near the end of the second B section at bars 102–103, which consisted of repeated dominant-seventh chords. So here is another clear way in which A on its final appearance seems to respond to B, to take some of its most salient features and interpret them in its own terms. Thus we might seem to have a model instance of the reciprocal interaction of different musical materials and their associated affects. The movement's behavioural contrasts, which are so extreme to start with, are mollified as it unfolds; William Kinderman notes how the final outburst from bar 148 sums up the gradual integration of the two opposed impulses.[17]

Yet we need not hear a complete rapprochement of A and B at the end; the very understated, modest ending that follows our dissonant chordal outbreak at bar 148 suggests that the spirit of A remains in control, and the fact that this highly sectional structure occurs in the first movement of a sonata may strengthen the sense of a fundamental incompatibility of utterance; such sectional structures may occur in any part of a multi-movement instrumental work except, with rare exceptions, its first movement. Lawrence Kramer, for one, does not hear a meeting of minds in this piece. He nicely describes the B sections as 'outbursts of bearish, surly aggressiveness', though his comment that the A sections 'elaborate on a placid little tune'[18] seems rather less acute, showing the usual critical unease with simple charm. Kramer also fails to notice how the events of the last page in particular modify the initial opposition, yet his overall verdict – that the 'expressive polarities' of the movement 'are conceived too crudely and

---

[17] William Kinderman, *Beethoven*, 2nd ed. (New York, 2009), p. 107.
[18] Lawrence Kramer, *Music as Cultural Practice, 1800–1900* (Berkeley, 1990), p. 38.

too starkly'[19] – has something to be said for it. We should bear in mind that a sense of interplay is more fundamental to sociable music than agreement; the discussion counts for more than the conclusion, as it were. In the case of Op. 54's first movement, therefore, it does not ultimately matter whether one hears resolution or a continued (at least partial) estrangement; and in offering up such a structure Beethoven is clearly challenging the listener to take an active part in making sense of the musical experience.

The handling of assertive and gracious elements in the first movement of the Sonata in F sharp Major, Op. 78, is more indirect and long-range, so much so, in fact, that most scholars have noticed no such thing. Instead, this movement, introduced by means of a Quiescenza schema[20] in a four-bar Adagio cantabile, is commonly characterized as a pastoral idyll.[21] It may be that in large part, but a three-chord unit quickly stands out from the lyrical fluency found elsewhere. It is first heard at bars 12 and 14, bar 12 being *subito piano* after a previous *crescendo*, and these two bars are interspersed with separated crotchet chords on first and third beats of bars 13 and 15 to give an effect of hesitant uncertainty. This is heightened by the fact that bar 12 seems to function as a cadential completion of an eight-bar theme, albeit relatively weak given the way it climbs by step to finish on scale degree 3 on the third beat of the bar; what is unexpected is the way in which that figure then generates a continuation in kind. Bar 12 also recalls the melodic progression from $f\sharp^1$ to $g\sharp^1$ to $a\sharp^1$ in the first two bars of the Adagio cantabile opening, and in fact the complete bars 12–15 seem to give us a ghosted version of that opening's ascent from $f\sharp^1$ to $c\sharp^2$, strengthening the sense that they stand somewhat apart from the musical flow.

This three-chord unit is then reworked later in the exposition so as to fall across the bar line at 31–32 and 33–34: again here it comes twice and is spaced two bars apart. On the other hand, the articulation is different – the first two notes of the unit are slurred, with a separate attack on the third note, which is now on the downbeat and marked *sforzando*. In addition, the dynamic is now (*subito*) *forte*, the opposite of the earlier sudden *piano*. These changes give the gesture a quite different character; it is now assertive, whereas earlier it clearly fell on the gracious side. Given this

---

[19] Ibid., p. 39.

[20] For a definition and an exemplification of the Quiescenza see Gjerdingen, *Music in the Galant Style*, pp. 181–95.

[21] See, for example, Elaine Sisman, 'After the Heroic Style: *Fantasia* and the "Characteristic" Sonatas of 1809', *Beethoven Forum 6*, ed. Glenn Stanley (Lincoln, NE, 1998), pp. 67–96, at pp. 93–5, and Hatten, *Musical Meaning in Beethoven*, p. 83.

transformation, one might even question whether this later pair of three-chord gestures can be related to the earlier pair, given how different they sound. However, the rhythmic resemblances are strong, not just in literal duration (three consecutive unembellished crotchet chords), but in the self-contained nature of the gesture each time, and in both passages the three chords undercut the lyrical fluency with which they are surrounded. In that sense both instances, while they partake of the assertive–gracious dualism, are on the same side relative to the rest of the exposition. This illustrates how the process of give and take that underpins this interactive aesthetic can readily spin off into different levels of reciprocity.

The interrupting character of the three-note idea, relatively understated in the exposition, is much more dramatically realized in the recapitulation. The originally soft passage from bars 12 to 16 is from bar 66 broken up into an internal loud–soft assertive–gracious alternation. The equivalent of bar 12 is transformed into three *fortissimo* chords, thicker in texture and wider in tessitura, which is then countered by an equivalent of bar 13 that reverts to a gentler, hesitant character and in which the register is compressed back to its original dimensions. The shock of the unexpected *fortissimo* assertion in bar 66 is augmented by its harmonically disruptive nature, as the three-chord unit now enters in E major, rather remote from the tonic key of F sharp. These pairs of suddenly contrasting one-bar units now alternate four times – twice the duration of what we heard in the exposition – in the service of a rising melodic sequence in the right hand. At the fourth time of asking, the soft rejoinder mimics the shape of the previous *forte* bar, including its contrary motion between the hands (see bar 73), and this leads to a very understated, simplifying close at bar 75. The greatly increased prominence of the three-chord gesture in the recapitulation then seems to spill over into the Allegro vivace finale, which opens with a near-equivalent sequence of three isolated chords.[22]

The first movement of the Sonata in E Minor, Op. 90, immediately offers in its first eight bars the more recognizable compact alternation of assertive and gracious elements – an ebb and flow of confident statement and retraction. In light of the composer's performance indication, 'Mit Lebhaftigkeit und durchaus mit Empfindung und Ausdruck', one might rebrand our conceptual dualism as 'Lebhaftigkeit' versus 'Empfindung', though the latter may not quite cover the sense of concession that is at the heart of my formulation. On the other hand, it would make clear that the concessive

---

[22] Kinderman recognizes the similarity of the finale's opening motive to the figure we have discussed in the first movement: see *Beethoven*, p. 159.

gesture does not just have a negating or palliating force, but carries as much expressive potency as the material with which it is in dialogue. There is a particular focus to the dualism in this movement: a two-note cell (x) involving note repetition over the bar line.

The assertive–gracious schema in fact operates on two levels at the start. Bars 1–8 clearly alternate different versions of the same two-bar phrase unit. The first and third are *forte*, and the repeated-note upbeat-downbeat cell x is strongly articulated through the upbeat's being realized as a full-textured quaver chord followed by a quaver rest. The second and fourth represent the softening lyrical rejoinder. The dynamic level drops to *piano*, and the initial anacrusis chord now lasts a full crotchet. In addition, the voicing of the second and fourth versions is quite different: the parts are close together in a middle register, as opposed to the more expansive range of versions one and three, and the parts move exclusively by step. At the same time, these alternating phrase units work together: the last melodic notes of each unit describe a rising stepwise line – from a^1 to b^1 to $c\sharp^2$ to d^2. This is coordinated with a 5-10 linear intervallic pattern that takes us from V to I of G major and then from V to i of B minor. It is most odd to have such sequential behaviour in conjunction with opening function, plus it means that III and v are tonicized while the tonic has not been similarly affirmed: E minor simply acts as the point of departure. Thus we have a harmonic cycle to go with the gestural-expressive cycle already outlined.

The eight-bar phrase that follows from bar 8^3 is more stable harmonic-ally, but stable in what will turn out to be the wrong key – G major. All of the textural-rhythmic gaps that featured in the first eight bars disappear, and we hear continuous sound. The phrase outlines a falling trajectory to counteract the rising line of the first eight bars, and gives us a second-level gracious riposte: what in the first eight bars was an internal alternation can be heard in retrospect as a single larger-scale 'hard' statement that is now countered by the far more yielding 8^3–16^2. As well as the more continuous texture and falling contour, these bars feature more even rhythms (the dotted value heard in bars 1, 3, 5 and 7 has gone) and, above all, the two-note upbeat-downbeat cell x is treated differently. With the exception of bar 10, no melodic downbeat is sounded, since the note that had entered on the third beat of the previous bar is now consistently tied over the bar line. This undercuts the energetic attack given by the reiteration of the pitch from upbeat to downbeat in the first eight bars, in effect suppressing this rhythmic impulse. A more direct equivalent of the two-crotchet cell then in fact emerges over the course of the phrase: as heard in bars 10, 12,

13 and 14, this shifts the repeated notes to beats two and three (the second of which is then sustained), a gentle metrical recontextualization.

After this phrase has finished quietly on a low B major chord, E minor is finally established in what follows, and both tied ('suppressed') and original forms of *x* are heard in the melodic line. After a pause in bar 24, *x* re-emerges in its most naked state, played in matching octaves by both hands as it rises up in 'empty' intervals of a fourth and a fifth that outline a mode-less tonic of E. However, the second note of the cell is now held for longer, creating a crotchet–minim rhythm. This passage mediates between the two affective typologies presented thus far: it marries the hard, downbeat-oriented version of *x* with the consistently soft dynamics of bars 9–16 (now in fact *pianissimo*), as well as the longer duration they apply to the second note, which is itself a kind of softening. The mysterious effect of the open intervals is swept away on the third beat of bar 28 as *x* returns to its original form and affect: full chords on upbeat and downbeat, with a quaver rest in between, and sudden loud dynamics. This is considerably more assertive than the original version, since *x* here plays an interrupting, not to say confrontational, role. The chords are much higher in register than they were at the outset, and they are succeeded by a flamboyant falling scale that is in turn followed by a version of *x* that retains its rhythm but not the repeated-note contour. In fact, bars 28^3–32^2 act like a heightened version of the first two-bar unit, with the descending scale representing a lavish expansion of the falling-third shape of bar 1; thus the relatively contained aggression of the first two-bar unit is now more overt. This complete unit is then reiterated in sequence, creating a 7-10 linear intervallic pattern that is comparable to the 5–10 sequence that energized the opening statement.

A further sequential repetition follows, beginning on a surprising B♭. If in that sense this third version continues the process, in every other way it counters the super-assertive embodiments of the main material that we have just witnessed. This one is abruptly *piano*, there is no quaver rest between upbeat and downbeat, the linear intervallic pattern as such is abandoned (the bass joins in with the upper voice's B♭), and the right hand's falling scale (now marked with a slur) is a little slower and covers a narrower range. This melts into a series of imitative entries of the crotchet–minim version of cell *x*, a sort of stretto effect as the texture builds up from one to four voices, and this suddenly thickens to seven parts to confirm the enharmonic reinterpretation of the B♭ as A♯, which forms the root of a diminished seventh on the leading note to B minor. The build-up of this chord through successively higher notes of the diminished harmony echoes the bare rising E 'arpeggiation' heard from bar 24^3, and indeed the fact that the fifth entry of x is suddenly chordally fuller exactly matches the sequence of events from that point.

This material guides us into a root-position B minor together with a *forte* dynamic, and a thumping repeated-quaver accompaniment enters, altogether giving the feeling that momentum is finally being achieved after so many short-lived, contrasting gestures. From bar 47 this takes us into rising chromatic lines in both outer parts and a 6-6 linear intervallic pattern, with the right hand playing pairs of notes in the rhythm [♪ ♪ ♪ ♪]. There is no note repetition here, but given the two-note duration of this figure, occurring on successive beats of the bar, it can readily be understood as a version of cell x. However, the placement has shifted, as the cells now occupy the first and second beats of the 3/4 bar, meaning that the accentual weight has now been reversed, with the stress falling on the first of the two notes. Hatten also notes the derivation of bars 47 ff. from the opening gesture, which he defines as 'two sound events in an upbeat-downbeat, short-long, and released-held articulatory configuration'[23] – what I have encapsulated as cell x.

The rising sequence culminates in dramatically declaimed F♯ minor-ninth chords that take us to a second subject in B minor, and a return to the tied-note version of cell x, though this now starts on the second beat of the bar and lasts a full three crotchets (bars 55–58). Through this further permutation in a short space of time Beethoven reminds us that the versatility of utterance on which this interactive style of music is based can include a flexible handling of accentual weight; once more, even the seemingly smallest details of diction may form a focus of interest. More specifically, the melodic line is based on falling 'bare' intervals ($f\sharp^3$ to b^2 to $f\sharp^2$ to b^1) and so is a mirror image of what we heard at the start of the transition (bars 24–28). But what was there mysterious and uncertain now sounds lyrically fluent. In the decorated reiteration of this phrase (forming part of a parallel period) a further variant of x is arguably heard: the grouping weakens this, but note how from bars 61^3 to 62^1, for instance, we hear a repeated F♯, but with both notes now heard off the beat, as quavers.

The codetta from bar 67 returns us to a more direct, compact form of exchange, an assertive rising scale in octaves giving way to a melody supported chordally, at a *subito piano* level after a *sforzando*. As part of this, x returns in its original rhythmic disposition, anacrusis to downbeat,

---

[23] Hatten, *Interpreting Musical Gestures*, p. 178.

but in its softer tied guise, joined to a minim so that the initial note lasts three beats altogether. Thus we hear yet another way of delivering the movement's basic cell, and a new affect, as x turns into a lamenting suspension. After this four-bar unit has been symmetrically repeated, followed by a silence, the tied form of x is repeated as an isolated fragment, though now over a tonic chord. A further repetition sees a stepwise rise on the third beat of bar 78, rather than a stepwise fall, and leads to a V-i close in B minor, which chord is softly played three times on the downbeats of bars 79–81 – another form of note repetition, and a kind of augmented, rhythmically 'neutral' version of x.

These three *pianissimo* B minor crotchet chords are immediately echoed by a single *pianissimo* dotted-minim b^1 that is also played three times, which forms a smooth link into the central section of the movement. This contrast in itself – crisp and detached versus sustained – encapsulates the argument we have been party to, even though the dynamics are now uniformly soft. The interplay of the rough and the smooth, in association with our two basic forms of x, is sustained through the rest of the movement, before a kind of liquidation occurs near the very end. The opening material returns from the upbeat to bar 232, but the earlier marked differences between two-bar segments are flattened out as the whole is performed *pianissimo* and *ritardando*, and in fact the phrase peters out into silence before the fourth limb can even be heard. While this might suggest a rapprochement of the two main forces that have driven the movement, it does not sound much like it, especially when this halting rendition of the opening gambit is succeeded by a verbatim return of the passage first heard at bars 16^3–24^2. This represents a play with formal function: while the passage had already acted as an ending, this was an internal one within the exposition. When it is here rankshifted so as to end the entire movement, the effect is disconcerting. Thus the ending hangs in the air, with the outcome of the basic dualism of rhythm and gesture unclear. Once again here, we may wish to conclude that the process of discussion is more fundamental than arriving at any firm agreement. Along similar lines, rather than emphasizing the motivic-cellular unity of this movement, we might instead place more weight on the sheer versatility of musical behaviour: the varied forms of cell x suggest a ready ability to adapt to changing circumstances. By thus placing the emphasis on the behavioural capacities of his music, as viewed through these movements from his piano sonatas, we may be able to appreciate the extent to which Beethoven continues to maintain an interactive, sociable musical style.

3 | Beethoven's Unfinished Symphonies

BARRY COOPER

Approaching the Unfinished Symphonies

Beethoven's symphonies form such an important part of our musical heritage that any he began but did not complete deserve detailed attention. They are, however, scattered in so many different sources that locating them all has proved challenging. In 1875 Gustav Nottebohm, having studied a large number of Beethoven's sketchbooks, made the following claim: 'Had Beethoven written as many symphonies as were begun in the sketchbooks, we would possess at least fifty of them.'[1] The wording was rephrased when the article reappeared posthumously in 1887, omitting 'in the sketchbooks',[2] perhaps in recognition that some of the sketches might have been on loose leaves rather than in actual sketchbooks; but the suggestion that there were at least fifty remained unchanged. Nottebohm's comment that 'we would possess' these sketches implies that he discounted any lost manuscripts, but he was presumably including even short sketches of only a few bars – in other words, symphonies barely begun – provided they were sufficiently different from other symphonies, finished or unfinished. Thus he estimated there were over forty unfinished symphonies; but with so many thousands of sketch pages surviving, it is hardly surprising that this figure has never been either refuted or confirmed.

Thus it is high time, over 140 years after Nottebohm's initial estimate, to establish whether it is reliable. A few of the unfinished symphonies have been discussed fairly extensively. The earliest, in the so-called Kafka Sketchbook,[3] is known as Hess 298, since Willy Hess considered it sufficiently substantial to be included in his list of works not published in the

---

[1] Gustav Nottebohm, 'Sechs Skizzenhefte aus den Jahren 1825 und 1826', *Musikalisches Wochenblatt*, 6 (27 August 1875), pp. 425–30, at p. 429: 'Hätte Beethoven so viel Symphonien geschrieben, als in der Skizzenbüchern angefangen wurden, so besässen wir ihrer wenigtens fünfzig.'

[2] Gustav Nottebohm, *Zweite Beethoveniana* (Leipzig, 1887), pp. 12–13.

[3] GB-Lbl, Add. MS 29801; see Joseph Kerman (ed.), *Ludwig van Beethoven: Autograph Miscellany from 1786 to 1799 ... (The 'Kafka Sketchbook')*, 2 vols. (London, 1970).

old *Gesamtausgabe*.[4] A batch of sketches distantly related to the *Eroica* Symphony has been examined in detail by Lewis Lockwood, who has recently dubbed this work as *Ur-Eroica*,[5] perhaps by analogy with Goethe's *Urfaust*. Some D minor symphony sketches of 1812 were regarded by Nottebohm as 'prophetic' of No. 9, a view echoed by others such as Michael Broyles and William Kinderman,[6] and they have been explored by Peter Cahn and Erica Buurman.[7] A verbal sketch for a new symphony in 1818, beginning 'Adagio cantique', was first noted by Nottebohm and has been discussed in several recent biographies.[8] Two other unfinished symphonies were sketched so extensively, one from before No. 1 and one from after No. 9, that they have become known as No. 0 and No. 10, as indicated in the title of a book published by the Beethoven-Haus, which translates as *From No. 0 to No. 10: Ways to Beethoven's Symphonies*.[9] A few others have been discussed briefly by Buurman,[10] but many have only ever been mentioned in passing or even overlooked altogether.

The first attempt to produce an inventory of them was made only in 2015, when Lockwood published a 'provisional list' of 'symphonic concept sketches and movement plans'.[11] This list includes numerous abandoned symphonies, plus the early batch of sketches related to the *Eroica*, but also very early sketches for each of the last five completed symphonies (not, however, Nos. 1 and 4, since their sketches are largely lost; and not No. 2, since the earliest known sketches for this are relatively advanced).[12] A few

---

[4] Willy Hess, *Verzeichnis der nicht in der Gesamtausgabe veröffentlichten Werke Ludwig van Beethovens* (Wiesbaden, 1957); revised as James F. Green, *The New Hess Catalog of Beethoven's Works* (West Newbury, 2003).

[5] Lewis Lockwood, 'Beethoven's Earliest Sketches for the *Eroica* Symphony', *The Musical Quarterly*, 67/4 (1981), pp. 457–78; Lewis Lockwood, *Beethoven's Symphonies: An Artistic Vision* (New York, 2015), pp. 59–61.

[6] Nottebohm, *Zweite Beethoveniana*, p. 111; Michael Broyles, *Beethoven: The Emergence and Evolution of Beethoven's Heroic Style* (New York, 1987), p. 235; William Kinderman, *Beethoven* (Oxford, 1995), p. 265.

[7] Peter Cahn, 'Beethovens Entwürfe einer d-moll Symphonie von 1812', *Musiktheorie*, 20/5 (2005), pp. 123–9; Erica Buurman, 'Beethoven's Compositional Approach to Multi-Movement Structures in His Instrumental Works' (PhD thesis, University of Manchester, 2013), pp. 163–6.

[8] Nottebohm, *Zweite Beethoveniana*, p. 163. See also, for example, Kinderman, *Beethoven*, p. 265; Barry Cooper, *Beethoven* (Oxford, 2000), p. 265 (2nd ed., New York, 2008, p. 285); Lewis Lockwood, *Beethoven: The Music and the Life* (New York, 2003), p. 425.

[9] Michael Ladenburger and Bernhard R. Appel (eds.), *Von der Nullten bis zur Zehnten: Wege zu Beethovens Symphonien* (Bonn, 2008).

[10] Buurman, 'Beethoven's Compositional Approach'.

[11] Lockwood, *Beethoven's Symphonies*, pp. 231–4.

[12] The earliest sketches are in Landsberg 7, page 38; see Karl Lothar Mikulicz (ed.), *Ein Notierungsbuch von Beethoven aus dem Besitz der Preussischer Staatsbibliothek zu Berlin* (Leipzig, 1927).

early sketches for individual movements for other symphonies are included as well, such as a G major Andante that was considered for the Second Symphony. So too are a few unlabelled sketches that may be for a different genre. When all these extra items are discounted, there are only twenty-two items in Lockwood's list that seem clearly to represent independent unfinished symphonies. Thus either his list has omitted several items or Nottebohm has overstated the total number.

Obtaining a more accurate total than Nottebohm's rough estimate or Lockwood's provisional list is a legitimate aim. The precise figure, however, is less important than what these sketches show. How closely do they relate to the completed symphonies, or to each other? Do any of them suggest unusual structures, keys or rhythmic/melodic qualities? Many are very short, but what proportion of them show more than just the opening, and which ones are the most substantial? Which ones have been least explored? Apart from those noted above, were there any others that were sketched extensively but then abandoned, as happened with a Triple Concerto in D of 1802 and a Sixth Piano Concerto of 1815?[13]

Criteria

Establishing definitive criteria for what counts as an unfinished symphony amongst Beethoven's sketches is not easy, although the main criteria are self-evident. One problem is that Beethoven sketched many disembodied themes, some of which may have been planned as the beginnings of symphonies. Thus there needs to be convincing evidence that any such theme was intended for a symphony, rather than some other genre, before it can qualify. For example, there are two sketches in Landsberg 5 that Clemens Brenneis has suggested may be symphonic.[14] These are included as a single item in Lockwood's list, but neither work has any instrumental indications or distinctively orchestral textures, and it is unclear how many of the 'movements' in the first set of sketches actually belong together. In

[13] On the triple concerto, see Richard Kramer, 'An Unfinished Concertante of 1802', *Beethoven Studies 2*, ed. Alan Tyson (London, 1977), pp. 33–65; on the piano concerto, see Nicholas Cook, 'Beethoven's Unfinished Piano Concerto: A Case of Double Vision?', *Journal of the American Musicological Society*, 42/2 (1989), pp. 338–74.

[14] Clemens Brenneis (ed.), *Ludwig van Beethoven, Ein Skizzenbuch aus dem Jahre 1809 (Landsberg 5)*, vol. 2 (Bonn, 1992–93), pp. 35–6. All sketchbooks will be referred to here by the name used in Douglas Johnson, Alan Tyson and Robert Winter, *The Beethoven Sketchbooks: History, Reconstruction, Inventory*, ed. Douglas Johnson (Oxford, 1985).

order to qualify as a symphony sketch, there needs to be either a heading such as 'Sinfonia' or 'Sinfonie', or else a clear indication of a multi-movement orchestral work without a solo part. This latter situation rarely arises except in sketches for completed symphonies.

The second criterion is that the sketch must be substantially different from other known sketches for either finished or unfinished symphonies, in order to count separately. There is potentially a grey area here, however, where connections are tenuous but clearly evident. Judgement has to be made about their similarity to other symphonic sketches, and for present purposes a sketch will be counted as a separate item only if it is deemed to have sufficiently little in common with other sketches. An important element here is the proximity between two sketches. The sketch for Hess 298 begins with the same six notes as appear as notes 2–7 of the main theme of the third movement of the Fifth Symphony (though at a different octave), and both movements are in C minor and 3/4. Had Hess 298 appeared amongst other sketches for the Fifth Symphony, therefore, it could not be considered as a separate unfinished symphony; but as it appeared nearly twenty years earlier it can legitimately be regarded as unrelated. On the other hand, when Beethoven was starting to work on Symphony No. 0 he drafted several themes on adjacent pages, all in C major. These could be regarded as separate unfinished symphonies, but it seems preferable to regard them as alternative beginnings for what is essentially one symphony. Again, then, there is potentiality for grey areas that could result in a different total number. Other individual cases will be discussed below.

A third issue is the question of later movements. Abandoned ideas for middle or final movements are to be discounted if a symphony was already in progress, or a first-movement sketch had been drafted shortly before the sketch for a later movement, since it can be assumed that the two would belong together. Thus the abandoned Andante for the Second Symphony, mentioned above, will be discounted, since the first movement had already been begun. Nor can one include an abandoned slow movement for the Eighth Symphony, sketched briefly in the Petter Sketchbook[15] and differing significantly from the scherzando movement that replaced it. A 'Sinfonia' in E, sketched in the Kafka Sketchbook (folio 81v), will also be discounted. It is clearly a slow movement and therefore presumably belongs with the first movement of No. 0 in C, sketched elsewhere around

---

[15] D-BNba, HCB Mh 59, ff. 49r–52r.

the same time. It cannot be regarded as an independent symphony, though Lockwood lists it separately. Since Beethoven nearly always sketched his movements in chronological order, any idea for a new symphony would normally be for the slow introduction or opening allegro, though there could be ideas for later movements too. A sketch for a later movement without any indication of what might come before it, however, is by no means impossible.

Using these criteria, a list of thirty-three unfinished symphonies emerges, numbered as U1 to U33 in the Appendix (pp. 76–81), which indicates their sources. Eleven are not in Lockwood's list and have rarely if ever been mentioned in the literature. The Appendix also includes a few sketches that might be counted as separate unfinished symphonies but do not quite fulfil the criteria outlined above. The list is still provisional in that more such sketches might yet be found, but it is the result of a comprehensive search. Assessment of these sketches is best done in small chronological groups that can be related to the completed symphonies, as follows.

Before the First Symphony

As mentioned above, the earliest known Beethoven sketch for a symphony is Hess 298, a 'Sinfonia' in C minor, which anticipates some motivic, tonal and emotional characteristics of the Fifth Symphony. It was first noted by Nottebohm,[16] and consists of a fully written-out two-stave score of 111 bars, reaching nearly the end of the exposition. Two variant sketches appear on the verso of the leaf. The draft (but not the variants) was first published by Fritz Stein.[17] A better transcription, with the variants, was published by Joseph Kerman in 1970,[18] and Douglas Johnson has dated the manuscript to 1786–90, on the basis of Beethoven's handwriting.[19] Lockwood has proposed 1788,[20] which seems the most likely date. As Nottebohm pointed out, the opening theme also appears, in E flat minor, in Beethoven's Piano Quartet, WoO 36 No. 1. After bar 7, however, the two works differ completely, and the symphony draft uses the relative major for

---

[16] Nottebohm, *Zweite Beethoveniana*, p. 567.

[17] Fritz Stein, 'Eine unbekannte Jugendsymphonie Beethovens?', *Sammelbände der Internationalen Musikgesellschaft*, 13 (1911–12), pp. 127–72, at pp. 131–2.

[18] Kerman (ed.), *Autograph Miscellany*, vol. 2, pp. 175–6.

[19] Douglas Johnson, *Beethoven's Early Sketches in the 'Fischhof' Miscellany: Berlin Autograph 28*, vol. 1 (Ann Arbor, 1980), p. 222.

[20] Lockwood, *Beethoven's Symphonies*, p. 26.

its secondary key area whereas the quartet uses the dominant. The quartet was an earlier work, dating from around 1785, and had evidently been discarded by the time Beethoven came to borrow the theme for the symphony draft. The draft has been mentioned by several recent writers,[21] but perhaps the most penetrating discussion is by Michael Broyles, who draws attention to important differences between it and the relevant movement in the quartet, including the use of overlapping phrases, absence of pianistic figuration and less complex rhythms. All these features are more characteristic of symphonies than chamber music with piano.[22] Broyles also notes that the draft continues to the foot of the page (folio 70r) and therefore may have continued elsewhere. What has not previously been noticed, however, is that the draft begins on what appears to have been originally a verso, and so could have continued on to an opposite page now lost, which would form the other half of the bifolio. A suggestion that Beethoven could have intended the symphony as a memorial to his mother, who died on 17 July 1787,[23] is possibly supported by an inscription on the present verso, 'dir folgen meine Thränen' ('my tears follow you').

Beethoven's next known attempt at starting a new symphony (U2) probably dates from about October 1790, for the leaf also includes sketches for the Leopold Cantata (WoO 88) of that date. Lockwood describes it briefly as a 'curious and humdrum' sketch,[24] but it is otherwise scarcely mentioned in the literature. It is indeed rather unsophisticated, like the preliminary sketches for many Beethoven works, but it contains several interesting features. The sketch is in C major, anticipating Symphony No. 1, and consists of an introductory Allegretto and ensuing Presto. This opening Allegretto, which consists of a substantial two-stave draft of fifty-six bars (including marked repetitions), is unusual, for it functions as a slow introduction despite its relatively fast tempo marking. Its five-bar opening phrase ends on a strange D flat, presaging some unexpected tonal excursions. The indication of wind instruments ('blasende In.') in bar 12 anticipates the prominent use of wind at the start of the First Symphony, and after a brief reprise of the opening theme the music suddenly

---

[21] See, for example, David Wyn Jones, *The Symphony in Beethoven's Vienna* (Cambridge, 2006), pp. 155–6, which notes the influence of *Sturm und Drang* style and Beethoven's unusually varied phrase patterns; and Barry Cooper, *Beethoven*, pp. 23–4 (2nd ed., pp. 24–5), which comments on the intensity and ingenuity of Beethoven's motivic development.

[22] Broyles, *Beethoven*, pp. 40–3.   [23] Cooper, *Beethoven*, p. 23 (2nd ed., p. 24).

[24] Lockwood, *Beethoven's Symphonies*, p. 27; he does not comment on the unusual tonal elements, nor mention the Presto that follows the Allegretto.

shifts to C minor in bar 28, before working dominant-wards to G minor, D minor, A minor and the dominant of A minor. The Allegretto introduction thus finishes on an E major chord, followed immediately by contrasting C major at the start of the Presto. Preparing for the fast section with the dominant of the relative minor is not unknown elsewhere: Haydn does something similar in Symphonies Nos. 99 and 103, but these postdate Beethoven's sketch. Moreover, Beethoven's route to the chord is uncommonly circuitous and has no obvious parallels in his later music.

The following Presto, not mentioned by Lockwood or other writers, begins with solo horns in octaves. A seven-bar theme is followed by an unsketched passage, represented by Beethoven's characteristic 'usw' (= etc.), and then a transition dominated by rapid scales, leading to what is apparently a second subject in G major. Altogether over thirty bars of the Presto are sketched, including marked repetitions, but there is no clear motivic connection with the First Symphony or other later works. Impressive as it is, with nearly a hundred bars altogether, this composite sketch has been largely overshadowed by Hess 298 and the Symphony No. 0 that followed it.

Beethoven retained C major in this next known attempt (U3). This was a much more determined and long-lasting effort, and more sketches survive for it than for any other Beethoven work before 1798, finished or unfinished. It was begun in 1795 or earlier, and continued intermittently until at least 1797, before giving way to the actual First Symphony in 1799–1800. These sketches have been described in detail in Douglas Johnson's unpublished doctoral dissertation, but most of his description was unfortunately omitted from his published version.[25] Some of them had already been surveyed by Nottebohm and John Shedlock in the nineteenth century,[26] and Lockwood includes a short account of the work, but in general 'scholarly interest has been slight'.[27]

There is no explicit heading such as 'Sinfonia' in these sketches; but Johnson demonstrated that their location, key, date and style imply that they all relate to plans for a symphony, and he established their overall

---

[25] Douglas Johnson, 'Beethoven's Early Sketches in the "Fischhof Miscellany": Berlin Autograph 28' (PhD thesis, University of California, Berkeley, 1978), pp. 785–1037; *Beethoven's Early Sketches*, vol. 1, pp. 461–9 (incorporating pp. 785–97 of the dissertation).

[26] Nottebohm, *Zweite Beethoveniana*, pp. 228–9; J. S. Shedlock, 'Beethoven's Sketch Books', *The Musical Times*, 33 (1892), pp. 591–2.

[27] Johnson, *Beethoven's Early Sketches*, vol. 1, p. 461; see vol. 2, pp. 163–76, for transcriptions of the sketches not in Kafka. Those in Kafka are transcribed in Kerman (ed.), *Autograph Miscellany*, vol. 2, pp. 166–74.

chronology on the basis of handwriting, position and paper types.[28] There is not always any motivic connection between the different sketches, however, and it could therefore be argued that Beethoven actually made a start on at least five symphonies, for in the first five attempts at an opening (U3a–e), only the last two are somewhat related, and they are followed by different allegro material. Both these two outline the pattern C – E – A, which was preserved in later sketches,[29] and the motif also appears at the start of the first page of a full score for the symphony.[30] This is the only full score fragment that survives for any of Beethoven's unfinished symphonies, and it shows a mere twelve bars, though it continues to the end of the page, a verso, and probably continued further. How much further is uncertain, but he seems to have abandoned this score in 1796 while in Berlin, where he added sketches for the cello variations Op. 66 on the recto, and sketched material for a greatly altered opening for the symphony.[31]

For the main allegro in the first movement Beethoven again sketched several themes so different that they could be regarded as ideas for different works. The first five, which are situated after the five slow introductions represented by U3a–e, have very little in common with each other, or with any of Beethoven's later works, in terms of actual motivic outline.[32] Only the sixth, which is first sketched with a version of U3a before reappearing in several later sketches, relates directly to later work (see Example 3.1), for it was taken up as the basis for the main theme of the finale of the First Symphony in 1799–1800, as was noted by Nottebohm.[33] Although these themes could have formed the basis for any of six symphonies, one cannot

Example 3.1 Kafka, f. 159r

[28] Johnson, *Beethoven's Early Sketches*, vol. 1, pp. 461–9. See also Johnson, 'Beethoven's Early Sketches', p. 823.

[29] It is possible that U3d preceded U3c, as Johnson proposes, on the grounds that the harmony has 'broader, more colorful strokes' ('Beethoven's Early Sketches', p. 803). Here we follow the order proposed by Kerman (*Autograph Miscellany*, vol. 2, pp. 166–7), where U3d and U3e are motivically related.

[30] Kafka, f. 71v; transcribed in Kerman (ed.), *Autograph Miscellany*, vol. 2, p. 169.

[31] Johnson, *Beethoven's Early Sketches*, vol. 1. pp. 464–8; vol. 2, pp. 163–4.

[32] They appear in Kafka, ff. 127v/12, 127v/15, 128r/15, 158v/10, 128v/8; see Kerman (ed.), *Autograph Miscellany*, pp. 166–8.

[33] Nottebohm, *Zweite Beethoveniana*, p. 228.

Example 3.2 Kafka, f. 127v

Example 3.3 Symphony No. 1, 1st movement, bars 13–17

imagine Beethoven developing all six. They are there to establish the character of the Allegro theme, rather than its actual motivic shape,[34] and the first five share certain rhythmic qualities with each other, including explicit or implied use of common time, and mainly crotchet movement. Thus it seems more legitimate to regard them as six attempts at the same symphony. Moreover, their character and certain aspects of their rhythmic qualities were actually preserved in the Allegro of the First Symphony. Any attempt at genetic criticism for this symphony, where it is seen in relation to other works, should take into account not only the late symphonies of Haydn and Mozart, as is often done,[35] but also more specifically these five themes. If the second of them, for example, is compared with the Allegro theme of the First Symphony, conspicuous similarities are apparent (Examples 3.2 and 3.3). Both emphasize the tonic on the first beat of the first two bars, through repetition of the opening gesture, with a dotted-rhythm upbeat, and both use a parade of crotchets before the end of the phrase; the similarity of gesture is even more apparent if the third bar in Example 3.3, which looks suspiciously like a late insertion, is omitted. Thus all these abandoned symphony sketches could be regarded as preliminary work on the First Symphony, as well as being ideas that could have been used independently.

Later sketches for the main Allegro show work on the rest of the exposition and part of the coda, but relatively little on the development and recapitulation. Nevertheless, Beethoven was already considering what three movements would follow. All three are represented more than once

---

[34] Johnson, 'Beethoven's Early Sketches', p. 817.

[35] See, for example, Broyles, *Beethoven*, pp. 64–5; Lockwood, *Beethoven's Symphonies*, pp. 23–5; although Lockwood goes on to mention these sketches in general, he does not draw any link to the theme of the symphony's first movement. On genetic criticism that brings earlier material to bear on later works, see for example, William Kinderman, 'Beyond the Text: Genetic Criticism and Beethoven's Creative Process', *Acta Musicologica*, 81/1 (2009), pp. 99–122, esp. pp. 116–19.

amongst the sketches of 1795–97, and Johnson quotes eight concept sketches that may well have been intended as possible slow-movement themes.[36] In addition, the 'Sinfonia' in E mentioned earlier is an almost complete draft for a slow movement,[37] made in 1796 on paper Beethoven evidently obtained in Berlin. It was later marked to be transposed to F, and although it shows no direct motivic connection to later symphonies, the idea of changing a slow movement from E to F within a C major work re-emerged in early sketches for the 'Waldstein' Sonata.[38] The draft could easily have been expanded into a complete movement in rondo form, with the aid of two episodes sketched briefly on the opposite page. Instead, Beethoven jotted down a new adagio theme as part of a synopsis of themes for the last three movements of the symphony – perhaps the earliest such synopsis sketch that has come down to us.[39] This adagio theme, too, was abandoned, but a complete minuet draft and almost complete trio can be found in sketches from late 1796 or 1797, after Beethoven had returned to Vienna.[40]

Thus the main stumbling block to completing the symphony appears to have been the finale. Beethoven had sketched at least nine possible finale themes, culminating in the one in the synopsis sketch. Johnson lists four of them and transcribes two more, marked 'anstatt leztes allegro' ('instead of the last allegro') and 'zulezt presto' ('for the final presto').[41] Three more themes are in the right key, have a finale-like character, and are situated close to one or more of the other movements of the work: Kafka folios 128r, 56v, 57r. Moreover, since Beethoven was still working on the minuet after returning to Vienna in 1796, one might expect to find occasional finale sketches from 1796–97. One that has been identified that fulfils all the necessary criteria is on Kafka, folio 43r.[42] It is situated on the same page as an unfinished song, recently identified as the long-lost 'Ich wiege dich in meinem Arm',[43] and other sketches for the same song appear on folio 67v, where is found a sketch headed 'andante zur sinfonie', in the

---

[36] Johnson, *Beethoven's Early Sketches*, vol. 2, pp. 174–5. Johnson's dissertation, however, devotes relatively little space to the later movements ('Beethoven's Early Sketches', pp. 896–912).

[37] Transcribed in Kerman (ed.), *Autograph Miscellany*, vol. 2, p. 176.

[38] See Lewis Lockwood and Alan Gosman (eds.), *Beethoven's 'Eroica' Sketchbook*, vol. 1 (Urbana, Chicago, and Springfield, 2013), p. 69.

[39] Fischhof, f. 16v; see Buurman, 'Beethoven's Compositional Approach', pp. 63–4.

[40] Kafka, f. 59r; see Kerman (ed.), *Autograph Miscellany*, vol. 2, p. 174.

[41] Johnson, *Beethoven's Early Sketches*, vol. 1, p. 463; vol. 2, p. 176.

[42] See Cooper, *Beethoven*, p. 69 (2nd ed., p. 75).

[43] See Mark S. Zimmer, '*Liebe*: The Discovery and Identification of a Beethoven Song Lost since 1822', *The Musical Times*, 157/1937 (Winter 2016), pp. 13–34.

Example 3.4 Kafka, f. 43r

unlikely key of B minor. Both leaves have the same paper type and probably date from around the end of 1797.[44] The putative finale sketch shows a lively 2/4 theme, with the second phrase beginning the same as the first (see Example 3.4), as in the finale of the First Symphony, and a planned rondo form with episodes in A minor and C minor. Thus Beethoven was still working on his symphony around late 1797, and still struggling with both slow movement and finale.

The leisurely pace of progress and the repeated attempts to work on this symphony, even after returning to Vienna, indicate that Beethoven did not abandon it for practical reasons related to possible performance in either Prague or Berlin, as has been suggested.[45] There is no evidence of any pressing deadline for such a performance, such as occurred with his Piano Concerto in C in 1795, where he was hurrying to complete the finale two days before the premiere.[46] He evidently remained dissatisfied with his ideas for the slow movement and finale, and perhaps the other movements, until around the end of 1799, when he decided the ideal finale theme was one derived from what he had originally sketched for the first movement of his projected symphony (Example 3.1). Thus he began again, using almost entirely new material, and it is preferable to think of this as a separate work rather than a completion of his previous sketches.

Work on the First Symphony was not begun, however, until he had drafted a synopsis for an entirely different symphony in C (U4) on folio 46r of the Fischhof Miscellany, a leaf that can be dated to around early 1798.[47] This synopsis sketch is not mentioned by other commentators, although its heading, 'Sinfonie mit einem adagio worin der Zweifel ausgedruckt ist' ('Symphony with an Adagio in which doubt is expressed') is transcribed by Hans-Günter Klein.[48] Only three movements are represented: a fast movement in common time (eight bars), followed by an Andante in A minor in 6/8 (four bars), and a final Presto in common time

---

[44] Johnson, *Beethoven's Early Sketches*, p. 185.   [45] Broyles, *Beethoven*, p. 63.

[46] This was reported by Franz Wegeler: see Franz Wegeler and Ferdinand Ries, *Remembering Beethoven*, trans. Frederick Noonan (Arlington, 1987), p. 38.

[47] Johnson, *Beethoven's Early Sketches*, vol. 1, pp. 190 and 344–5.

[48] Hans-Günter Klein, *Ludwig van Beethoven: Autographe und Abschriften: Katalog* (Berlin, 1975), p. 106.

(sixteen bars). Although new three-movement symphonies were not unknown in Vienna at this time,[49] Beethoven probably envisaged four movements, as was normal. There are other cases where an early set of sketches omits the minuet/scherzo movement, such as one for his Seventh Symphony (Petter Sketchbook, f. 5r).[50] The reason is probably that, as with sketches for No. 0, he was initially more concerned with establishing character than precise motivic details. Whereas the characters of outer movements and slow movement vary greatly from one work to another, that of the minuet/scherzo is much more limited and consistent, and therefore could be assumed in any initial synopsis. The question of character is certainly to the fore in the sketch under consideration, for it is specifically mentioned in the heading. It seems that Beethoven was using the word 'adagio' to mean slow movement, and then indicated that this particular one was actually an Andante. The somewhat tentative nature of the Andante theme, with its soft staccatos and sudden sforzandos, could easily be perceived as expressing doubt or hesitancy, as in the heading. It does not resemble any of his other symphonic slow movements, though it might recall that of the third 'Razumovsky' quartet (another Andante in A minor and 6/8). The following Presto uses regular four-bar phrases and tonic/dominant harmony, suggesting renewed confidence that erases previous doubts. This is his first known symphony sketch to use an explicit 'characteristic' element – an idea he returned to repeatedly in later years. There are, however, no other conspicuous links between this sketch and later symphonies.

Between Nos. 1 and 5

After the premiere of his First Symphony in April 1800 Beethoven moved on to sketches for his Second in the winter of 1800–01, but before he had progressed significantly beyond the first movement he interrupted work to compose his ballet *The Creatures of Prometheus*. Curiously, however, amongst the sketches for this is one for a new symphony in C (U5), in Landsberg 7.[51] The key is a surprising choice, even to follow No. 2 in D, since he had already written one symphony in C (although Nos. 6 and 8 share the same key with only a single symphony between them). The sketch could not have been written before 1800 on a leaf subsequently

[49] See Buurman, 'Beethoven's Compositional Approach', pp. 39–40.
[50] Transcribed in ibid., p. 159.   [51] See Mikulicz (ed.), *Notierungsbuch*, p. 110.

integrated into Landsberg 7, as occasionally happened with other sketches,[52] for the sketch appears beneath some for *Prometheus*. Another possibility is that it was intended as a possible 'sinfonia' within the ballet, like the 'Siegessinfonie' in the music for *Egmont* (1810). In this case it could be an early idea for Nos. 7, 8 or 9 in the ballet, for its opening motif resembles that of No. 7, while No. 9 appears in adjacent sketches. The sketch in question, however, does not unfold in the same way as these numbers, but more resembles an idea for an independent symphony. Its first three bars are detached spatially from a twenty-bar continuation, and Karl Mikulicz regards them as two separate sketches,[53] but the continuation seems to represent a transition in G minor, following the dynamic opening theme after an unspecified number of bars before linking into a more lyrical secondary theme in G major (thus recalling the tonal direction of the transition in the C major piano sonata, Op. 2 No. 3). Nothing like this occurs in this part of the ballet or sketches for it.

No further sketches for possible symphonies are known until the plan for an E flat symphony mentioned earlier (U6), which dates from autumn 1802 – probably just after Beethoven had returned from his ill-fated stay in Heiligenstadt. The bold plan might even represent part of his response to the turmoil expressed in his Heiligenstadt Testament of 6 and 10 October 1802. The relevant sketches were first connected to the *Eroica* by Nathan Fishman in his edition of the Wielhorsky Sketchbook, and have been much discussed since, especially by Lockwood.[54] There are extended sketches for the first three movements but none for the finale, and it is widely accepted that Beethoven had decided from the outset that he would reuse for the finale a theme from *Prometheus* that he had just been using for a set of piano variations (Op. 35). Thus he needed to sketch only the first three movements at this stage. Several writers have drawn links between the batch of sketches and the finished work.[55] For example, Lockwood observes that one version of the main first-movement theme in the 'Ur-Eroica' uses the notes from the *Basso del tema* of the finale (which also permeates some other sketches less directly).[56] In addition, one short passage in one exposition draft (Example 3.5) bears a strong resemblance

---

[52] Johnson, *Beethoven's Early Sketches*, vol. 1, pp. 190–1.

[53] Mikulicz (ed.), *Notierungsbuch*, 'Einleitung', p. 30.

[54] Nathan L. Fishman (ed.), *Kniga eskizov Beethovena za 1802–1803 gody*, 3 vols. (Moscow, 1962); Lockwood, 'Beethoven's Earliest Sketches'; Lockwood, *Beethoven's Symphonies*, pp. 59–62. The sketches are on pp. 44–5 of the Wielhorsky Sketchbook.

[55] See Buurman, 'Beethoven's Compositional Approach', pp. 107–11.

[56] Lockwood, 'Beethoven's Earliest Sketches', pp. 467–8.

Example 3.5 Wielhorsky, p. 44

to bars 144–151 of the *Eroica*. In general, however, the sketches have so little direct melodic connection with the finished work as to represent a largely different symphony, and thus qualify for inclusion amongst the unfinished ones. Rather than emphasizing the connections here, therefore, it is worth highlighting some of the striking features that never found their way into later works.

The set of sketches includes an extended slow introduction, unlike the *Eroica*: thirteen bars are shown, with more implied by an 'etc.' The other three of Beethoven's first four symphonies all have a slow introduction, as do most of Haydn's and several of Mozart's late symphonies, and the sketch takes after Haydn's 'Drum Roll' Symphony in the same key by beginning in the bass clef. None of Beethoven's completed symphonic slow introductions begins in the bass clef, though several of his later unfinished symphonies do, as will be seen. The second movement is a gentle, lyrical 6/8 Adagio in C major – a key relationship already used by Beethoven in his Piano Sonata Op. 7. Lockwood points out the thematic resemblance to the slow movement of the String Quartet Op. 135,[57] but omits to note that the accentuation is different: the figure that appears in the weakly accented bar 2 in the sketch appears in the strong bar 3 in the quartet, giving a very different effect.

The following Menuetto is marked 'serioso', a term Beethoven rarely used elsewhere.[58] Almost as rare is his use of three consecutive triple- or compound-time movements in a multi-movement instrumental work.[59] The term 'serioso' implies a slower speed than might be expected, and certainly slower than the 3/4 first movement. This is confirmed in the equally serious Trio section in G minor, where rushing semiquavers preclude a speed any faster than that of the stately Tempo di Menuetto in his Eighth Symphony.

---

[57] Ibid., p. 470.

[58] It appears in his String Quartet, Op. 95, and Var. 6 of the Diabelli Variations; see Kurt von Fischer, '"Never to be Performed in Public": Zu Beethovens Streichquartett op. 95', *Beethoven Jahrbuch*, 9 (1973–77), pp. 87–96, at p. 87.

[59] The only other cases are Op. 7, Op. 18 No. 1, Op. 29, Op. 127 and (if one counts the finale introduction) Op. 135.

There is nothing conspicuously heroic here – no enlarged size is evident (the sketches imply an opening exposition of well under 100 bars, as opposed to over 150 in the *Eroica*). The Adagio is gentle, not portentous, and even the serious minuet with minor-key trio does not imply overall grandeur or heroism. Thus despite motivic similarities, this is no 'Heroic' Symphony (the name *Eroica*, it will be remembered, did not appear until the printed edition, long after the first performances), nor a work particu-larly suitable for a supposedly enlightened French general (Napoleon) or a commemoration of the death of General Ralph Abercromby, as alleged by Joseph von Bertolini.[60] If Beethoven was aiming for such a work from the outset, rather than just allowing it to develop that way during sketching, he had much rethinking to do in the six months or so before he began the main series of *Eroica* sketches. Nevertheless the extent of the sketching is remarkable for such a preliminary stage, and may suggest that Beethoven was aiming far higher than he achieved here. This was certainly no mere passing thought like some of his other abandoned symphonies.

After completing the *Eroica* Beethoven soon started sketching ideas that were to feed into his Fifth and Sixth Symphonies, both of which are repre-sented in his 'Eroica' Sketchbook, Landsberg 6.[61] This also contains ideas for two other symphonies that did not get off the ground. The first (U7) is headed 'lustige Sinfonia' ('merry symphony'), which as Lockwood notes contrasts neatly with the serious Fifth Symphony sketched on neighbouring pages.[62] Lockwood and Gosman unaccountably transcribe the sketch in the bass clef (which Beethoven rarely used in concept sketches without some clear sign such as a two-stave score or the clef itself), but it was surely intended in the treble clef. This places it in F major instead of A, thus foreshadowing the *Pastoral*, which portrays 'lustig' folk in the third movement. Unlike sketches on pages 64 and 96 of the sketchbook, however, there is no motivic connection with this symphony, in either melodic or rhythmic shape.

The second abandoned symphony in Landsberg 6 appears on page 177. The two bars shown as U8 are all that were sketched at this point, supported by repeated D quavers in the bass clef. Its heading 'Sinfonia in d moll' leaves no doubt about the missing key signature, and reveals that Beethoven was contemplating a minor-key symphony to follow the *Eroica*. It is puzzling,

---

[60] Carl Czerny, *On the Proper Performance of All Beethoven's Works for the Piano*, ed. Paul Badura-Skoda (Vienna, 1970), p. 13.

[61] See complete transcription in Lockwood and Gosman (eds.), *Beethoven's 'Eroica' Sketchbook*, vol. 1, part 2, pp. 80–3, 56–7.

[62] Lockwood, *Beethoven's Symphonies*, p. 82.

however, that he should consider D minor when several sketches for the Fifth Symphony in C minor appear earlier in the sketchbook, on pages 155–8. The probable explanation is that the chronology is not what it seems. Lockwood and Gosman have convincingly demonstrated that the sketches for the Fifth, which relate to its first and third movements, postdate a synopsis for three movements of this symphony found in Autograph 19e in Berlin.[63] William Meredith suggests that Beethoven had 'some sort of three-movement symphony in mind',[64] but sketches showing only three out four movements were not unusual, as noted earlier. The first two movements of this synopsis correspond to those of the final version, but the 'ultimo pezzo' ('final movement') is in C minor, in 6/8, and incorporates the D minor 'Sinfonia' from Landsberg 6, transposed down a tone.[65] Thus the probable chronology is that the D minor idea came first, before being incorporated into a possible C minor finale; sketches matching the first and third movements of the Fifth (and possible ideas for the other two movements) were then added on pages 157–8 and 155–6 respectively of Landsberg 6 (and probably in that order, since the heading 'Sinfonia' appears on page 157). The fact that they are mostly squeezed in at the foot of the relevant pages, below pre-existing sketches for *Leonore*, confirms that their apparent chronology is misleading, and that they could have been added many weeks later. The zigzag pattern of the D minor sketch later became smoothed out into a plain arpeggio to form the opening theme of the third movement of the Fifth. The prospect of a possible D minor symphony, however, must have remained at the back of Beethoven's mind until he set to work on the Ninth over a decade later. Thus the sketch can be regarded as feeding into two separate symphonies, although the connections are tenuous.

Between Nos. 6 and 7

After completing his Fifth and Sixth symphonies in 1808, Beethoven's next known attempts at beginning a new symphony occurred in 1809. The early

---

[63] Lockwood and Gosman (eds.), *Beethoven's 'Eroica' Sketchbook*, vol. 1, part 2, pp. 82–3.

[64] William Meredith, 'Forming the New from the Old: Beethoven's Use of Variation in the Fifth Symphony', *Beethoven's Compositional Process*, ed. William Kinderman (Lincoln, NE, 1991), pp. 102–21, at p. 108; his view is convincingly challenged in Buurman, 'Beethoven's Compositional Approach', p. 118.

[65] Meredith ('Forming the New', pp. 108–9) suggests this passage should be read in C major, not C minor; but in view of its D minor origins and absence of change of key signature, this theory seems untenable.

part of the year was devoted mainly to work on his Fifth Piano Concerto, but after the French invasion of Vienna in May he found himself so disrupted mentally that he was unable to concentrate on composing. In a letter dated 26 July 1809 he lamented:

We have lately been suffering really concentrated misery [zusammengedrängtes Elend] ... since 4 May I have brought into the world little coherent work, practically just a fragment here or there. The whole course of events has for me affected both body and soul.[66]

The sketchbook for this period, Landsberg 5, confirms this picture, for after coherent work on the concerto and the first movement of the *Lebewohl* Sonata (autograph dated 4 May) there are many pages consisting mainly of unrealized fragments. As mentioned above, Brenneis considered two of these to represent symphonies, describing the first as 'concept sketches for a multi-movement work (symphony?) in F minor / F major', and the second as 'symphony movement or overture in F major, with slow introduction in F minor'.[67] They are listed as U11a and U11b in the Appendix below, but there is nothing to confirm that they are not sketches for some other genre. The first consists of the start of an allegretto in F minor, followed by a 6/8 movement in F major labelled 'leztes all[egr]o' ('last allegro'). Thus it is clearly a multi-movement instrumental work but could equally be a sonata rather than a symphony. The same applies to the second group of sketches, starting with an 'Eingang Largo' ('Introduction Largo') in F minor (providing a tonal connection with the previous allegretto), followed by an allegro probably in F major, then a 'fuga' in C and later C minor. The uniformity of script suggests this group represents a single work, although the result would be a very strange structure more like a fantasia. Perhaps it is significant that the group was sketched shortly before Beethoven began work on his Piano Fantasia, Op. 77.

Three other fragments in Landsberg 5, however, are explicitly labelled as symphonies. The one on page 104 (U11) is minimal, indicating merely keynote and mode: 'A moll / Sinfonie'. None of the adjacent sketches is in A minor. The 'erstes All[egr]o einer Sinfoni[e]' on page 55 is not much more substantial – four bars in G major (U9), with tonic harmony provided for the first two. This looks like just a passing thought from a clearly disrupted mind struggling to produce anything substantial and coherent. The tentative label, 'first Allegro' of some indeterminate symphony, also suggests a chance idea rather than a definite project. By the time he reached page 87, however,

---

[66] BG, no. 392.   [67] Brenneis (ed.), *Landsberg 5*, vol. 2, pp. 35–6, 43.

Example 3.6 Landsberg 5, p. 87

around September 1809, Beethoven had regained his momentum and had sketched much of his String Quartet, Op. 74, when he noted some further ideas for a 'Sinfonia' (U10). The slow introduction is in G minor, with a bold unison figure that is repeated a semitone higher in bar 3. He seems to have been particularly drawn to this type of opening, for it appears in some form in several of his minor-key works around this period – the 'Appassionata' Sonata of 1804–06, the second 'Razumovsky' quartet of 1806 and the F minor Quartet, Op. 95, of 1810 – but not in any of his symphonies. The opening bar is answered by a short motif for viola in bar 2, and it is this motif that is developed in the later bars of the slow introduction, leading to some rather anguished chromaticism. The main Allegro provides a sharp contrast in G major, somewhat in the manner of some of Haydn's symphonies (such as Nos. 101 and 104), with a cheerful theme in rising quavers starting on the dominant (Example 3.6) and recalling the main first-movement theme of Haydn's Symphony No. 101, as well as Beethoven's own No. 0. Though initially marked *f*, Beethoven altered this to *pp*, giving a wispy effect that is continually floating upwards. This eight-bar theme is extended on the next four staves, along with an idea for developing the rising scales in a brief excursion to E minor, which prepares for an A major chord that would presumably herald a second subject in the dominant as usual. Compared with the Fifth and Sixth symphonies, therefore, this is all much more traditional, and there is no sign of later movements. Nevertheless this group of sketches extends to nearly fifty bars, including a marked repeat, and if Beethoven had developed them in his customary manner they would have yielded a symphony very different from any of the nine he completed. Its echoes of Haydn place it in the same field as Beethoven's Eighth Symphony, which is often regarded as Haydnesque, and it suggests that he was already trying to revert to a more classical style than in his previous two path-breaking symphonies.

During Nos. 7 and 8

Beethoven made no further sketches for symphonies, as far as is known, until late 1811, when he began making copious sketches for his Seventh

Symphony in the Petter Sketchbook.[68] At what stage he decided to write a set of three symphonies rather than just the one is unclear, but the plan was explicitly mentioned in his letter to Breitkopf & Härtel of late May 1812: 'I am writing three new symphonies, of which one is already finished.'[69] His claim is confirmed by his sketches, two of which are marked as the second symphony in the group (U14, U16), while two others are marked as the third (U20, U23). It has never been realized just how many abandoned symphonies were sketched during this period. Lockwood mentions only five and discusses none in detail, while Buurman, who is concerned just with those where more than one movement is sketched, assesses only three.[70] There are actually at least twelve (U12–U23). In addition, on the stave directly beneath U17 is another possible symphony sketch (U17a), headed '·/.'. Since this sign was normally used by Beethoven to denote repetition, it is likely that he was using it as a kind of ditto mark below the heading for U17, thus indicating another possible symphony. Of the twelve, nine are in the Petter Sketchbook and two others are on leaves formerly belonging to it,[71] while the remaining one (U23) is on a leaf containing sketches for the Eighth Symphony but not from the sketchbook. Ironically the Eighth Symphony, completed in October 1812, is based on none of these twelve ideas but on some sketches originally intended for a piano concerto.[72] And neither the Seventh nor the Eighth ever appears in a sketch labelled as a symphony. It is almost as if Beethoven used the label only for symphonies that he probably would not compose.[73]

The three D minor sketches can be linked to the Ninth Symphony not only by key, as Nottebohm noted (see above), but by some actual motivic similarities.[74] For example, all three D minor symphony sketches begin with a descending figure and the answering phrase begins on a B flat (see

---

[68] For dating of the Petter Sketchbook, September 1811 to December 1812, see Johnson (ed.), *The Beethoven Sketchbooks*, pp. 207–15.

[69] BG, no. 577. The 'finished' symphony was No. 7, whose autograph is dated 13 April 1812: see Johnson (ed.), *The Beethoven Sketchbooks*, p. 212.

[70] Lockwood, *Beethoven's Symphonies*, pp. 173–4, 233; Buurman, 'Beethoven's Compositional Approach', pp. 163–71. Buurman discusses the same three ideas plus one more (thus U20–U23) in 'Three Symphonies in One Year? Beethoven's Sketches of 1812', *Ad Parnassum*, 16/31 (2018), pp. 35–48.

[71] D-BNba, BH 120 and BH 119; their original position in the Petter Sketchbook is indicated in Johnson (ed.), *The Beethoven Sketchbooks*, pp. 217–18.

[72] Sieghard Brandenburg, 'Ein Skizzenbuch Beethovens aus dem Jahre 1812. Zur Chronologie des Petterschen Skizzenbuches', *Zu Beethoven: Aufsätze und Annotationen*, ed. Harry Goldschmidt (Berlin, 1979), pp. 117–48, at pp. 135–8.

[73] See Barry Cooper, *Beethoven and the Creative Process* (Oxford, 1990), p. 121.

[74] See Cahn, 'Beethovens Entwürfe'.

U14, U19, U20). Both these features recur in the opening theme of the Ninth. Thus these three sketches confirm that Beethoven had in mind the germ of an idea that was eventually to grow into the Ninth after much transmogrification. Yet D minor was not the only key considered at this stage. Three of the other sketches are in C major (U12, U16, U17), the first beginning with a rising scale from the dominant, recalling the Haydnesque allegro theme in U10 (Example 3.6). The second also suggests echoes of Haydn, for it bears the heading '2te Sinfonie leicht C', implying a light, perhaps whimsical symphony with a character similar to what was emerge in the Eighth. Though starting in C as shown, it appears to move towards F and then B flat after a few bars – a seemingly improbable progression which nevertheless anticipates the Eighth, which also moves towards the subdominant of the subdominant (bars 20–25). U17 has an energetic theme in the bass clef but is less than five bars long. It is followed by a short theme in the treble clef in 3/4, which could have been drafted as a possible second movement, though its precise role is unclear.

The equally brief U15 is in B flat and bears no obvious connection to any of Beethoven's other symphonies. U18 is also in B flat but with a slow introduction in G minor, where the prominent E flat at the start of the second phrase recalls those prominent B flats in the D minor sketches. The B flat section of eight bars bears no connection with the Eighth Symphony beyond its 3/4 time signature. However, the use of two different keynotes, forming relative major and minor, is a novel idea, the first sign of a plan resurrected ten years later in the sketchbook Artaria 201 and developed in sketches for the Tenth Symphony, where an Andante in E flat major adjoins a fast movement in C minor.[75] After the B flat section and a double bar appear two bars in 2/4 in F major, which probably represent the start of a second movement; but an alternative movement marked 'Adagio', also in 2/4 and F major, appears on the stave beneath. Again there is no obvious relationship to any known Beethoven work.

Other keys tried out for symphonies in 1812 were E minor (U21), C minor (U22) and E flat major (U23), while U17a is in D major. Thus, unlike Beethoven's attempts at a first symphony in 1795–96, where his multiple ideas had similar characters and were all firmly set in C major, on this occasion his thoughts for a second and third symphony in the group display an almost bewildering diversity of possible keys, characters and figurations, with D minor being merely *primus inter pares*. A pattern of development can

---

[75] See Sieghard Brandenburg, 'Die Skizzen zur Neunten Symphonie', *Zu Beethoven 2: Aufsätze und Dokumente*, ed. Harry Goldschmidt (Berlin, 1984), pp. 88–129, at pp. 110–11.

be observed, however, in that nearly all the sketches for the second symphony in the group were in major keys, whereas once he had fixed on F major for this, the sketches for the third symphony were nearly all in minor keys, following his habit of using one minor key in a group of three works.

U21 is noteworthy not only for emphasizing once again the flattened sixth but for actually using a motif (bars 3–4) that ended up almost unchanged in the Ninth Symphony (bars 25–27). The four main notes of its melodic outline (B E C D sharp) also recall Mozart's C minor Fugue (K. 426), which in turn echoes certain Baroque fugues such as Handel's 'And with his stripes' (*Messiah*); thus the use of imitation in the opening bars of the symphony sketch, before a descending unison passage, reminds of these earlier fugues. Although he abandoned this sketch, he later rearranged these four notes into several other orders (in different keys) in his late quartets, Opp. 131 and 132, without using the same rhythmic pattern. U22 is a much more isolated concept, with no connection to the C minor motifs that were sketched some ten years later in connection with the Tenth Symphony; but U23 does show a connection, emphasizing the notes G and A flat at the start – notes that became an important feature in the sketches for No. 10.[76]

U21 and U23 are also important for showing, like U18, more than just the first movement. The E minor sketch is immediately followed by a C major theme which was presumably intended as a possible second movement. This key would be surprising, since all Beethoven's other multi-movement works in E keep the same tonic for every movement; but this was not inevitable, as shown here. The theme actually resembles that of the Trio in the third movement of the Eighth Symphony, and it appears to have been adapted for that purpose almost immediately afterwards.[77] The sketch for U23 in E flat is even more substantial with over thirty bars, containing themes for all four movements, including a 'tempo di Menuet' in C major, an adagio in A flat and a fugal rondo finale begun by the bass instruments.[78] The idea of having non-tonic keynotes for both the central movements was new for Beethoven's symphonies, but the key scheme here exactly replicates that in his Piano Trio, Op. 70 No. 2 (there, however, the minuet movement is placed third instead of second). It is unusual to find such a substantial synopsis for an unfinished work, and it

---

[76] See Barry Cooper, 'Subthematicism and Metaphor in Beethoven's Tenth Symphony', *Ad Parnassum*, 1/1 (2003), pp. 5–22, at pp. 19–20.

[77] See Buurman, 'Beethoven's Compositional Approach', p. 167.

[78] The four themes are transcribed in ibid., p. 170.

suggests that Beethoven was seriously considering a new symphony in E flat instead of, or as well as, one in D minor, in preference to all the other keys recently sketched. Thus, when he began work on a companion to the Ninth Symphony, the idea of using E flat was already firmly in his mind. In fact, the relationship between the 1812 sketches and those of 1822–25, which also include a fugue among the later movements,[79] is almost as close as that between U6 and the *Eroica*.

One other noteworthy feature of the 1812 symphony sketches is the frequent reference to instrumentation, especially any that is slightly unusual. Already in 1809 Beethoven had sketched a prominent viola motif in bar 2 of the opening theme (U10). Now one finds references to a symphony with piccolo (U12), a symphony without timpani (U13, which contains this description but no themes), and a further reference to the piccolo in U23. The Adagio associated with U18 is even more precise: 'due oboe 2 corni uno clarinetto viole' ('two oboes, 2 horns, one clarinet, violas'). This type of comment is far more common in his later symphony sketches than in the earlier ones.

Between Nos. 8 and 9

By the end of 1812 the idea of composing a third symphony in the group seems to have dissipated, and no abandoned symphony sketches are known from 1813 or early 1814. Between the completion of the revision of *Fidelio* in June 1814 and the start of work on his large-scale cantata *Der glorreiche Augenblick* around October, however, Beethoven had no major project occupying him, and the possibility of writing another symphony re-emerged. During this period, probably in late August, he sketched a new idea for a symphony (U24). As in U18 he chose to use two main keys, for the main Allegro is in E minor (Example 3.7) but the opening Adagio is in C major ('C dur anfang'). Both themes remained undeveloped ideas of only

All[egr]o

[etc.]

Example 3.7 Dessauer, p. 141/6

[79] Brandenburg, 'Die Skizzen', p. 111.

a few bars, and neither is related to those of other symphony sketches. Further down the page there is an Andante in E flat and an Allegro in D minor (U24a). Buurman and Lockwood imply that the latter is an alternative symphony sketch to the E minor one,[80] but there is no clear indication of this. Beethoven did, however, explicitly indicate that a sketch at the top of the page was for the second movement of the symphony ('Sinfonia 2tes Stück'), with a 9/8 theme for 'Corni' – another of his growing number of specific instrument indications.[81] The key, F major, could go with a first movement in either E minor or D minor. The Andante in E flat is evidently orchestral, since one motif is marked 'timpany', but it seems less likely to fit well into the projected symphony.

Two further abandoned symphonies were sketched later in 1814. The first (U25) is on a leaf that also contains sketches for *Der glorreiche Augenblick* (first performed on 29 November 1814[82]) and therefore dates from October–November. The first four bars were quoted by Alfred Kalischer in 1895,[83] but the sketch has not been discussed since and is not listed by Lockwood. The four bars are doubled at the lower octave and followed by four more bars, but there is nothing very substantial or significant here, except as an indication that Beethoven was still thinking of composing symphonies. From about the same time and not noted hitherto is a sketch 'Sinfoni auf 2erlei Horn' ('symphony with two different horns') (U26) – another interesting instrumental indication. The comment appears beneath a sketch in D flat (shown under U26) which may be an idea for the symphony, although there is no certainty that it is. There are no instances where Beethoven used only two horns crooked in different keys, and so he was probably planning to use four horns. Before 1813 he had only ever used four in stage works (*Leonore, Egmont, Die Ruinen von Athen* and *König Stephan*), where they were normally crooked in two different keys. In the *Eroica* the three horns are all in the same key except in the slow movement (horns 1 and 2 in C and 3 in E flat) and in two short passages (I.408–416 and IV.270–273) where the two types are not heard simultaneously. From 1813, however, Beethoven began introducing four horns (two different crooks) in concert works – *Wellington's Victory*

[80] Buurman, 'Beethoven's Compositional Approach', pp. 158 and 174; Lockwood, *Beethoven's Symphonies*, p. 233.
[81] The theme is quoted in Nottebohm, *Zweite Beethoveniana*, p. 199, though Nottebohm makes no mention of the other sketches on the page.
[82] BTW, vol. 1, p. 896.
[83] Alfred Kalischer, 'Die Beethoven-Autographe der Königl. Bibliothek zu Berlin', *Monatshefte zur Musik-Geschichte*, 27/11 (1895), pp. 153–61, p. 157.

(1813), *Der glorreiche Augenblick* (1814), the *Namensfeier* Overture and *Meeresstille und glückliche Fahrt* (both completed in 1815 but begun earlier). Thus by late 1814 the idea of having horns 'of two types' in a symphony would have been attractive, and was indeed executed in the Ninth Symphony, begun in earnest in 1817. By that time he had also used four horns in the last movement of the incidental music for *Leonore Prohaska*, and six horns (four in D, two in B flat basso) in the military march WoO 24.

Beethoven's only known attempt at a symphony in B minor (U27) is a very brief theme that appears in a pocket sketchbook of 1815 and was quoted by Nottebohm.[84] Again it has an instrumental indication (partly indecipherable), stating that the timpani were to be tuned to D and A. In several of Beethoven's later works the timpani are tuned to notes other than tonic and dominant (such as F and A in the scherzo of the Seventh Symphony, or F octaves in the scherzo of the Ninth). Use of tonic and dominant of the relative major, as noted here, was another possibility.

Three more beginnings of symphonies were jotted down in the Scheide Sketchbook of 1815–16. The first (U28) is very rudimentary, with a curious blank space at the end of the first bar; and although its key signature has only one sharp, Nottebohm's suggestion of D major[85] may reflect Beethoven's intentions. The second (U29) is far more interesting. It contains a detailed verbal description of how Beethoven intended the symphony to begin. Nottebohm was sufficiently intrigued to quote it in two separate articles, and it has since received comments from other writers:[86]

Sinfonie erster anfang in bloss 4 stimmen 2 Vi[oli]n Viol[e] Basso dazwischen forte mit andern stimmen u. wenn möglich jedes andre Instrument nach u. nach eintreten lassen –

The sketch continues the trend in Beethoven's sketches to indicate instrumentation rather than specific melodic material, and here it is developed beyond the mere naming of instruments to an indication of how they would interact. The plan was to begin with just four-part strings, but with other instruments performing *forte* interjections ('among them *forte* with other instruments') and 'if possible' each other instrument gradually entering. Lockwood relates this procedure to the gradual entry of instruments at the start of the Ninth Symphony, but the differences are

---

[84] Nottebohm, *Zweite Beethoveniana*, p. 317.   [85] Ibid.

[86] Ibid., pp. 158 and 329. See also Brandenburg, 'Die Skizzen', pp. 91–2; Buurman, 'Beethoven's Compositional Approach', p. 181; Lockwood, *Beethoven's Symphonies*, p. 194.

considerable, for the symphony does not begin with four-part strings, nor do other instruments enter *forte* at that point.

The layout of the material on the page is confusing and is discussed in detail by Brandenburg.[87] The first, short, entry is unrelated, but the second is an extended draft of twenty-eight bars in B flat, 3/4 time, in apparently moderate tempo, while the third is the above inscription. Since the inscription is written directly beneath the B flat draft and even overlapping with it, Brandenburg suggests that the draft, which appears to be intended for orchestra, may be a slow middle movement for the symphony. It seems rash, however, to presume that a symphony from this period could not begin in moderate tempo. The sketches for the Tenth Symphony indicate an opening Andante, and the piano sonatas Opp. 101 and 110 both begin with a movement in moderate tempo. Thus the draft may well represent the beginning of the symphony, with bars 1–4 perhaps functioning as a slow introduction. Thereafter much of it contains one chord per bar, implying a fast tempo, not a typical slow movement.[88] Moreover, the draft matches Beethoven's inscription rather well, for bar 1 is in four-part harmony, probably intended for strings, while the sudden off-beat chords in bars 2–4 match the notion of other instruments entering *forte* intermittently. Thus it is easy to imagine bars 1–4 being orchestrated as outlined, with the other instruments then entering gradually in subsequent bars. Brandenburg rightly considers it less likely that the remaining material on the page is related to the symphony, since it was written later in different ink (or pencil). One sketch shows a D minor theme that re-emerged slightly altered in the second movement of the Ninth Symphony; but in the sketchbook it is simply headed 'Fuga', with no indication it was being considered for a symphony, and another version of this theme was used in an unfinished string quintet movement in 1817 (Hess 40). Another brief sketch in 3/4, in D major, could have been written as a possible addition to the symphony, since it is located on staves 11–12 between the B flat draft and the verbal inscription; but its purpose is doubtful.

The third idea for a symphony in the Scheide Sketchbook (U30) returns to E flat major, but the material is completely different from the four-movement synopsis of 1812 and shows no connection with other symphony sketches. An accompanying figure using dotted rhythms is supplemented by a single horn note before reappearing an octave lower.

---

[87] Brandenburg, 'Die Skizzen', pp. 91–2.

[88] The first nine bars are quoted in Nottebohm, *Zweite Beethoveniana*, p. 158, and Buurman, 'Beethoven's Compositional Approach', p. 182.

Example 3.8 Scheide, p. 106

A following passage that exploits demisemiquaver figuration is written in a different ink and may not belong. This ink is also used for a two-bar 'adagio' theme in C on the next two staves, which could represent a second movement for the symphony. Its theme (Example 3.8) seems to be derived from that of the first movement, with its dotted rhythm and triadic outline; and its key matches the second movement in the 1812 synopsis. Thus the sketches on this page confirm that E flat was still a likely key for a subsequent symphony, but they show no other connection with No. 10.

During and after No. 9

On 9 July 1817 Beethoven accepted a commission from the Philharmonic Society of London to compose two new symphonies.[89] By the end of the year he was making headway with one in D minor that was to become No. 9,[90] but there is no sign of the other one at this stage. Mention is made of this, however, in an oft-cited verbal sketch (U31) from about April 1818:

Adagio Cantique – Pious Song in a symphony in the old modes (Herr Gott dich loben wir, alleluja), either on its own or as an introduction to a fugue. Perhaps the whole second symphony characterized in this way, where then the voices enter in the last movement or already in the Adagio. The orchestral violins etc. are in the last movement increased tenfold. Or the Adagio is repeated in some way in the last movement, where first the voices enter gradually – In the Adagio text Greek myth, ecclesiastical canticle, in the Allegro festival of Bacchus.[91]

---

[89] BG, no. 1140.   [90] Brandenburg, 'Die Skizzen', pp. 95–103.

[91] 'Adagio Cantique / Frommer Gesang in einer Sinfonie in den alten Tonarten. (Herr Gott dich loben wir. alleluja) entweder für sich allein oder als Einleitung in eine Fuge. Vielleicht auf diese Weise die ganze 2te Sinfonie charakterisirt, wo alsdenn im lezten Stück oder schon im adagio die Singstimmen eintreten. Die Orchester Violinen etc werden beim lezten Stück verzehnfacht. Oder das adagio wird auf gewisse Weise im lezten Stücke wiederholt wobei alsdenn erst die Singstimmen nach u. nach eintreten – im adagio text griechischer Mithos Cantique Eclesiastique im Allegro Feier des Bachus.' D-BNba, BSk 8/56; dating from Brandenburg, 'Die Skizzen', p. 103.

This is the culmination of Beethoven's trend to concentrate on instrumentation and verbal description for new works, rather than actual themes. It revives the idea from U29 of instruments, or this time voices, entering successively rather than all at once, and surprisingly describes the last two movements rather than the opening one. The reference to the 'second symphony' shows that at this stage he did not contemplate a vocal finale to No. 9, but in the end some elements in the sketch were absorbed into that symphony, notably that 'the voices enter in the last movement'. Many features, however, were laid aside, including the use of modes, a tenfold(!) increase in the number of string instruments and the specific texts mentioned. These were replaced by Schiller's *An die Freude*, which conveniently includes Greek elements ('Tochter aus Elysium'), ecclesiastical canticle ('muss ein lieber Vater wohnen') and festivity ('Freude'). Nothing from this sketch found its way into a 'second symphony' that was to be paired with No. 9.

A later, supposed attempt at a second symphony was suggested by Nottebohm, who believed a 'Sinfonie allemand' in D (Artaria 201, page 119) to be a separate work.[92] Brandenburg showed that Nottebohm was right to assume Beethoven was contemplating two symphonies at that time; but the 'German symphony' was No. 9, and Beethoven would surely not write a pair of symphonies with one in D minor and the other in D major. The D major finale belonged from the start to No. 9.[93] Brandenburg went on to observe that a substantial batch of sketches did survive for a second symphony (U32), now known as the Tenth, which was to begin with an Andante in E flat followed by an Allegro in C minor. Some were found in Artaria 201 (pages 124–5), and a larger group appears on a loose bifolio along with some sketches for the Ninth Symphony. This latter group also includes a synopsis of the three later movements, though the longest, for the finale, was later absorbed into Beethoven's *Gratulationsmenuett* (WoO 3). Since this was performed on 3 November 1822, the sketches for the symphony probably date from September–October. At this stage the Ninth was far from complete, but after it had been performed Beethoven turned again to the projected Tenth in spring 1824,[94] and a batch of sketches survives from about October 1825 in Autograph 9/1.[95] This batch includes new ideas for later movements, but those for the first

---

[92] Nottebohm, *Zweite Beethoveniana*, pp. 167–8.   [93] Brandenburg, 'Die Skizzen', pp. 108–10.
[94] Ibid., p. 126.
[95] Barry Cooper, 'Newly Identified Sketches for Beethoven's Tenth Symphony', *Music & Letters*, 66/1 (1985), pp. 9–18.

movement correspond to the earlier ones. To these may be added a further sketch for the first movement, probably from late 1825, in the Kullak Sketchbook, f. 13r. It is unclear which, if any, of the later movements would have been incorporated into the symphony, but the sketches for the first movement changed relatively little over a period of over three years. They consist altogether of about 250 bars of sketches for this composite movement (along with about 100 for possible later movements), and they display strong motivic and expressive coherence between the different ideas. Particularly notable is the tension between the motifs 3–5–8 and 3–2–1 that can be observed in most of the sketches, and the foregrounding of the notes G and A flat.[96] A few earlier sketches survive showing the C minor theme transposed to D minor and the E flat one to B flat, for possible use in the Ninth Symphony,[97] but this idea was quickly abandoned. Although the sketches contain much melodic material, they also continue Beethoven's attention to instrumentation, for there are references to horns, string instruments, timpani and *Harmonie* (wind group). There are also structural indications, showing that the E flat section was to be in '2 Theile' ('2 parts') which lead into the C minor Allegro, which in turn leads back to a varied reprise of the first section.

Nottebohm was clearly unaware of most of this material, and of the fact that it so closely matches Karl Holz's description of a movement that he heard Beethoven play on the piano: a gentle introduction in E flat followed by a stormy Allegro in C minor, which Holz reported was the first movement of the projected Tenth Symphony.[98] What Nottebohm did observe was two sketches in Autograph 9/1 that had been annotated by Schindler as 'Scherzo zur 10ten Symphonie' and 'Andante zur 10. Symphonie'. On their own these sketches amount to no more than the many other abandoned symphony sketches that Nottebohm had seen, and therefore held no particular significance except in postdating the Ninth Symphony. He therefore concluded, perfectly reasonably, that these were the source of the 'fable' of the Tenth Symphony. This conclusion in turn gave rise to his claim that

---

[96] See Cooper, 'Subthematicism'. A completion of the movement, giving an 'artist's impression' of how the sketches interrelate, is published by Universal Edition: Ludwig van Beethoven, *Symphonie Nr. 10: Erster Satz,* completed and ed. Barry Cooper, 2nd ed. (Vienna, 2013).

[97] See Nicholas Marston, 'Beethoven's "Anti-Organicism"? The Origins of the Slow Movement of the Ninth Symphony', *Studies in the History of Music, Vol. 3: The Creative Process* (New York, 1992), pp. 169–200.

[98] Klaus Martin Kopitz and Rainer Cadenbach, *Beethoven aus der Sicht seiner Zeitgenossen* (Munich, 2009), p. 463.

Beethoven began at least fifty symphonies.[99] It was only when the extent and coherence of the first-movement sketches were recognized in the 1980s that it became apparent that the material for the Tenth Symphony is very different, in quantity and recurrence, from earlier passing thoughts.

A final sketch for a possible symphony dates from summer 1826 (U33). It is particularly difficult to decipher with confidence, but it is concerned, like U31, with the end rather than the beginning of the work. Again it features an important instrumental reference – this time to an off-key timpani roll on E flat in a D major context. It is clearly just a passing thought – the end of an unspecified symphony – rather than the beginnings of an eleventh symphony.

Conclusions

Beethoven's unfinished symphonies can generate almost as much fascination as his nine completed ones. Hitherto, however, the overall image of them was very blurred, and only through a diligent search, followed by spotlighting each one in turn, has it been possible to produce a clear overview. Since thirty-three have been identified, the total number of Beethoven's projected symphonies is not far short of Nottebohm's estimated fifty, when the nine completed ones are included. If the sketches identified as possible symphonies (U11a, U11b, U17a, U24a) are added, and the five symphonic ideas listed as U3a–3e are counted separately rather than as versions of a single symphony, the total comes to exactly fifty. There is also the likelihood that some other sketches were intended for symphonies but were left unlabelled and therefore not identifiable as such. Thus Nottebohm's estimate of 'at least fifty' is exactly right. In addition there were probably a few others noted down on leaves now lost or not yet discovered, which were not included in Nottebohm's total. On the other hand any figure higher than Nottebohm's would be speculative, since there is no firm evidence of others.

None of the abandoned symphonies resembles any previously completed. This is in line with Beethoven's habit of making all new works, especially new symphonies, very different from any previous one. Some of the sketches, however, anticipate later symphonies, as has been noted. This applies particularly to U1 (anticipating No. 5), U3 (forming some of the basis for No. 1), U6 (which feeds into No. 3) and both U19 and U20 (which

---

[99] Nottebohm, *Zweite Beethoveniana*, p. 12; Nottebohm silently amended Schindler's spelling of 'Simphonie'.

anticipate No. 9); a few others have more tenuous connections, as indicated above and in the Appendix. Apart from the themes listed in U3, there is rarely any connection between different abandoned symphony sketches, although U12 picks up on an idea from the Allegro section of U10, shown in Example 3.6 above. What is striking, therefore, is the great diversity of ideas that Beethoven had for forming symphonies, and many include at least brief indications of harmony. Keys are also quite varied. C major occurs most often (eight times), while there are also several in D minor, E flat major or other keys used elsewhere. On the other hand several keys were considered but never used in a completed symphony: E minor, G major, G minor, A minor, B minor and perhaps D flat major. Also noteworthy is the increasing use of verbal description and names of instruments, rather than just musical notation.

Among the more striking or bizarre openings are U2, with its five-bar phrases and curious flattened second in bar 5; U10, with a strident G minor opening and rapid modulation towards D flat major; U21, starting in the bass clef with imitation based on echoes of a Baroque theme; U27, another bass-clef opening with a dynamic opening gesture; and U30, which shows a strange combination of figurations and implied textures. The well-known U31 is remarkable for its implied structure and massive increase in sonority for the finale. And U33 reveals the timpani creating tonal confusion rather than the usual reinforcement of tonal stability.

Most of the symphonies sketched show the main allegro theme, while about a dozen of them contain a slow introduction, usually in addition (such as U10 and U24); in a few cases the theme sketched might represent either introduction or main movement. As for later movements, they may occasionally be represented by an adjacent theme, as in U18, but they are not usually indicated. The four-movement synopsis in U23 is exceptional in this respect, and the heading 'Sinfonia 2tes Stück' in U24 is also noteworthy, but the only ones with extensive indications of later movements are the three large-scale attempts – Nos. 0 and 10 and the *Ur-Eroica* (U3, U32 and U6 respectively). Apart from these, most of the projected works were probably little more than passing thoughts that Beethoven did not expect to develop but jotted down nevertheless, in case they might prove useful. This was very much part of his normal practice, and what he advised to his composition pupil Archduke Rudolph.[100] The only other lengthy attempt is U1, which displays an intention for a symphony at a time when Beethoven surely knew

---

[100] BG, no. 1686; cf. Johnson (ed.), *The Beethoven Sketchbooks*, p. 4.

he was not ready to complete such an ambitious task, and he was still aware of the magnitude of such an undertaking when he laboured on U3 in 1795–97.

The three large-scale attempts are therefore qualitatively different from the thirty other 'symphonies' abandoned. Yet they are also very different from each other. Whereas U3 shows repeated attempts at constructing a symphony in C, and several extended drafts for a first movement plus a selection of ideas for later movements, U6 is a single attempt, confined to a double-page spread. U32 resembles U3 in being repeatedly revisited over an extended period, but its two main themes remained much more consistently intact than those of U3, even though Beethoven did not make any extended written drafts but only an extemporized one reported by Holz. All three large-scale attempts include a synopsis of all the movements except those whose themes were apparently already in place (the first movement of U3 and U32, and the finale of U6).

It is significant that none of these three large-scale attempts is headed 'Sinfonie' whereas each of the other thirty has this or a similar label. The three can be confirmed as symphonies only through their internal content, consisting of groups of sketches for a multi-movement orchestral work that is not a concerto. The same applies, incidentally, to the early sketches for most of Beethoven's completed symphonies, which rarely have a genre label (exceptions are No. 5, which is headed 'Sinfonia' in Landsberg 6, page 157, and No. 6, headed 'Sinfonia pastorella' in Landsberg 12, page 48). Thus Beethoven's use of 'Sinfonia' may sometimes have been deliberately written to indicate a work that was probably not going to be developed to completion.

Although Beethoven's symphonic jottings are scattered almost throughout his composing career, from about 1788 to 1826, it is now clear that far more symphonies were begun during 1812 than at any other time – representing about a third of the total. Some of these were precursors of the Eighth Symphony, but after having converted sketches for this from a piano concerto to a symphony, he seriously considered forming a set of three symphonies. A comment found on the same page as the E minor symphony sketch (U21) perhaps betrays some of the underlying thinking: 'Absolutely no piano things such as concertos' ('gar keine Klawir sachen als Konzerte').[101] It seems that his deafness had finally dissuaded him from composing more piano concertos, and he had just transformed his latest attempt into the Eighth Symphony. Thus his next *Akademie* would not include a piano concerto and two symphonies, like his previous one of

---

[101] Cited in Hans Schmidt, 'Die Beethovenhandschriften des Beethovenhauses in Bonn', *Beethoven-Jahrbuch*, 7 (1969–70), pp. 1–364, at p. 312.

1808, but perhaps a set of three symphonies, forming a triptych like his three 'Razumovsky' quartets. An approximation to this plan emerged in his *Akademie* of 27 February 1814, when his Seventh and Eighth symphonies were performed along with *Wellington's Victory* (his so-called 'Battle Symphony'). Hence *Wellington's Victory*, which begins in E flat but ends in D major – two of the keys considered for symphonies in 1812 – could be interpreted as a realization of his plans for a 'third symphony' in the group.

It is worth remembering that Beethoven had little external incentive to write symphonies – only three are known to have been commissioned (Nos. 4, 5 and 9), and the difficulties in mounting benefit concerts where they could be performed and generate much-needed income were considerable, as he repeatedly experienced. Yet he kept returning to the genre and contemplating new ones, far more often than previously realized. He regarded it as the supreme instrumental genre, as he indicated in a letter of 20 December 1822, when he said he wanted to write just operas, church music and symphonies, adding quartets almost as an afterthought.[102] Performance and publication could be arranged somehow, but they were not the immediate incentive. This attitude is reflected in a note relating to a new overture and the Tenth Symphony: 'This overture with the new symphony, thus we have an *Akademie* at the Kärntnertor[theater]' ('diese Overture mit der neuen Sinfonie so haben wir eine Akadem[ie] im Kärntnerthor').[103] The symphony was to come first and thoughts of a performance second. Thus the numerous abandoned sketches could be interpreted as representing whole works in the highest instrumental genre, for which Beethoven simply lacked the time to work out the details.

No other composer is known to have begun nearly as many abandoned symphonies. Beethoven stands out in this way, as in so many others, as being in a league of his own. If even two or three of these works had been brought to completion they would surely have had a profound impact on the subsequent development of the symphony, and they reveal endless potential for the genre. Most literature on Beethoven's sketches has concentrated on those for completed works, but those for unfinished works are in their way equally significant. A comprehensive examination of the unfinished symphonies reveals much about his working practices and the context in which the nine completed ones were composed; and the unfinished symphonies themselves form a major contribution to what is arguably the most celebrated genre in Beethoven's output.

---

[102] BG, no. 1516.   [103] Autograph 9/1, f. 2v; see Cooper, 'Newly Identified Sketches', p. 11.

Appendix 3.1 | Thematic Inventory of Unfinished Symphonies Sketched by Beethoven

The reference number is followed by the title as given in the manuscript, the key (lower-case for minor), the date, the source, and any necessary comments, including the number given in BTW, if any. In sketches written on two staves, only the upper stave is shown.

U1 'Sinfonia', c, c. 1788 (Kafka, f. 70). Anticipates No. 5. Hess 298; Unv 1 in BTW.

U2 'Sinfonia', C, 1790 (Kafka, f. 88v). Anticipates No. 1.

U3 (no title), C, 1795–97 (Kafka/Fischhof passim). No. 0. Anticipates No. 1. Unv 2 in BTW. Several possible later movements, and at least five possible introductions as follows (U3a–e):

U3a (Kafka, f. 127v/12)

U3b (Kafka, f. 127v/14)

U3c (Kafka, f. 128r/13)

U3d (Kafka, f. 158v/9)

U3e (Kafka, f. 128v/5)

U4 'Sinfonie mit einem adagio worin der Zweifel ausgedruckt ist', C, c. 1798 (Fischhof, f. 46r)

U5 'Sinfonia', C, 1801 (Landsberg 7, p. 110)

U6 (no title), E♭, 1802 (Wielhorsky, pp. 44–5). First three movements ('Ur-Eroica'). Anticipates No. 3

U7 'lustige Sinfonia', F, 1804 (Landsberg 6, p. 159). Anticipates No. 6

U8 'Sinfonia in d moll', 1804 (Landsberg 6, p. 177). Anticipates Nos. 5 and 9

U9 'erstes All[egr]o einer Sinfoni', G, 1809 (Landsberg 5, p. 55)

U10 'Sinfonia', g/G, 1809 (Landsberg 5, p. 87)

U11 'A moll Sinfonie', 1809 (Landsberg 5, p. 104). Title only, no music.
U11a (no title), f/F, 1809 (Landsberg 5, p. 50): all[e]gr[e]tto / leztes all[egr]o

U11b (no title), f/F, 1809 (Landsberg 5, p. 59): Eingang Largo / all[egr]o

U12 'Sinfonia con fl: piccolo', C, 1812 (Petter, f. 15v)

U13 'eine Sinfonie ohne Pauken', 1812 (Petter, f. 23r). Title only, no music
U14 '2te Sinfon d moll', 1812 (Petter, f. 29v). Anticipates Nos. 8 and 9

U15 'Sinfonia', B♭, 1812 (BH 120, f. 1r, originally after Petter f. 29).
  Anticipates No. 8

U16 '2te Sinfonie leicht C', C/F, 1812 (Petter, f. 35r). Anticipates No. 8

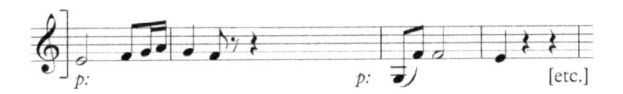

U17 'Sinfoni', C, 1812 (Petter, f. 42v/5)

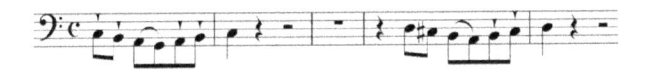

U17a (no title), D, 1812 (Petter, f. 42v/6). Sign ·/. perhaps means repeat previous title (f. 42v/5 above)

U18 'Sinfon', g/B♭, 1812 (Petter, f. 42v/13–14)

U19 'Sinfonie in d moll', 1812 (Petter, f. 44r). Anticipates No. 9

U20 '3te Sinfon', d, 1812 (Petter, f. 45r). Anticipates No. 9

U21 'Sinfonia', e, 1812 (BH119, f. 1r, originally situated after Petter f. 52)

U22 'Sinfonie c moll', 1812 (Petter, f. 61v)

U23 'Sinfon 3', E♭, 1812 (HCB Mh 86). Four movements. Anticipates No. 10

U24 'C dur anfang Sinfonia', e, 1814 (Dessauer, p. 141/3)

U24a (no title), d, 1814 (Dessauer, p. 141/14). Possibly alternative to U24

U25 'Sinfonia', C, late 1814 (aut.19e, f. 6v)

U26 'Sinfoni auf 2erlej Horn', D♭, late 1814 (Mendelssohn 6, p. 91)

U27 'Sinfoni in h moll', b, 1815 (Mendelssohn 1, p. 25)

U28 'Sinfonia', G, 1815 (Scheide, p. 33)

U29 'Sinfonie erster Anfang in bloss 4 Stimmen...', B♭, late 1815
(Scheide, p. 51)

U30 'Sinfonia', E♭, 1816 (Scheide, p. 106). Key anticipates No. 10

U31 'Adagio cantique – Frommer Gesang in einer Sinfonie in den alten
Tonarten ...', 1818 (BSk 8/56, f. 1r). Description only; no music.
Anticipates Nos. 9 and 10

U32 (no title), E♭/c, 1822–25 (Kullak, f. 13r, and earlier sketches).
No. 10. Unv 3 in BTW. Several possible later movements

U33 'Am Ende einer Sinfoni', D, summer 1826 (Paris Ms 66, f. 6a/v)

4 | Beethoven as Sentimentalist

MICHAEL SPITZER

An astonishing scene from Abel Gance's monumental film *Napoleon* depicts the Siege of Toulon in 1793, in which the young captain helped capture the port from the British. It is Napoleon's first success, and sends him on his way to First Consul and Emperor. Carl Davis, who compiled the score for *Napoleon*, leans heavily on Beethoven's *Eroica*; indeed, he draws mostly from the finale, despite the first movement being much more dominant in the symphony's reception history. For this particular scene, Davis uses the music of the finale's second fugato section. Although the crassness of Davis's score has been much criticized, and justly so, in this particular scene I think Davis gets it right. Music and imagery come together in an expression of the violent, group emotions of war, an experience well captured by the late-nineteenth-century French military historian, Commandant Henri Lachouque's report on Waterloo:

Much has been written about mass hysteria. These men gone berserk, drunk with fear, rage, enthusiasm, blood; killing one another regardless of nationality, shouting with joy, cursing, crying for vengeance in five languages, were victims of an emotion neatly summed up in the imprecation attributed to Cambronne on the evening of 18 June 1815.[1]

There are two versions of what General Cambronne is heard to have said. The famous inscription on his monument records that it was 'La garde meurt et ne se rendent pas!' ('the guard dies but does not surrender'). On the other hand, Victor Hugo says it was, simply, 'Merde!' Here we have, then, two versions of glory: something magnificent which is also enmired in the dirt of war. If this episode is the chaos, then other side of glory is the apotheosis of the theme just afterwards. These two sides constitute an emotional script, which looks, from the outside, like battle leading to victory; and from the inside, as a move from heroic self-sacrifice to public recognition. Or from 'Merde!' to 'Meurt'.

---

[1] Henri Lachouque, *The Anatomy of Glory: Napoleon and His Guard, A Study in Leadership* (Pickle Partners Publishing, 2015), p. 106.

The topic of this essay is the glory script as expressed in the slow movement and finale of Beethoven's *Eroica*: glory as both a timeless emotion, going back to Homer and Plutarch, and a historically very specific instantiation. First, we must ask whether glory is actually an emotion at all. Talking about emotion in Beethoven runs against the grain of German Idealism, which has governed nearly all reception of his music as organically unified, and organized by a quasi-Hegelian *Idee*. One version of this chapter might go deeper down this path, because if you scrape away the surface of German Idealism, you find emotion. The emotion of glory lurks at the basis of dialectical synthesis: the drama of the self willing itself to go to ground, to emerge sublated at a spiritual level.[2] Just like Beethoven, the young Hegel was immensely impressed by Napoleon's victories. In more sober middle age, Hegel wrote more circumspectly about glory in his *Philosophy of Right*. Hegel links glory to violence; recognizes that glorious death can be willed and volitional; wonders whether glory is always posthumous; and asks pointedly whether a republic is ever actually worth dying for. I won't go down this path here, however, because my agenda is how Beethoven fits within the history of emotion, a rising discipline in the humanities and social sciences, yet one which musicology has virtually ignored. There are two main strands to this approach. First, the idea that there is a link between emotion and cognition; more properly, between the structural features of the musical object and its affective properties. This claim runs counter to Kant's and Hanslick's outlawing of emotion from their definition of an object's formal beauty. For them, emotion sits in the subject, not the object. The second strand is that these formal, emotional features were historically mutable.

Let's begin with history. Two books are especially relevant. William Reddy's *Navigation of Feeling*,[3] a study which explores sentimentalism in French eighteenth-century politics, from its origins as a critique of artificial etiquette, and then, provocatively, as the source of the Jacobin Reign of Terror. Reddy only touches upon Napoleon, who had little interest in sentiment, which is where I turn to a second book by Robert Morrissey on the economy of glory.[4] Whilst Napoleon is the centrepiece of Morrissey's book, he also argues that glory had a far wider historical significance,

---

[2] Katrin Pah, *Tropes of Transport: Hegel and Emotion* (Chicago, 2012).
[3] William Reddy, *The Navigation of Feeling* (Cambridge, 2001).
[4] Robert Morrissey, *The Economy of Glory: From Ancien Régime France to the Fall of Napoleon* (Chicago, 2014).

especially in France, stretching as far back as Homer and Plutarch, an author with whose heroes Napoleon was obsessed.

According to Reddy, the history of emotion in eighteenth-century France progresses in three main steps: sentimentalism; its mutation into Jacobinism; and its efflorescence into Napoleonic glory. So, sentimentalism first. The sentimentalist attack on courtly etiquette as artificial, hypocritical and stifling, fed on familiar ideas of Shaftesbury, Hume, Smith, Diderot, Rousseau and many other thinkers. Reddy's new angle is that confining the expression of sincerity to intimate private spaces – what he terms 'emotional refuges' – created 'emotional suffering'. In a hydraulic metaphor of pressure and release, this claustrophobic emotional suffering is relieved when sentiment is discharged into a wider social and political arena; in other words, there was a yearning to reform the state on the basis of natural human feeling. Is this audible in Beethoven's music? The finale is a set of variations, and its theme is, ostensibly at least, extremely simple, especially when introduced as a naked bass-line, the so-called *basso del tema*. David Hume's notion of emotional 'sympathy' seems relevant here.[5] For Hume, people are brought together by resonating sympathetically with each other's sentiment, what we would nowadays call 'emotional contagion'. In Humean terms, Beethoven's theme is sociable because it is so conventional, made up of simple tonics and dominants, the building blocks of music. The audience resonates with the clarity and symmetry of the form. But the theme also enacts sociability through the subject–answer periodicity of its form; the way the phrases answer each other sympathetically, a dynamic with which the listener also resonates. This resonance is repeated at rising hierarchical levels.

Now, Beethoven was obsessed with this so-called *contredanse* theme. He explored it in his earlier Variations for Piano, Op. 35, and in his ballet, *The Creatures of Prometheus*. The Promethean narrative of brute, natural material being gradually brought to life, ennobled and refined, of course maps naturally onto variation process. This is exactly how the symphony operates: a playful, childishly simple theme is set on the path of spiritual growth and heroic apotheosis. Critics have compared this childish tone to Schiller's play drive,[6] and a sense of the ridiculous turns on the absurd

---

[5] David Hume, *A Treatise of Human Nature* (London, 1985). First published 1739. See also John Mullan, *Sentiment and Sociability: The Language of Feeling in the Eighteenth Century* (Oxford, 1988).

[6] See Stephen Rumph, *Beethoven after Napoleon: Political Romanticism in the Late Works* (Los Angeles, 2004).

empty bars and peremptory B♭s. This is music of pure contingency, of *hazard*. With a child's lightness of spirit and lack of consequence, the grown-up hero will throw his life away, as if in a game. Not for nothing does Gance's film begin with a snowball fight, with the child Napoleon outmanoeuvring a rival gang of schoolboys.

The second moment of Reddy's story tells how sentiment is politicized, even weaponized, by the Revolution. Appealing to emotional authenticity, the Jacobins sought to transform all of society into a private enclave, a vast salon, an emotional refuge. In short, to render private emotion into public emotion. We hear something of this eruption from inner to outer in Clara's song ('Freudvoll und leidvoll') in Beethoven's music for *Egmont*. When the orchestral tutti bursts in, there is a vertiginous opening up of emotional space. Nevertheless, Reddy easily demonstrates how the Jacobin project was riddled with contradictions, in a narrative through which an emotional regime based on natural sentiment led to terror and mass murder. The logic of turning white into black was ineluctable. The Republic used their machinery of violence to purge feelings it saw as unnatural so as to purify emotion. The terror was destined to fail because it assumed that everyone was heroic and ready to die for the Republic. If they did not, then this was a failing of sincerity and a marker of guilt. There thereby emerged a vicious circle through which emotion consumed itself and the Revolution devoured its children. To be afraid of death damned you as insincere; and the fear of being detected of being frightened made you even more frightened and insincere. The definition of terror is the terror of being discovered in your terror. This made literally everybody into a traitor. Can we detect this emotional suffering in the music of the Revolution? I hear it in the monotonous euphony and overbearing uniformity of its soundscape, as in Gossec's grand symphony of 1793, *Le Triomphe de la République*. Like Beethoven, Gossec ends with a *contredanse*. Such music is unbearable because it doesn't comprehend dissonance or real drama. Its sanitized consonance typifies what Frolova-Walker calls the officially sanctioned *boredom* of revolutionary music, as in Soviet Russia in the 1930s.[7] The paradox is that state terror needs to expunge representations of terror in its cultural materials. A vision of hell is to hear this consonance for all eternity. The broader contradiction of the Jacobin emotional regime is

---

[7] Marina Frolova-Walker, 'Stalin and the Art of Boredom', *Twentieth-Century Music*, 1/1 (2004), pp. 101–24.

that it attempted to make an essentially private emotion, sentimentalism, into a public one. Similar conceptual problems beset Adam Smith's theory of sentiment. Smith's notion of the 'impartial spectator' leads to a conformist, right-wing view of emotion as governed by the social status quo and the financial market.[8]

And so we come to the third moment in Reddy's story, Napoleonic glory. Here are the Emperor's final words to his troops before departing for his brief exile at Elba: 'Do not lament my fate. If I have decided to go on living, it is to serve your glory.'[9] And here is a key passage from Neufchâteaux's elegy for General Desaix, killed at the battle of Marengo in 1800: 'Existence is nothing, for them glory is all ... Those who defy death are the masters of the world.'[10] Several strands can be picked out from the rich economy of glory. First, glory, as conceived by Napoleon, was a public emotion which could bring together every level of society – aristocrats, financiers, common soldiers – in what Morrissey calls 'the politics of fusion'.[11] The whole nation could rally around the heroic individual, decked out in a suitable display of splendour – a role incarnated by Napoleon himself. Napoleon achieved this through the democratization of warrior values, whereby anyone could be a soldier, and every soldier was noble. The hard, practical, basis of that was universal military conscription, the bulwark of his army. Napoleon's war economy succeeded, but relied on continuing military victories, so it of course had a limited future. On the debit side there is also the cynicism of the cult of appearance, shading into the glory of gold, the lustre of which so impressed the heroes of Wagner's *Ring*. The crucial point is that the unifying function of national glory allowed Napoleon to leapfrog the chasm between private and public emotion, a chasm that had swallowed up the Jacobins. The Terror had also attempted to expunge fear, but glory changed the terms of the equation. Now seduced by the glory of a charismatic leader, the nation gladly put fear to one side. In a neat inversion of the Jacobins' terror of concealed terror, voluntary self-sacrifice, seduced by the charisma of a Leader, surmounted the terror of death.

---

[8] Adam Smith, *The Theory of Moral Sentiments* (London, 2007). First published 1759.

[9] Munro Price, *Napoleon: The End of Glory* (Oxford, 2014), p. 243.

[10] Judith Miller, 'Fratricide: Tragic Brothers, Masculine Violence, and the Republic on the French Stage, 1799', in *Republics at War, 1776–1840: Revolutions, Conflicts, and Geopolitics in Europe and the Atlantic World*, eds. Pierre Serna, Antonino De Francesco and Judith A. Miller (London, 2013), pp. 189–211, at p. 205.

[11] Morrissey, *The Economy of Glory*, p. 147.

There is of course a history of glory before Napoleon, and the outline of this history marks a coming to terms with the virtue of self-sacrifice. Glory was not just a gloss justifying death retrospectively – although this of course remained. Glory was also a reflection of what military martyrs really felt, a true nobility of the spirit. In the early modern period, Thomas Hobbes establishes the contrarian, brutally realist position. For Hobbes, the thirst for glory was the engine of human endeavour in the 'war of all against all'.[12] As with David Hume's emotion of pride, a close cousin of glory, and Hume's principal passion, glory was the very cornerstone of human subjectivity, echoing Spinoza's *conation*, and anticipating Darwin's survival instinct. Hobbes's map of glory makes some revealing distinctions. True glory serves the self. Against that, 'vainglory', or false glory, isn't properly earned by battle; it is propaganda.[13] There is also cowardice, when one refuses to struggle; and finally, and most important for my argument, there is recklessness, which is to sacrifice yourself in battle. The nihilism of Hobbes has no time for glorious self-sacrifice; this is exactly what becomes sanctioned in the eighteenth century. Compare these words by Montesquieu, from his *Persian Letters*:

The desire for glory does not differ from that instinct which all creatures have for their self-preservation. It seems that we extend our very being when we can exist in the memory of others. We acquire through it a new life.[14]

Now, Montesquieu wrote these words extolling the French monarchy in 1721. Nevertheless, his advocacy for a moral economy based on what he calls 'that general passion of the French for glory' lays out the basis for Napoleonic glory some eighty years later. This is the crucial step: the idea that we 'extend our being' when we die for a higher cause. In other words, the unit of the self is raised from the single human subject, to the unit of the nation, or the species, just as with the tension in evolutionary theory between genes and organisms, when a creature dies for the greater good of the species or gene pool. The slow movement and finale of Beethoven's *Eroica* stage glorious self-sacrifice in two moves, respectively that of death and resurrection. The idea that the second and fourth movements represent the demise of the hero and his return to life is of course hardly new, notwithstanding the (narratologically) problematic buffer of the *Scherzo*. Nevertheless, the history and psychology of emotion can shed new light on Beethoven's glory.

---

[12] Thomas Hobbes, *Leviathan* (London, 2011). First published 1651.   [13] Ibid., p. 74.
[14] Morrissey, *The Economy of Glory*, p. 59.

Marcia funèbre

Beethoven titled his slow movement a funeral march. In reality, the music is a hybrid of two funerary genres popular in revolutionary France: march and hymn. In its discursive complexity, it also evokes the third genre of the funeral eulogy, with its joint responsibilities both to mourn and to praise the deceased. Although it is unlikely that Beethoven experienced these French rituals at first hand, he was extremely fluent in the republican musical style. Claude Palisca's fine study of the movement has revealed it to be saturated with traits from funeral marches and hymns by Gossec and Cherubini.[15] Beethoven might also have known Paul Wranitzky's *Grand Characteristic Symphony*, a direct precursor in its assimilation of this style into the Viennese symphony. Wranitzky's slow movement is a funeral march for Louis XVI. And more broadly, as Nicholas Mathew observes, at this time 'the sound of the Viennese public sphere [was] one of marches and fanfares.'[16]

What are these funerary traits? Palisca lists drumrolls, the frequent unisons, fanfares, the wind writing and the demisemiquavers in the strings, which imitated the sound of muffled drums, the *caisse roulante voileé*. There are also many direct borrowings from specific works, such as Gossec's *Marche lugubre* and his *Hymne à l'égalité*. Formally, Beethoven's C major trio section is more characteristic of hymns than of marches (see the trio of the funeral march from his Op. 26 piano sonata). Nevertheless, although one might imagine the square, syllabic melody of the *minore* section being sung, it doesn't conform to the verse–refrain structure David Charlton finds typical of revolutionary hymns.[17] Indeed, stepping back, the *Marcia funebre* proves to be just as formally problematic as the *Eroica*'s finale. Our sense of the form starts with deceptive simplicity but quickly slips through our fingers. An opening, tonally closed (cadencing on the tonic) eight-bar phrase seems to forecast a steady march-like tread of similar periods. But the answering phrase (bars 9–16) drifts into E flat major, where it cadences. The third phrase begins in E flat, quickly hits the buffers on a diminished seventh chord with rhetorical silences, and passes through F minor to sit on the dominant for eight bars, stretching the

[15] Claude Palisca, 'French Revolutionary Models for Beethoven's "Eroica" Funeral March', in *Music and Context: Essays for John M. Ward*, ed. Anne Shapiro (Cambridge, MA, 1985), pp. 198–209.

[16] Nicholas Mathew, *Political Beethoven* (Cambridge, 2013), p. 50.

[17] David Charlton, 'Revolutionary Hymn', in *New Grove Dictionary of Music and Musicians*, 2nd ed., vol. 21, ed. Stanley Sadie (London, 2001), pp. 240–2.

phrase to fourteen bars. The expectation that the march/hymn would proceed in stately eight-bar units is smashed. The aftermath of this formal crisis is even more irregular, beginning with a reprise of the opening phrase now in F minor, squeezed into six bars, and ending, at bar 56, with what sounds like a variation on the theme, quickly nipped in the bud. The subsequent C major episode is, locally, a trio since it is framed by an abbreviated refrain of the march theme. Architectonically it functions as a quasi-second group, even though it is never recapitulated, just as the central F minor fugato is analogous to a sonata-form development section. That said, although the movement is not a sonata form by any normal standards, one needs to seek beyond standard *Formenlehre* to understand why it holds together so well (infinitely better, say, than Wranitzky's rambling effort); why it makes such compelling *affective* sense. I'll approach this question, respectively, from psychology and history.

The basic point to make is that the march's funerary aspect assembles the building blocks of sadness, as described by a vast literature on the psychology and philosophy of this emotion. If *eudaemonia*, happiness, indicates human flourishing, then sadness and its many cognate emotions – melancholy, grief, mourning and depression – point to its opposite. According to Philip Fisher, sadness is a foretaste of death and an elaboration of our own mortality. It is a 'boundary condition of existence as finite, mortal, and limited'.[18] Whereas anger has the positive virtue of expressing strength of the human spirit, sadness seems utterly negative in this regard, marking a radius of our power and a 'humiliation of the will'. Anger can avenge, but nothing can restore the loss of a loved one. For the neuroscientist Jaak Panskepp, the 'separation anxiety' induced by the death of a partner or child is the most painful emotion of all.[19] And yet just like the other negative emotions, sadness does in fact possess many virtues, to the extent that the ancients believed that it was the only emotion which ought not to be therapeutically controlled, but allowed to run its natural course. Aristotle thought that melancholy was a creative force, and a trace of this long-lived idea is Dürer's celebrated engraving of *Melancholia*, which shows symbols of artistry and science strewn around the central image of the seated thinker. The intimate link between sadness and rumination is natural, given that the resignation of the will leads to the contraction of the world around the lost object. This is why sad cognition

---

[18] Philip Fisher, *The Vehement Passions* (Princeton, NJ, 2001), p. 205.
[19] Jaak Panskepp, *Affective Neuroscience: The Foundations of Human and Animal Emotions* (Oxford, 1998).

sharpens the focus on detail. David Huron usefully terms such analytic, detail-orientated cognition 'depressive realism'.[20]

What we call 'sadness' actually runs together two distinct emotions, each with its own properties. Sadness proper has low energy, is mute rather than vocal, and can be mistaken for boredom, neutrality, or indeed thoughtfulness. In the psychologist Nico Frijda's terms,[21] to say that this emotion is static and has no 'action tendency' (i.e., is not associated with an adaptive behaviour) would be wrong because rumination is itself an activity, and its goal is reparative or therapeutic. Grief has quite different properties to sadness. In contrast to the exhaustion of sadness, grief has high energy and is expressed through weeping or keening. If sadness is inward-looking and contemplative, grief points outwards, soliciting recognition and comfort from others. Sadness might be taken as the action tendency, grief as the action itself, with one portending the other. Grief's high energy can be suggestive of rage; this is significant, given Fisher's claim that grief is anger turned against the subject when there is no external party to blame. This is why grief can end in self-murder (famously, in Dido's lament).

The family of sad emotions has familiar acoustic cues. According to Patrik Juslin and Renee Timmers, sad music displays slow tempo, legato articulation, small variability of articulation, low sound level, dull timbre, large timing variations, soft contrasts of duration and slow attack.[22] It is a common perception that sad melodies tend to fall, mimicking the listlessness of a sad body. Huron argues that the small intervallic pattern of sad music reflects the muffled articulation of sad speech, the exhausted voice's tendency to mumble. Sad – or, more properly, grieving – music can also 'weep', as in the standard musical figure of the *pianto* (plaint, or sigh). Finally, sad music tends to be more atomized, just as it induces analytic, detail-orientated perception in the listener.

Beethoven's opening melody – low, slow, *pianissimo*, darkly orchestrated, and with its small intervallic patterns (mostly in step) – is quintessentially sad. But the movement climaxes with the higher energies of grief: the dense, *fortissimo* textures of the fugato, culminating with the blazing fanfares of the retransition. These fanfares, projecting blood-curdling submediant and diminished-seventh harmonies, express rage and terror: it is

[20] David Huron, 'Why Is Sad Music So Pleasurable? A Possible Role for Prolactin', *Musicae Scientiae*, 15/11 (2011), pp. 146–58.

[21] Nico Frijda, *The Emotions* (Cambridge, 1986).

[22] Patrik N. Juslin and Renee Timmers, 'Expression and Communication of Emotion in Music Performance', in *Handbook of Music and Emotion Theory, Research, Applications*, eds. Patrik N. Juslin and John Sloboda (New York, 2010), pp. 453–92.

typical of the chemistry of emotion that a ruling emotion – in this instance grief – can regulate others in its cause. This also includes the emotion of glory, as in the C major trio's glorification of the hero. Sad music typically slides into *maggiore* memories of the lost loved one – this is why the beginning of the march vacillates between C/F minor and E flat major. Such memories are grist to sadness's mill, sharpening its pangs when the *maggiore* phrases are snuffed out by the returning gloom. The apotheosis of the hero in the trio intensifies this principle with the military regalia of brass and drums, as well as the rising tonic-triad arpeggiations suggestive of victory (see the finale of Beethoven's Fifth Symphony).

The chemistry of musical emotion lends itself very well to the psychology of expectation. This is why so much research on emotion is conducted in the realm of experimental music perception. Whilst the science can be daunting, much of it speaks to common experience. Low-energy sadness tends to explode into high-energy grief, which is exactly what happens in Beethoven's fugato. In psychological terms, the beginning of the march is implicative of (i.e., portends) its climax. Likewise, the trio must precede the fugato to give the latter something to grieve about: that is the role glory plays in the 'system' of sadness. The fugato also has a hydraulic motivation to 'explode' out of the cramped registral space of the march's opening. Everything about the fugato projects a vast acoustic space: not just the orchestral tutti in itself, but the contrary motion of the counterpoint, the wide register of the thematic material, and the resonance of the wind and brass. The sound of the latter in particular connotes an open plain, perhaps a camp of battle or a field of commemoration. One can also drill down to motivic detail. The fugato's incipit is a liquidation of the march's opening melody, compressing its contour into its scale from C to F. This compression intensifies the emotion, in counterpoint with the simultaneous expansion of acoustic space. One can also pick out the notes of the trio's C–E–G apotheosis implied, yet buried, within the opening march melody. The Landsberg sketchbook shows that the melody at bar 3 originally began with a D, not a G. By substituting a G, Beethoven created a background C–E♭–G arpeggiation (see Example 4.1).[23]

In shifting our perspective to history, we must be wary that its boundary with psychology is a fuzzy one. Take the emotional reserve of the march's opening, an effect of its melodic, harmonic, and metrical plainness and simplicity. Such plainness and simplicity was a hallmark of revolutionary

---

[23] Landsberg 6, pp. 6 and 42, as cited in Palisca, 'French Revolutionary Models', p. 205.

(a)

Example 4.1a Landsberg 6, p. 6

(b)

Example 4.1b Landsberg 6, p. 42

(a)

Example 4.2a Beethoven, Symphony No. 3, 2nd movement, bars 1–2

(b)

Example 4.2b Beethoven, Piano Sonata in C Minor, Op. 13 (*Pathétique*), 1st movement, bar 1

hymns to allow a crowd of mourners to join in the singing. Equally, the metre needed to be regular so that the procession could move in lockstep. Palisca discovers in the *Eroica*'s march 'the telltale feminine pattern of many French songs', as in Gossec's *Hymne à la liberté*.[24] I would contend, however, that Beethoven's thematic line strikingly *avoids* such characteristic *pathétique* appoggiaturas at crucial moments. Indeed, in comparison with the introduction to the *Sonate pathétique* (an obvious comparator, not mentioned by Palisca), the line at bar 2 of the march stands out for eschewing an appoggiatura. Instead of resolving down to D, the E♭ 'plods', as it were, a minor third to C (see Example 4.2).

This fingerprint is admittedly tiny; but it encapsulates a sense both of weight and a stoic refusal to display pathos. In the same stoic spirit, the

---

[24] Palisca, 'French Revolutionary Models', p. 204.

march doesn't permit itself the *Sonate pathétique*'s indulgent use of diminished-seventh chords. And whilst the Grave of the sonata runs away with itself, ascending and accelerating sentence-like towards the Allegro di molto con brio (as of course it must: it is an introduction), the march's period sticks stolidly in the tonic. Such emotional reserve chimed with Napoleonic disapproval of individual expression, epitomized in Jacques-Louis David's chilly neo-classical paintings, especially of ancient Rome. Whilst this quality can be pinned down historically, it is also characteristic of ceremonial or group emotions in all times and places. By their nature, rituals or crowds level emotions down in order to conform with an external standard. We are dealing here, however, with a very particular and much chronicled standard of the republican state funeral.

Cherubini's *Hymne funèbre sur la mort du general Hoche, 1797* commemorates Louis Lazare Hoche (1768–97), a dashing young general of the Revolutionary army famed for his defeat of the Royalist forces in Brittany. If any youthful martyr fits Beethoven's idealized portrait of a dead hero, it is Hoche (it obviously couldn't have been Napoleon, since he was alive and well). After an address by the president of the Directoire, forty young students of the Conservatoire sang the first strophe at the mausoleum at the Champs de Mars in Paris. This was followed by a eulogy given by Daunou, after which a group of altos sang the second verse in unison accompanied by trombones, horns, bassoons and serpents. The third strophe was sung in unison by baritones, with flutes and muted trumpets. Finally, all the men's voices sang together accompanied by a full orchestra.[25]

It goes without saying that Cherubini's hymn is nothing like Beethoven's slow movement. Although the hymn accompanies a procession, it singularly lacks musical process – the hallmark of Beethoven's music. It is strophic. In terms of choreography, Hoche's funeral also departs from the earlier pattern of republican funeral processions, which typically conveyed the body towards the Panthéon, the state-sanctioned repository for France's Great Men. In short, the Panthéon operated as the terminus of the funeral's trajectory. On arrival, the funereal tone would shift to an emotion of joy. The painter David, who crafted the plan for the funeral of the child soldiers Bara and Viala on 10 Thermidor (28 July) 1794, instructed that the mood during the procession was to be sombre, after which 'Everything changes: the grief disappears; it is replaced by public joy;

---

[25] I am summarizing Palisca, 'French Revolutionary Models', p. 201.

and the people cry three times: "they are immortal . . .", the trumpets blow, and the celebrations commence.'[26] By contrast, the Champs de Mars was an open-air field: the republic came to reject the Panthéon for its secrecy and lack of public transparency in favour of the open space of nature (once the coffin had entered the building, the public was shut out). Moreover, the Champs de Mars was circular, conditioning the rotation of the ceremony around four sacred objects (a pyramid, a statue of liberty, an altar of the fatherland and a bust of the dead general). Cherubini's circular, strophic hymn fitted Hoche's non-linear funeral. The most striking aspect of Hoche's funeral, however, was that there was no body. Hoche had fallen in German territory, and his body would never be repatriated.

Although bodies were not always missing in action, Hoche's physical absence typified a drift in the compressed history of republican state funerals. According to Avner Ben-Amos, this history proceeded in three stages. The first stage, featuring the funerals of non-military Great Men such as Voltaire in 1791 and Rousseau in 1794, were 'integrative': they celebrated a great life so as to reinforce the shared values of the common French people.[27] The second stage, the funerals of military commanders interred in the Panthéon, was 'exclusive', in that their purpose was to whip up emotions for armed revenge against external enemies. Key ingredients of the exclusive funeral were to rehearse the manner of the martyr's death and to exhibit his wounds. Hoche's funeral exemplified the third phase, shifting the focus from death to patriotic theatre publically displayed in the Champs de Mars.

Beethoven's *Marcia funebre* cleaves towards the second of these three models: the exclusive funeral for a dead military hero as a procession towards the Panthéon. The hero's apotheosis is disposed of early in the C major trio. Instead of glory, the march's centre of gravity is the intense negative emotions of the fugato and retransition, which evoke battle and a moment of death. There is also the astonishing return of the theme in the coda at bar 238, broken up into its constitutive atoms. It is as if Beethoven is displaying the hero's broken remains, the religious trope borrowed by the revolution to whip up grief. From a psychological perspective, the atomized theme, as the quintessence of mourning, epitomizes Huron's notion of 'depressive realism': the association of sadness with a sensitivity for analytic detail. In other respects, Beethoven's march points in two

---

[26] Cited in Avner Ben-Amos, *Funerals, Politics, and Memory in Modern France, 1789–1996* (Oxford, 2011), p. 44.

[27] Ben-Amos, *Funerals, Politics, and Memory in Modern France*, p. 28.

directions. On the one hand, its gradual opening up of acoustic space, from the cramped register of the *minore* to the vastness of the trio and fugato, seems to side with the republicans' rejection of the Panthéon in favour of the open-air Champs de Mars. This chimes with the common perception that the *Eroica* is a pastoral symphony. On the other hand, the re-enactment of the hero's death and the exhibition of his atomized remains refer to the older type of funeral, the procession towards the Panthéon. In short, Beethoven's *Marcia funebre* is simultaneously 'closed' (Panthéon) and 'open' (Champs de Mars). One could even say that its musical architecture figuratively recreates a Panthéon in sound in which his hero is interred. After all, a symphony is akin to the third phase of republican funerals, when they had devolved into ceremonial theatre without a body. There is no real body inside the symphony, which is how it invites the listener in. There being no body of the hero, the listener's body will do in its stead.

Finale

If the funeral march is designed to provoke a battle of revenge, then this battle arrives in the finale. Let us return to the glory script, and focus on the finale's form. The glory script captures the two strands of the finale: the music of battle and the music of triumph. These two elements are relatively straightforward in themselves. However, it is their interaction that has foxed generations of critics and theorists, because the *Eroica* finale has resisted analysis, even by the likes of Hepokoski and Darcy, who don't even touch it. The form of the piece is *sui generis*, an original fusion of variation, fugue, rondo and sonata. Let's take the two strands in turn, beginning with battle.

There are actually two waves of battle, both in fugato style; the music Davis uses for the Siege of Toulon is the second, more extreme episode. The two fugatos are based on the same tonal model, both starting with a chord of G, and climaxing with a dissonant harmony featuring a powerful A♭. The first fugato cuts in after variation three, after an emphatic caesura on two chords of G as dominants of C minor. This instigates sixty bars of fugato, cycling away from, and returning to, the key of C minor. This climaxes on a diminished-seventh chord of C minor, with a powerful A♭ in the bass. The second wave is bigger and more extreme in every sense. The harmony of G minor is powerfully tonicized, for the first time in the movement, by bringing the theme back in D major, the dominant of G, and then in G minor itself, ending with an emphatic cadence at bar 256. There follow seventy bars of fugato climaxing with an extraordinary, twenty-bar prolongation of a B♭7 chord. The pitch A♭ is now posited as the seventh of the dominant, the normative tactic at the end of sonata-form retransitions. In Schenker's classic graph of this movement, the fugato unfolds a simple neighbour-note progression from G, the primary tone, to A♭, the upper-neighbour, supported by a dominant.

I want to focus on this second, more extreme, fugato, the music for the Siege of Toulon. Why do I hear it as a sonic metaphor of glorious self-sacrifice? Let's unpack the fugato bit by bit.

First and foremost, what is striking is the absence of fear. The music lacks any of the topoi of frightening music: no mystery, no vagueness, no tremolando, no unusual or particularly dissonant harmonies.[28] It sounds quite different from the development of the first movement. The music is not chaotic: on the contrary, it is marshalled extremely tightly towards a climactic goal, the dominant seventh of the tonic. And it doesn't wander off into any alien keys, such as the E minor of the first movement. I want to underline in triplicate this absence of fear for various reasons. We have got used to invoking Burke and Kant's category of the sublime for all music which sounds loud, overwhelming or deceptively chaotic. The links between the sublime and fear are well known. But the defining feature of this music – what makes it 'glorious' – is the very lack of fear. Indeed, self-sacrifice must be fearless. How does Beethoven achieve this, without it sounding boring or sanitized? In three main ways.

First, he uses fugal texture. This Baroque idiom is appropriately object-ive and selfless, and parallels Napoleon's taste for the coldly rational emotions of seventeenth-century classical painting, especially as imitated by the neo-classicism of David. See, for instance, David's *The Oath of the Horatii*. As with the Spartan discipline of David's soldiers, Beethoven's subject submits selflessly to the objectivity of the contrapuntal texture.

Second, he uses sentence technique at an architectonic level. The phrase structure which Schoenberg termed 'sentence form', as in the *locus classicus* first theme of Op. 2 No. 1, is as fascinating as it is undertheorized.[29] The sentence is a little machine for accelerating time and condensing material (see Example 4.3).

---

[28] Clive McClelland, *Ombra: Supernatural Music in the Eighteenth Century* (New York, 2012).
[29] William Caplin, *Classical Form: A Theory of Formal Functions for the Instrumental Music of Haydn, Mozart, and Beethoven* (Oxford, 1998).

'melodic residues'

Example 4.3 Beethoven, Sonata in F Minor, Op. 2 No. 1, 1st movement, bars 1–8, sentence form

Its rising arc of intensification exemplifies Goethe's theory of *Steigerung*, and I have elsewhere theorized it as a vehicle for a metaphorics of personification, the gradual incarnation of the subject, a technique which fits the *Eroica*'s Promethean narrative like a glove.[30] Now, whilst sentences are normally considered at the level of the phrase, Beethoven also likes to apply their processes of *Steigerung* to entire sections. Thus one might term the second fugato a 'grand sentence', as it unfolds a progressive acceleration of phrase structure and harmonic rhythm. The unit of repetition begins with the eight-bar phrase, and is whittled down to four bars, two bars, single bars, and ultimately to single crotchets, or quarter-bars (see Example 4.4).

So, an eight-bar phrase. Then a four-bar phrase. Then two bars, elided into one-bar sequences. Finally, half a bar and a quarter of a bar. Note the acceleration of harmonic rhythm; and the liquidation of the octave motives into quavers. The telos of this drive is the B♭ V7 chord. The music submits itself to this single point, just as it submits to the discipline of fugato counterpoint, and just as an individual soldier submits to a military strategy commanded by a general.

Third, the really unusual aspect of the music, and the secret of its glory, is that it features three cumulative returns of the theme in the tonic E♭, first on flute, a military instrument; then on horns; and climactically on full brass and wind. Of course, this is implicit in fugato style, in the alternation

---

[30] Michael Spitzer, *Metaphor and Musical Thought* (Chicago, 2004).

Example 4.4 Beethoven, Symphony No. 3, 4th movement, liquidation in the second fugato

between tonic subjects and dominant answers. This is why, unlike a proper development section, a fugato cannot wander too far away from the tonic; the tonic is kept in sight at all times. But that is exactly the point: Beethoven embeds a tonic-centred fugato within a sentence-style drive to the dominant. Let me emphasize how counter-intuitive it is to mix up a drive to the dominant with premature tonics. The music is engaged in a massive teleological push towards a dominant-seventh climax; any reference to the tonic within that drive should, in principle, be avoided because that risks short-circuiting this drive to the dominant. Certainly, the second halves of development sections in sonata forms avoid pre-empting the climactic dominant sevenths. I simply don't know of any other work in the repertoire that does this. And yet Beethoven brings the theme back in the tonic three times, with cumulative emphasis. This cuts across the incredible energy of the music. Beethoven compounds that with striking metrical and harmonic displacements. First, the refrains are displaced by half a bar, creating dramatic conflict between layers of the counterpoint. At the climax, the horns, trumpets and wind even cut into the harmony of the strings: the strings play a subdominant harmony; the brass and wind superimpose a tonic over that. The effect is one of powerful assertion, stamping the authority of a leader onto the contrapuntal texture. This metrical energy disguises the fact that, tonally speaking, nothing much happens in this music other than a conventional alternation of tonics and dominants, just as in the theme itself. There is no real dissonance, no true hazard. It is all a rhetorical trick, perhaps the ultimate truth of glory.

I venture, then, that the secret of Beethoven's glorious self-sacrifice is hidden in this tonal and formal paradox: a drive to the dominant short-circuited by tonic refrains. The tonic fanfares assert authority, reassurance, fearlessness and also a certain feeling of timelessness. The three tonic returns are little islands in the stream of time. They are extremely suggestive for unlocking Beethoven's dialectic of glory. On the one hand, the music is rushing purposefully towards its climax, a military goal. On the other hand, true nobility doesn't have a purpose; it sacrifices itself because that is the right thing to do. To coin a phrase, it is purposive without purpose. These three sincere, authentic-sounding tonic fanfares express a true ethical content: they meld the beautiful with the good.

Now let's look at the second half of the glory script, the triumph of glory. If the first half, the battle, expresses the earthy imprecation ascribed to General Cambronne, this second half is the inscription on the monument: the radiant, more leisurely, mostly posthumous emotion that memorializes the sacrifice. This is what we hear in the slow apotheosis of Beethoven's theme, just after the fugato climax. In many ways, its emotion of pride is much more straightforward to decode. As with pride, Hume's principal passion, the theme puffs out its chest. We are reminded of the stately march of a proud French overture by Lully; or even of a Chopin polonaise; also of Siegfried's horn leitmotif decked out in clanking armour at the court of the Gibbichungs. The tempo is slow, because the music is heavy. The weight exudes sheer power, a mixture of heaviness and difficulty. This power is demonstrated in the effort needed to lift those heavy French horn semiquaver scales up to the high A♭s. We empathetically feel with those horns, pushing up the scale, and leading the orchestra. And of course, the brass of the horns gleams with the glory of gold, of money.

The apotheosis is recognized not only in itself, but as a justification for the battle. It also crowns the sentimental education of the original theme: its growth from playfulness to heroism. Most broadly, it puts the stamp on the apparent inevitability of the process, why this is musical form and not improvisation. This inevitability can be reverse-engineered back to the theme. The fearlessness of the battle music, the absence of real dissonance, is already implicit in the theme's harmonic simplicity, the naïve reduction to tonics and dominants. We can also imagine those bizarre, empty bars in the theme as a kind of chthonic cave, out of which emerge the music's powerful heroic forces. Whilst all these things might be true, and may emerge on reflection, I don't think we hear the music as inevitable. The power of Beethoven's battle is that it is made to sound precarious and contingent – like an improvisation – and also goal-driven at the same time. How these contradictory forces are made to coincide is exactly the music's glory: we can feel it; but it is harder to analyse it.

There are similar issues when we explore the effect of glory in everyday life. Psychologists of emotion are fond of erecting walls between aesthetic emotion and what they term 'utilitarian' emotion.[31] This distinction doesn't work, particularly for glory, an emotion which passes easily across art and life. We don't need to go to battle to experience glory, so I won't go down the road, with critics such as Susan McClary, for apologizing for the heroic style as murderous or blood-soaked, even given Napoleon's insouciance towards military casualties.[32] In our everyday lives, we experience glory when we achieve something against the odds, for instance, when we overcome a disability such as deafness. There is also glory when this victory is recognized by other people. But, as a codetta to this essay, let's end by taking the battle into the enemy camp, indeed to consider a battle as a kind of work of art.

Beethoven famously said to a French officer, 'If I, as general, knew as much about strategy as I, the composer, know of counterpoint, I'd give you something to do.'[33] On the other side of the looking glass, one is tickled to discover that scholars analyse Napoleon's battles, just as we analyse Beethoven symphonies. Military historians agree that Napoleon's strategic masterpiece – his *Eroica* – was the Battle of Ulm in 1805, a campaign in which he encircled and captured the Austrian army with hardly a single shot being fired.[34] The operation unfolded in two waves,

---

[31] Marcel Zentner, Didier Grandjean and Klaus Scherer, 'Emotions Evoked by the Sound of Music: Characterization, Classification, and Measurement', *Emotion* 8/4 (2008), pp. 494–521.

[32] Susan McClary, 'Getting Down off the Beanstalk: The Presence of a Woman's Voice in Janika Vandervelde's Genesis II', *The Minnesota Composer's Forum Newsletter* (1987), p. 7.

[33] Rumph, *Beethoven*, p. 100.

[34] See for instance David Chandler, *The Campaigns of Napoleon* (New York, 1966).

not unlike, perhaps, the two fugato episodes in Beethoven's finale, and there are many graphic analyses of the attack in military histories. Not being tied to immobile food depots, like the army of Frederick the Great, Napoleon's troops lived off the land as they moved, often in harvest time, with an ability to disperse and concentrate rapidly with multiple routs of advance. At Ulm, the French turned the Austrian flank and positioned themselves between their army and its base. This manoeuvre usually leads to the total destruction of an army because it cuts off its line of retreat. The interesting thing is that Napoleon had trialled exactly the same manoeuvre five years earlier at the battle of Marengo in 1800. A battle, like a symphony, can have a conventional form which can be repeated and improved. Although Napoleon won at Marengo, on that occasion it was largely through sheer luck, but that is not how the propaganda after the battle presented it. Napoleon's publicity machine portrayed a seamless unity between planning and execution; for instance, presenting a chaotic rout as a tactical retreat. Napoleon's victory at Marengo was crucial in burnishing his reputation as a First Consul on the way to becoming an Emperor. Yet glory in this case was the force which holds together planning and execution. This is what Hobbes calls 'vainglory'. By contrast, the glory of Ulm was fully justified. In Beethoven's case, imagine that the triumph of the theme wasn't fully motivated by the fugato battle; simply put, that it was composed badly, as in, for instance, his later potboiler, *Wellington's Victory*. The vainglorious *Wellington's Victory* was Beethoven's most successful work in his lifetime. It was his Marengo moment. By contrast, the *Eroica* finale is his masterpiece; it is Beethoven's Ulm.

Putting the Music Back into Politics

Beethoven's funeral march and finale interact as in the game 'paper–stone–scissors'. Paper wraps stone; scissors cut paper. A glorious apotheosis is shunted aside by death in the fugato (funeral march); glory overcomes death in the fugato episodes (finale). The history and psychology of emotion has helped us see how formal processes in the *Eroica* resonate with ritualized behaviours in the world of politics – state funerals and battles. Otherwise put, funerals and battles can be as formalized as music. I would like, in conclusion, to modulate into a polemical key. In recent years, there has been a fashionable drift in Beethoven studies away from looking at the scores 'in themselves' – critically or analytically – to considering the composer as fully engaged in the political world.[35] This shift in focus from 'music as aesthetic text' to 'music as historical document', as Dahlhaus would have put it, has certainly produced many welcome contextualizations. Yet the price of this has generally been to concentrate on Beethoven's occasional or minor works; indeed, potboilers such as *Wellington's Victory*. The bathwater has been thrown out together with a very large baby, the music of Beethoven which we cherish. I hope to have shown in this essay that there is a way of putting the politics back into the music without this compromise. The idea that we need to circumvent masterworks such as the *Eroica* in order to get at 'the real world' rests on a fallacy – that a composer is only ever political when he or she directly addresses their music to events. This fallacy was debunked with particular pungency by Helmut Lachenmann, a living exponent of the Austro-German musical tradition:

Writing music ... always has a political aspect. But for me a Webern bagatelle is much more subversive and politically significant than all those requiems, cantatas and oratorios dedicated to the Holocaust, to 9/11 or to oppression in the Third World using depressive clusters, aggressive noises, threatening percussion orgies and sad nostalgic quotations.[36]

In essence, Lachenmann means that composers mediate their political stances through the musical material. A common way of revealing that used to be Adorno-inspired critical theory, and it is possible that this approach is tired and needs to rest.[37] Critical analysis of Beethoven has fallen prey to the critique that it is overly hermetic – an ironic echo of how the revolution rejected the closed Panthéon for the open Champs de Mars. In this essay, I have put aside critical theory for another tool, emotion theory. It is perfectly valid to contextualize Beethoven in the politics of his time. But, please, let us keep the music.

---

[35] The finest and most illuminating of these studies is Mathew's *Political Beethoven*.

[36] Abigail Heathcote, 'Sound Structures, Transformations, and Broken Magic: An Interview with Helmut Lachenmann', in *Contemporary Music: Theoretical and Philosophical Perspectives*, eds. Max Paddison and Irène Deliège (Farnham, 2010), pp. 331–48, at p. 341.

[37] See my *Music as Philosophy: Adorno and Beethoven's Late Style* (Bloomington, 2006).

5 | Beethoven's Nature: Idealism and Sovereignty from an Ecocritical Perspective

KEITH CHAPIN

Few assertions about Beethoven are better known than E. T. A. Hoffmann's exuberant defence of the composer's control: 'In truth, he is fully the equal of Haydn and Mozart in rational awareness, his controlling self detached from the inner realm of sounds and ruling it in absolute authority.'[1] Although Hoffmann levelled his pen specifically at doubting critiques of the composer's fecund fantasy, the statement is indicative of a view of the composer's rationality as standing above nature – both the nature of tones and his own natural inspiration. To wit, Beethoven has a rational autonomy that allows him to dictate the ways of tones and to control the irrational side of his own imagination. More broadly, the quotation gestures towards the various ways that the composer and his music demanded autonomy, providing, in Lydia Goehr's words, a 'Beethoven Paradigm' that models the separation of compositional activities and composed works from social, economic, political and aesthetic conditions.[2]

Idealist aesthetics provided ideological support to each of these claims of autonomy, for each could be perceived as a celebration of the power of human will to rise above the ties and traditions in which people find themselves. When composers went without traditional patronage forms of employment (social autonomy), traded their works in the market (economic autonomy), wrote music without overt uses for representative ends (political autonomy), or wrote music whose quality did not depend on its usefulness (aesthetic autonomy), they could appear to be demonstrating freedom from constraint, to demonstrate the power of spirit over matter. As freedom bred insecurity, musicians themselves, including Beethoven, had mixed feelings about these shifts in practice and orientation, but they tended to appreciate the valorization of music that occurred through the emphasis on spirit given in Idealist accounts.

---

[1] E. T. A. Hoffmann, *E. T. A. Hoffmann's Musical Writings: Kreisleriana, the Poet and the Composer, Music Criticism*, ed. David Charlton, trans. Martyn Clarke (Cambridge, 1989), p. 98; *Fantasie- und Nachtstücke* (Düsseldorf, 1996), p. 44.

[2] Lydia Goehr, *The Imaginary Museum of Musical Works: An Essay in the Philosophy of Music* (Oxford, 1992), pp. 205–42.

In various ways, recent commentators have worked towards differentiated perspectives on the various types of autonomy claimed for Beethoven. To take two examples, Nicholas Mathew has noted the political associations of monumentality and the glorification of popular melodic strains in Beethoven's symphonies. The autonomy of the music from politics is a matter of sublimation rather than exclusion.[3] For his part, Michael Spitzer has argued that the musical processes of Bach, Mozart and Beethoven (and the musical styles for which they stand) manifest three types of metaphor (radial, hierarchical and processual).[4] Their musical processes are not autonomous from musical meaning, but rather engage the structures of understanding that govern all human thought.

Beethoven's relationship to nature also bears reconsideration. Hoffmann's depiction of Beethoven's 'absolute authority' or ruling ego suited the writer's defence of a style deemed by contemporaenous critics as eccentric and uncontrolled. It also suited Romantic ideals of the composer as a genius who stands far from the mortal crowd. Finally, it suited modernist ideals of the composer as a radical innovator gifted with an imaginative rationality.

However, the model of the ruling ego does not sit well with current approaches to human agency, post-humanist or otherwise, which emphasize multilateral interweavings within the world rather than control over it. Nor, for that matter, does it sit well with what we know of Beethoven's own life and activities. Finally, it does not sit well with a more considered perspective on the practices of Idealist writers themselves. Idealist aesthetics were a specific response to the situated and embodied nature of human agency. This essay reviews Beethoven's compositional engagement with themes of nature, his attitudes towards nature as expressed in writing and in contemporary reports on the composer, and, finally, Beethoven's aesthetics as a response to his own physical embodiment in nature. Beethoven provides an opportunity to examine notions of sovereignty associated with Idealism from an ecocritical standpoint.

Over the years, ecocriticism has shifted from a Romantic fixation on 'wild' or 'rural' nature towards a more varied concern with a wide variety of environments and differing ways that they and human participants interact in specific locales. At the same time, Romantic ideals continue to exercise a strong pull on the popular imagination, and it is through these ideals that Beethoven's practices can be examined.

[3] Nicholas Mathew, *Political Beethoven* (Cambridge, 2013), pp. 102–35.
[4] Michael Spitzer, *Metaphor and Musical Thought* (Chicago, 2004), pp. 54–9.

Beethoven was no prescient harbinger of future ecocritical consciousness, but rather much the child of his age in his dualistic approach to a
world conceived as divided between city and country, urban and 'natural'.
As problematic as this dichotomy was, it could also be worked out in
different ways, either to emphasize human control over a static world or,
on the other hand, to emphasize human participation in larger processes.
In works that named nature as their subject matter – in particular the
Symphony No. 6 in F Major, Op. 68, 'Pastoral' and the song cycle *An die
ferne Geliebte*, Op. 98 – Beethoven marked human agency as limited, as
part of a process.

His representations of situated agency took place within traditions that
had once idealized human control of nature. In the Pastoral Symphony,
Beethoven built upon both iconographic traditions of ancient pedigree and
recent genre traditions. From the time of classical antiquity, poets and
painters imagined Arcadian idylls in which shepherds and shepherdesses
faced torments of love but never of physical hardship, disease or poverty.
As Raymond Williams noted, these idylls reflected the ease of aristocratic
life more than they did the harsh realities of country life. Neo-pastoral
poetry, as he termed it, presented as a Golden Age the values and exploitive
practices that regulated rural life. Throughout the history of English
literature, this Golden Age always tended to be located one or two generations before any particular poet's writing, and functioned as an object of
nostalgic yearning.[5]

Equally oblivious to ecological or rural realities, musical traditions of the
pastoral also focused on ideals and idylls. While the pastoral had a long
history in music, David Wyn Jones notes that Beethoven would have
known little of it. Rather, his inspiration would have lain close to hand,
in traditions of the pastoral mass, the Austrian and Bohemian pastorella
and the pastoral symphony as found within church services (that is, with
pastoral moods but without programmatic titles).[6] Such traditions associated the pastoral traditions inherited from antiquity with states of especial
religious grace, in particular the Nativity. Non-liturgical works with pastoral content, such as Joseph Haydn's oratorios *The Creation* and *The
Seasons*, might focus on prelapsarian idylls. Although the religious pastoral
reminded human beings of the limits to their sovereignty, they still emphasized revealed religion and a divine order in which human beings were
masters of the created world. The rhythms of this created world were

---

[5] Raymond Williams, *The Country and the City* (London, 1973), pp. 9–45.
[6] David Wyn Jones, *Beethoven: Pastoral Symphony* (Cambridge, 1995), pp. 15–16.

dominated by cycles of seasons and religious festivals, and were thus also fundamentally static. Each year resembled the last, always patterned by the same natural phenomena and sacred events. In this respect, the Pastoral Symphony represents an 'idyllic pastoral', as Aaron Allen has noted, marshalling musical features ranging from relaxed tempos, the major mode and sustained harmonies to the inflection of styles in narrative directions.[7]

Yet the pastoral tradition was not always static, nor the religious traditions associated with it always focused on the human domination of nature. The pastoral tradition changes in significance depending on the position it takes within the range of ways that people can engage with the world. By the end of the eighteenth century, intellectuals, artists and others who engaged with the pastoral began to pay greater attention to the natural world beyond garden and park walls. They did this in part in response to the pressures of urban growth and the beginnings of the industrial revolution. This is not to say that they paid greater attention to the needs of people who lived in rural places – they still idealized nature – but it does indicate that the tradition, even as it held to long-established iconography, could lend itself to reinterpretation. If the pastoral had once allowed people to imagine original innocence, it increasingly functioned as an outlet for the pressures of modernity. As Beethoven wrote in the Tagebuch he kept 1812–18, 'A farm, then you escape your misery!'[8] Even as the modern world might confuse as it pressed in on individuals, the pastoral world allowed individuals to imagine moments of wholeness.

As Richard Will and Raymond Knapp have emphasized with respect to the Pastoral Symphony, Beethoven framed his engagement with the pastoral in religious terms, but also in such a way as to de-emphasize Arcadian idyll and to emphasize the passage of time. The first two movements comply with pastoral traditions by emphasizing the static condition of nature. The final movements, joined together as a narrative sequence involving the reactions to a storm, emphasize dynamic temporal change and thus represent the advent of history into the pastoral.[9] As Will writes, 'Like the pastoral writings of Klopstock or Goethe, it dramatizes fundamentally human concerns about morality and about the effect of time's passage on the paradises, real or imagined, that people value.'[10] Knapp

---

[7] Aaron S. Allen, 'Symphonic Pastorals', *Green Letters*, 15/1 (2011), pp. 22–42, at pp. 25–8.

[8] Maynard Solomon, *Beethoven Essays* (Cambridge, MA, 1988), p. 269.

[9] Richard Will, *The Characteristic Symphony in the Age of Haydn and Beethoven* (Cambridge, 2002), pp. 156–87.

[10] Ibid., pp. 186–7.

emphasizes the transformations that happen over the course of the movement. The finale 'presents for the first time an integrated world embracing
nature, humanity and God. And, also for the first time, we are given a
movement that is constructed with a genuine sense of teleology, with
progress marked both tonally and through thematic development and
variation.'[11] Through its engagement with processes and progressive integration of human history into a pastoral environment, Beethoven gestures
towards what Kate Rigby calls the valorization of 'hybrid places that
manifest a life-enhancing collaboration – the "blended might" as
Wordsworth refers to it in "Home at Grasmere" – of human and other-
than-human beings and processes'.[12]

Beethoven's engagement with the pastoral tradition is relevant for a
consideration of Idealist aesthetics as it indicates the ways that idylls –
and ideals for that matter – had particular functions, both positive and
pernicious: the justification of a socio-economic order that separated a
privileged urban civilization from an ostensibly happy but undeniably
disadvantaged rural folk; a way to deal with the pressures of a complex
modernity; or a way for individuals to understand themselves as part of
larger process. I will return to the functional position of ideals below.

Beethoven also prominently engaged with themes of nature through vocal
music, especially Lieder, and again in ways that show both his adherence to
conventions and their intelligent manipulation. Nature provided a source
domain for metaphors and set scenes and it underpinned the symbolism of
simple melodies and heartfelt sentiment. In each case, nature offered a sheen
of authenticity that contrasted with the ostensible artificiality of urbanity.
Beethoven's striking song cycle *An die ferne Geliebte* serves to exemplify
both ways that Lieder conventionally thematized nature and ways that
Beethoven turned genre traditions to his own ends.

The cycle places itself firmly within the nature genre traditions of the
Lied in the most obvious way in its evocation of a natural setting. The poet
sits on a hill gazing out into the mist. In the distance, separated from him
by mountains and valleys, is his beloved. Such natural settings were an
extension of pastoral iconography and could suggest a similar idealized
imbrication of rural life and rural world. In addition, the natural setting

---

[11] Raymond Knapp, 'A Tale of Two Symphonies: Converging Narratives of Divine Reconciliation
in Beethoven's Fifth and Sixth', *Journal of the American Musicological Society*, 53/2 (2000),
pp. 291–343, at p. 337.

[12] Kate Rigby, 'Romanticism and Ecocriticism', *The Oxford Handbook of Ecocriticism*, ed. Kate
Rigby (New York, 2014), pp. 60–79, at p. 73.

suggested that whatever words were spoken or sung by the protagonist of a Lied were authentic, that human beings were closer to themselves outside of urban, civilized settings.

Central to song's link to nature is the use of similes and metaphors, in particular metaphors that describe the human passions – love, anger, sadness – or human gestures that spring directly from them, such as sighs. For instance, the poet compares his sighs to the vanishing of the sun's gleam – 'My sighs dissipate like the last rays of the sun' (No. 3). Metaphors perform many roles within lyrical poetry. They offered visual parallels to inner sentiments and thus strengthened the rhetorical efficacy of the text. They also offered composers the possibility of building upon such visual parallels through text depiction, especially if they were minded to go beyond the simple melodies and strophic forms associated with folk songs. Finally, they implied that the sentiments responded to something more than ulterior motives, or, more generally, instrumental rationality.

Metaphors were also central to the tradition of anthropomorphism: poets endowed animals and natural phenomena (clouds, winds) with human agency or sentiments. Although anthropomorphism owes much to an anthropocentric approach to the world – the world becomes an extension of human sentiments and aspirations – it can also emphasize the limits on human agency. The natural world may accomplish what human beings cannot or may oppose human action. For example, the poet of *An die ferne Geliebte* asks the brook, the birds and the clouds to communicate his pain to his beloved: 'And you, little brook, | if you can see my love, | greet her for me a thousand times' ('Und du, Bächlein klein und schmal, | Könnt mein Liebchen ihr erspähen, | Grüßt sie mir viel tausendmal').

Finally, Lieder thematized nature not just through textual references, but also through their musical style. Simplicity of melody suggested simplicity of character, even the simplicity of the character of a people, and were essential to the aesthetics of the Lied in the eighteenth century.[13] Although the melodies of *An die ferne Geliebte* were carefully composed, Beethoven alluded to the shapes of folk song – gentle stepwise motion and the avoidance of virtuosity in the melodies, and rounded strophes, though always modified, in the forms.[14] While the song cycle is one of Beethoven's most elaborate in terms of its artifices of cyclical thematic returns, plays of harmony to set the text, harmonic plan and many other details, Beethoven

---

[13] Heinrich W. Schwab, *Sangbarkeit, Popularität und Kunstlied: Studien zu Lied und Liedästhetik der mittleren Goethezeit, 1770–1814* (Regensburg, 1965).

[14] Joseph Kerman, *Write All These Down* (Berkeley, 1994), pp. 181–3.

yet gestures towards the ideal of folk song. Infused with motivic connections they may be, but the mostly stepwise melodies situate the songs far from the realm of opera. As Kerman notes, Beethoven quiets his melody to repeated Fs, ornamented only with a small neighbour motion, at the culminating point at which the poet describes his own songs as 'sung without art'.[15] The words offer a mise-en-abîme of the principle of melodic restraint in the cycle. For German artists in particular, the aesthetics of the folk song provided models of values of 'genius, authenticity and purity'.[16] So long as there was a perceived connection between artist and folk, the same values could also be seen to inhabit more elaborate works.

But it is perhaps the play of memory that most suggestively inflects the tradition of the Lied in such a way as to suggest the attenuation of sovereign thought. Throughout the cycle, the poet shifts between memories of his beloved and hopes for communication with her. Past and present intermingle, and spatial distance acts as a metaphor for temporal distance in the cycle. The poet – the fictional author and protagonist of the songs – perhaps addresses his memory of a past love more than one simply not present,[17] or the poet imagines his beloved as singing the songs themselves.[18] Particularly powerful is the moment at which the poet, after losing himself in the fading glow of the sun as the last rays disappear behind a mountain, addresses his beloved as singing the songs he has just sung ('und du singest', bars 283–284). Kerman, Rosen and Marston single out the moment as one of a delicate negotiation of past, present and future – of memory and longing.[19]

What bears emphasis in the current context is the degree to which memory acts as both a disruption and a spur to intentionality in the song. Memories can be called up, but they also come involuntarily, and in moments of reverie it is difficult to tell the difference between the two. Memories signal disruption of willed thought and a brake on instrumental reason. In the play of dualistic correspondences that flow from the opposition between nature and civilization, or between human nature and human rationality, memories stand on the side of nature. They function

---

[15] Ibid., p. 194.

[16] Matthew Gelbart, *The Invention of Folk Music and Art Music: Emerging Categories from Ossian to Wagner* (Cambridge, 2007), p. 196.

[17] Kerman, *Write All These Down*, p. 179.

[18] Nicholas Marston, 'Voicing Beethoven's Distant Beloved', *Beethoven and His World*, eds. Scott Burnham and Michael P. Steinberg (Princeton, 2000), pp. 124–47, at p. 142.

[19] Kerman, *Write All These Down*, p. 195; Charles Rosen, *The Romantic Generation* (Cambridge, MA, 1995), p. 172; Marston, 'Voicing', p. 138.

in a similar way to emotions, also associated with nature. It is no surprise that a song cycle that presents a play with memory emanating from strong emotion features nature imagery so prominently. However, because of their engagement with thought, memories suggest that the opposition between nature and its other is not rigid.

At this point, Beethoven's specific thematizations of nature begin to blur into cultivation of affects, musical processes and formal organizations. These were ostensibly unmarked, but sat close to the aesthetics of nature in the eighteenth century. Effects of intense emotion, memory and spontaneity were both ideal responses to nature, but they could also become central to works that did not name or paint their ties to the pastoral or draw on the aesthetics of the Lied. Examples include the play of memory which brings the meditative opening phrases of the Piano Sonata in A Major, Op. 101 back in its finale, or the staging of spontaneous creation that disrupts the opening Vivace ma non troppo of the Piano Sonata in E Major, Op. 109.[20] In such cases, the music suggests mental processes at the borders of rational control.

At this moment, E. T. A. Hoffmann may well brandish a warning finger, noting that it is only my 'inadequate understanding that fails to grasp' Beethoven's 'rational awareness' and that in truth Beethoven was in full control of his materials, ruling over them 'in absolute authority'.[21] Were he anachronistically to take up from narrative theory distinctions between the composer of the music and the protagonist that one reads into music, Hoffmann would be right to note that there is a difference between the composer's agency and the narratives of attenuated agency that the music presents. Yet, as one moves from the shape of works to the shaping process itself, as one slides into biography, that is, one is left with the question as to why a composer celebrated for rational control was so taken with slips of mind.

In an extensive study of such slips, Karol Berger has placed Beethoven's work in the context of the dualistic aesthetics common to German Idealism. The 'aesthetic state' can be a personal one, the presentation of a momentary slip of mind or fumble of the fingers and thus a slip from pianist as invisible medium to pianist as 'Beethoven', as in the slow

[20] Elaine Sisman, 'Memory and Invention at the Threshold of Beethoven's Late Style', *Beethoven and His World*, eds. Scott Burnham and Michael P. Steinberg (Princeton, 2000); Richard Kramer, *Unfinished Music* (New York, 2008), pp. 265–84.
[21] Hoffmann, *Musical Writings*, p. 98.

movement (bars 71–72) of the Piano Sonata in C Major, Op. 2 No. 3.[22] It can represent a retreat into private thoughts, as when characters fall into an extended moments of reverie as they meditate on an extended moment in the Act I Quartet 'Mir ist so wunderbar' (No. 3) in *Fidelio*. 'The content of timelessness is revealed as inwardness', writes Berger.[23] It can also be a reflection of a distinction between the phenomenal world (governed by laws of causation) and the noumenal world (the realm of freedom).[24]

This distinction between the phenomenal and the noumenal was fundamental to German Idealism, though it played out differently in philosophical and artistic accounts. In Kant's work, the distinction arose in part from epistemological questions with metaphysical implications. It was possible to explain a person's action either as an act of free will or as an event caused by some earlier event. But as much as free will was central to human self-understandings, it was resistant to the types of empirical analysis that lent itself to discussions of causation. This dual approach to issues was replicated in other domains. Just as our practical understanding of the world had two sides to it, our theoretical understanding mediated between between those aspects of the world that conformed to frameworks of space and time (and that thus lent themselves to empirical analysis) and those aspects resistant to our understanding (Kant's thing-in-itself).

Two things should be emphasized in this quick summary of Kantian Idealism. First, that Kant finessed the question of agency by distinguishing between phenomenal causation and noumenal free will, but viewed them both as operational in every action. They were proper to the 'antinomies' of pure reason, in which two contradictory statements could both be true. There is no need at this point to enter into the critical Idealism through which Kant dealt with this dual structure to human experience. It is sufficient to note that, although Kant set high store by sovereignty, he recognized that human agency was also constrained.

If Kant aimed at practical and theoretical philosophy, his distinctions could easily be turned in other directions. Romantics distinguished between phenomenal and noumenal realms in ways that paralleled the opposition between urban and rural. In particular, they could figure the noumenal realm (that of the unknowable 'thing-in-itself') as that of Christian heaven or some metaphysical land of fantasy. This parallel between natural landscapes (whether rural or 'wild') and noumenal realms hardly

---

[22] Karol Berger, 'Beethoven and the Aesthetic State', *Beethoven Forum 7*, eds. Lewis Lockwood, Christopher Reynolds and Elaine R. Sisman (Lincoln, NE, 1999), pp. 17–44, at pp. 17–18.
[23] Ibid., p. 33.   [24] Ibid., pp. 38–9.

stood on sound logic. For one thing, no worldly landscape could belong to the noumenal realm. For another, natural phenomena depended on the types of causal chain that Kant associated with the phenomenal world. Finally, one might cynically note that cultivated and financially secure residents in cities had more freedom of choice than those constrained by rural poverty.

Yet, feeling is more important than logic to symbolic associations. To educated urbanites, noumenal and the natural worlds seemed sublime and served as focuses of yearning. Writers could easily elaborate the unknowable world of the thing-in-itself with visual and sonic imagery. Forests and mountains easily stand as places of awful or awesome mystery. In Ludwig Tieck's story 'Der blonde Eckbert' (1796), the woman Bertha tells of losing herself in an unpopulated forest, which she compares to hell, and then coming to a no less unfamiliar or uninhabited region, which appears as a paradise.[25] Less given to nature descriptions, E. T. A. Hoffmann preferred to figure the noumenal world in musical terms. In 'Ritter Gluck' (1809), the narrator recounts his experiences in this other realm with imagery close to that used by Hoffmann to describe Beethoven's music.

The association of pastoral and Idealist traditions offered metaphysical weight to excursions to the land, but, more importantly, they may have shifted the ideal mode of experience that a person was to take. The escape from urban spaces had long been associated with relaxation and escape from the pressures of urban life. They no doubt continued to be so. However, part of the value of the Romantic approach was self-forgetting, an immersion in the world in which a person felt themselves part of a network of entities. This form of experience had a variety of functions. As Kate Rigby has noted, Romantics noted that the experience could be productively directed so as to allow participants to reconsider their place in the world, even as a spur to the protection of their environments, or could be eviscerated as a form of tourism.[26]

Beethoven was one with his contemporaries in his quest for strong personal connections with the countryside. David Wyn Jones has surveyed the principal ways in which Beethoven demonstrated this attachment.[27] In numerous letters, he noted his love of countryside and his distate for urban environments. In May 1810, for example, he wrote to Therese Malfatti,

---

[25] Ludwig Tieck, *Märchen aus dem 'Phantasus'* (Stuttgart, 2003), p. 34.
[26] Rigby, 'Romanticism and Ecocriticism', pp. 69 and 73.
[27] Jones, *Pastoral Symphony*, pp. 19–22.

How fortunate you are to be able to go out into the country so soon. I cannot enjoy this happiness until the 8th, but I look forward to it with childish excitement. How delighted I shall be to ramble for a while through bushes, woods, under trees, through grass and around rocks. No one can love the country as much as I do. For surely woods, trees and rocks produce the echo which man desires to hear.[28]

He took frequent walks, either in the open space that separated the centre of Vienna from its suburbs. In summers he, like many others with the means to do so, escaped to an outlying village or spa such as Hetzendorf, Heiligenstadt, Nussdorf, Mödling or Baden, where he could spend long hours in the countryside. On his walks he normally carried a sketchbook with him and would use the solitude to put his mind to compositional problems or new ideas. Finally, he read. Christoph Christian Sturm's *Betrachtungen über die Werke Gottes in der Natur* (1772–76) presented nature as a manifestation of God's benevolence and has been taken as essential to understanding Beethoven's attitudes to nature.[29] Nature was in essence a form of revelation.

That Beethoven attributed religious significance to nature testifies to the intensity of his experience there. 'Every tree in the countryside said to me: "Holy! Holy!" In the forest, enchantment! Who can express it all?', he wrote on a loose sheet of paper.[30] As Maynard Solomon and Jones have noted, Beethoven's religious feelings followed typical lines of the Enlightenment. God stands above the world, tweaking its workings as a watchmaker might do a watch. Given his general distaste for religious doctrine and ritual, nature may have provided Beethoven his greatest experience of situatedness.

While Beethoven believed in God as a being above nature, it is also significant that Beethoven interested himself in forms of religiosity that viewed God as existing within nature. Most likely Beethoven lifted the three inscriptions that he kept under his glass from Friedrich Schiller's historical essay 'Die Sendung Moses' (1790).

> I am that which is.
> I am everything that is, that was, that will be. No mortal man has lifted my veil.
> He is of himself alone, and it is to this aloneness that all things owe their being.[31]

---

[28] LOB, vol. 1, p. 274; BG, vol. 2, p. 122.   [29] Jones, *Pastoral Symphony*, pp. 21–2.
[30] Solomon, *Beethoven Essays*, p. 219.
[31] Ibid., p. 225; Friedrich Schiller, *Sämtliche Werke in 5 Bänden*, vol. 4, eds. Peter-André Alt, Albert Meier and Wolfgang Riedel (Munich, 2004), pp. 792–3.

These were translations of hieroglyphic texts from the Statue and Pyramid of Isis at Sais and from a hymn of initiation.[32] Eighteenth-century European intellectuals were fascinated with these statements, as they crystallized issues of divine omnipresence, the limits of human cognition, the relationship between Christian and pagan religions, religious mystery and the sublime.[33] Variously interpreted, the statements led theologians, philosophers and historians to question the accepted narratives of their disciplines.

To take Beethoven's likely inspiration, Schiller (1759–1805) presented the rituals and doctrines of Egyptian polytheism as ways to communicate religious truth in ways that could be comprehensible to the uneducated. As the line of thought went, the priests of polytheistic religions knew the truth of monotheism, but kept that truth to themselves. The antiquarian argument, drawing heavily on the interpretation of Karl Leonhard Reinhard (1757–1825), aimed in part at excavating the relationship between polytheistic and monotheistic religions, but it also had implications for the relationship between humanity, nature and divinity. The proclamation of omnipresence served as a profession of divine immanence in nature, just as the mystery of the veil pointed towards the magical incomprehensibility nature – its sublimity. Isis, following a long line of mythological mother figures, was its personification.

The book and its reception fit into the larger religious debate about pantheism, as it was called. At the end of the eighteenth century, many German intellectuals, including both Ephraim Lessing and Johann Wolfgang von Goethe, read the ideas derived from the seventeenth-century Dutch Jewish philosopher Baruch Spinoza. According to this view, God was not a being that stood above the world, but was rather the sum total of the cosmos. There was no fundamental difference between human society and the natural world, as they were both simply modes of God. Pantheism was controversial. For theologians who held to the doctrines and dogmas of revealed religion, it seemed tantamount to atheism and was indeed called thus.[34]

---

[32] The first phrase, reported by Voltaire, was commonly interpreted as synonymous with the statement of the burning bush ('I am that I am') in Exodus 3:14. The second was transmitted by Plutarch ('On Isis and Osiris'), and the third by Eusebius and Clement of Alexander. Jan Assmann, *Moses the Egyptian: The Memory of Egypt in Western Monotheism* (Cambridge, MA, 1997), p. 118.

[33] Ibid., pp. 91–143.

[34] Frederick C. Beiser, *The Fate of Reason: German Philosophy from Kant to Fichte* (Cambridge, 1987), pp. 44–108.

While Beethoven showed a strong taste for the poetry and other writings of German artists involved in the pantheism controversy, he was distant enough from the halls of debate not to concern himself with contradictions between the quotations on his desk, on the one hand, and his appeals in words and in music to divine beings, from the Gellert Lieder of 1802 to his two masses to the Ninth Symphony. Yet his intellectual play with such materials is important. If traditional religious thought up through the Enlightenment (and often to the present day) had always distinguished human beings from nature, assigning humans stewardship over divine creation, Beethoven tended to see his own actions as part of a larger system.

There is one final way in which Beethoven's love of nature channelled his life. When Beethoven wrote to his childhood friend Wegeler on 16 November 1801, he spoke wistfully of his childhood surroundings: 'Those beautiful parts of my native land, what did they give me but the hope of bettering my circumstances?'[35] Memories of Bonn and the Rhine valley were strongly inflected by his recollections of natural beauties there. These memories are particularly poignant as they also suggest that they are linked both to social connection and to physical health. Beethoven notes that his moments in the lap of the Wegeler family were among the happiest in his life. Fragmentary as they may be, Beethoven's own accounts of intense experiences of place suggest that he displaced the very human search for connection and solace from his everyday life to experience of the countryside and memories of childhood.

One might retort to Hoffmann, then, that Beethoven did not so much rule over tones as a sovereign arbiter as channel his sense of connection with his world. Yet the conviction of Idealist aesthetics – that men had the power to rise above their conditions to put their stamp on the world around them – was a stubborn one. While Romantics, Idealists, Classicists and others of the late eighteenth and early nineteenth centuries looked to nature and the arts for experiences of connection, for experiences of attenuated agency, it was very much on their own terms.

Or was it? Nature – that multifaceted concept – lies without and within. In the final part of this essay I turn to another motivation of Idealism, the bodily experiences of its protagonists. It is easy to read Idealism at face value, as a celebration of human ingenuity and spirit, but the exuberant claims read differently if one remembers the degree to which its most

---

[35] LOB, vol. 1, p. 67; BG, vol. 1, p. 89.

ardent champions were prey to ill health and physical pain. Idealism itself was in many cases a response to experiences in which individuals were hardly arbiters of their fates.

On 10 May 1805, when doctors performed an autopsy on Friedrich Schiller, they were aghast at what they found: ossified rib cartilage, a right lung turned to mush, spots of pus on the left lung, shrivelled heart, distended gall bladder, swollen spleen, growths around the liver – in fact, only the bladder and the stomach were in normal condition. The lead doctor concluded, 'With such conditions, one must wonder how the man could live so long.'[36] Such conditions were not recent. Throughout his life, Schiller battled against ill health. This history of ill health puts his optimistic claims about the power of the human spirit in perspective. As the 'first definition' of Schiller's Idealism, one of his most philosophically astute biographers, Rüdiger Safranski, suggests that it 'is when the power of enthusiasm [*Begeisterung*] permits one to live longer than the body allows'.[37] It is a definition in tune with Schiller's time, but also one whose optimism overshoots brute facts of corporeal existence. High spirits may extend the body's limits, but they cannot overstay them.

Beethoven faced similar travails. Thomas Palferman's sober survey of Beethoven's medical history notes recurrent depression and infections, chest symptoms and 'asthma', recurrent diarrhoea and abdominal pain and attacks of rheumatism. Many of these complaints affected Beethoven throughout his adult life, especially the diarrhoea and abdominal pains. Later in life Beethoven also experienced jaundice, eye pains, dropsy (which Palferman interprets as peripheral oedema and ascites) and an enlarged liver. And then there was Beethoven's deafness.

At a time before modern medicine, hygiene and sanitation, such health complaints were not uncommon, though Schiller and Beethoven may have suffered more than many. Such bodily experiences need to be taken as a context for any interpretation of claims for the power of spirit. Beethoven himself did so. In the Heiligenstadt Testament, he attributed his single-mindedness to his increasing deafness: 'I would have ended my life—it was only *my art* that held me back. Ah, it seemed to me impossible to leave the world until I had brought forth all that I felt was within me. So I endured this wretched existence—truly wretched for so susceptible a body which

---

[36] Walter Hinderer, *Schiller und kein Ende: Metamorphosen und kreative Aneignungen* (Würzburg, 2009), p. 179.
[37] Rüdiger Safranski, *Friedrich Schiller, oder, die Erfindung des deutschen Idealismus* (Munich, 2004), p. 11.

can be thrown by a sudden change from the best condition to the very worst.'[38] The hope to rise above the body was itself an expression of the extreme subjection to the physical condition.

Early in his life, Schiller himself expressly warned against attributing too much power to human agency. In his medical dissertation on the connection of animal and spiritual nature of man, he first set out two opposed philosophical views, one which viewed the body as the spirit's prison, and another that attributed the happiness of human beings to the state of the body. He, he noted, sought a middle road. 'But because the general tendency is to err on the side of mental powers insofar as they are considered beyond any dependency on the body, so the current essay will concern itself more with the remarkable contribution of the body to the actions of the soul.'[39]

Schiller went on to explore the positive functions of pain and pleasure in regulating the harmony of spiritual and physical existence. He did consider body and soul as distinct, and professed confidence in the continued existence of the soul after the dissolution of the body. Yet he emphasized they were bound together up to the moment of death. Although he later left medical matters far behind him, he continued to treat philosophical and aesthetic matters with a similar concern for the interpenetration of physical and spiritual existence.

The interpenetration of physical and mental/spiritual concerns was not just a matter of philosophical musing, but was also something that was consciously cultivated. Beethoven may have boasted stoically of turning his back on his suffering, but he actually falls into a long line of artists who consciously turned their ailments to productive ends. Immanuel Kant (1724–1804), for example, worried often about his health, specifically about 'a narrow and flat chest, which leaves little room for the movements of heart and lung', as he wrote.[40] He noted his own tendency to hypochondria, and perhaps reformed his own life in response to the condition. In the latter part of his life, Kant turned away from his early interests in playing cards, relaxed socializing and attending concerts and the theatre. Modelling himself on the regular habits of a new friend, the Englishman Joseph Green, whom he met around 1764 or 1765, he eventually developed a strict daily schedule with set times for eating, writing, reading and walks.

---

[38] Alexander Wheelock Thayer, *Life of Beethoven*, rev. ed., vol. 1, ed. Elliot Forbes (Princeton, 1964), p. 305.

[39] Schiller, *Werke*, vol. 5, pp. 290–1.

[40] Manfred Kuehn, *Kant: A Biography* (New York, 2001), p. 151.

Hypochondria may seem a strange card to play in any discussion of the interrelationship between the physical and the mental. It is and was associated with imaginary ailments. But it could also be recognized as having both physiological and psychological origins. As Kant described it, 'it is an evil, which probably intermittently migrates through the entire nervous system, regardless which part of the body is its main location. It attracts primarily a melancholic vapor around the seat of the soul', which explains the hypochondriac's taste for medical literature and tendency to feel the sickness of which he hears. The hypochondriac can behave as if nothing was wrong in society, laughing, eating and socializing as any person would, but can also fall prey to states of anxiety 'similar to insanity, even if there is no danger'.[41]

Kuehn notes that Kant, in offering this general description, could very well have been drawing upon his own experience. He could also draw upon the experiences of others around him, such as his Königsberg friends Johann Georg Hamann and Christian Jakob Kraus, who both described themselves as hypochondriacs. It was after all a fashionable ailment in the eighteenth century. Samuel Johnson and James Boswell also complained of it,[42] as did Jean-Jacques Rousseau and Karl Philipp Moritz.[43] It owed its popularity in part to the cultural prestige of melancholy and brooding, associated as they were with genius.[44] As with melancholy, hypochondria emerged from the ambiguous space that ostensibly separated mind and body.

If the blurred line between physiological afflication and imaginative projection could be lambasted as the self-serving bluffing of a healthy person, as in Molière's *Le malade imaginaire* (1683), it could also be used to dismiss easy physiological explanations for complex psychological operations. In E. T. A. Hoffmann's late story, 'Die Räuber' (1820–21), a riff on and ironic reversal of Schiller's early play of the same name, the protagonist Wilhelm disparages his doctors' diagnosis of hypochondria as an oversimplification of the complex relationship between mind and body.[45] The narrator later describes the condition as a 'ruinous mood to which physical pain can also be attributed'.[46]

---

[41] Ibid., pp. 151–2.   [42] Ibid., p. 152.

[43] Matthew Bell, *The German Tradition of Psychology in Literature and Thought, 1700-1840* (New York, 2005), p. 89.

[44] Cf. Elaine Sisman, 'Music and the Labyrinth of Melancholy: Traditions and Paradoxes in C. P. E. Bach and Beethoven', *The Oxford Handbook of Music and Disability Studies*, eds. Blake Howe, Stephanie Jensen-Moulton, Neil Lerner and Joseph Straus (Oxford and New York, 2016), pp. 590–617, at pp. 592–5.

[45] E. T. A. Hoffmann, *Späte Werke*, ed. Friedrich Schnapp (Munich, 1965), p. 436.

[46] Ibid., p. 440.

Hypochondria was but one of the ways that Beethoven's contemporaries discussed the interpenetration of mind and body. In both life and literature, Hoffmann placed great emphasis on mood [*Stimmung*] as the meeting point of the physical and the psychological. In his diaries, he tracks his own shifting mood as much as he does the events of his days. Produced by a kaleidoscope of psychological and physical catalysts, exalted and exhausted moods succeed each other with at times astonishing rapidity. They colour his experience of the world, offering him moments of enthusiastic embrace of the world and scurrilously ironic distance,[47] but also stretches of indifferent days that were sadly ordinary (and unproductive): 'dies tristes atque ordinarii' as he designated 3–4 January, 4–7 February and 19–22 February 1812, for example.[48]

Mood and *Stimmung* return us to the close relationship between individuals and their environment and thus to the central concern of this essay. As noted by Leo Spitzer, the term expresses 'the unity of feelings experienced by man face to face with his environment (a landscape, nature, one's fellow man), and would comprehend and weld together the objective (factual) and the subjective (psychological) into one harmonious unity ... *Stimmung* is fused with the landscape, which in turn is animated by the feeling of man—it is an indissoluble unit into which man and nature are integrated.'[49] The essential aspect of *Stimmung* is the melding of things normally considered seperate. The fusion might occur between individual and landscape (nature without), but it also involves the fusion of psychic and physical life. In an article that picks up chronologically where Spitzer ended – towards the end of the eighteenth century – David Wellbery notes both the integrative function of *Stimmung* and its central but varying role in the aesthetics of the late eighteenth and nineteenth centuries.[50]

Thus, if Hoffmann celebrated Beethoven's sovereignty, it was in spite of many aspects of his own experience and philosophical inclinations, not to mention the experiences and inclinations of many contemporaries, including Beethoven himself. In part, the hyperbolic terms of Hoffmann's

---

[47] Keith Chapin, 'Lost in Quotation: Nuances Behind E. T. A. Hoffmann's Programmatic Statements', *Nineteenth-Century Music*, 30/1 (2006), pp. 44–64, at pp. 45–6.

[48] E. T. A. Hoffmann, *Tagebücher und literarische Entwürfe*, ed. Hans von Müller, 2 vols. (Berlin, 1915), vol. 1, pp. 174, 180 and 182.

[49] Leo Spitzer, *Classical and Christian Ideas of World Harmony: Prolegomena to an Interpretation of the Word 'Stimmung'*, ed. Anna Granville Hatcher (Baltimore, 1963), p. 5.

[50] David E. Wellbery, 'Stimmung', *Ästhetische Grundbegriffe: Historisches Wörterbuch in sieben Bänden*, ed. Karlheinz Barck (Stuttgart, 2000–05), vol. 5, pp. 703–33, at pp. 704–5.

review can be written down to the polemical rhetoric natural to a defence against criticism. In part, it is due to Hoffmann's tendency to cultivate the yin–yang of Romantic irony by writing in either enthusiastically hyperbolic or satirically deflationary terms, and to favour enthusiasm when he turned to the music he liked.[51] But in part, the celebration is part of what can be called the practice of Idealism.

As much as they may seem to prove the point of Idealist aesthetics – that it is possible for a person to produce work in spite of their body – such histories of susceptibility point in the exact opposite direction. It is precisely as a response to their physical conditions that these writers and artists produced their striking work. At a time in which modern medicine had not yet mitigated the daily experience of pain and suffering, Idealism was as much a practice as it was a philosophy.

---

[51] Keith Chapin, 'Sublime Experience and Ironic Action: E. T. A. Hoffmann and the Use of Music for Life', *Musical Meaning and Human Values*, eds. Keith Chapin and Lawrence Kramer (New York, 2009), pp. 32–58.

6 | (Cross-)Gendering the German Voice

KATHERINE HAMBRIDGE

> Imagine a calm, really feminine form, fully formed, about thirty years old;
> with beautiful arms, white, gentle, German, reliable, unspoilt; whose lips
> are open so wide that a lightly expressive, rich, full voice can comfortably
> flow through: then you will see Madame Milder, who performed in
> Gluck's *Armida* yesterday. If in your mind you add to such a figure an
> inner life of pure naivety that, in its innocence, reminds you of Pallas von
> Velletri (if I have the correct name), then you will have Armida.
>
> That such a creature, who is inhibited by no rules or acquired knowledge
> of the art, flows along like a fine stream, who doesn't come and go and
> stand as if an audience were present, but is rather like a blacksmith [who
> stands] before a forge in order to pull out hot what was placed in cold;
> that such a creature causes confusion and conflict for the connoisseurs of
> our art will become very evident perhaps because one says: a pretty
> woman – but colossal; a beautiful voice – but not what one calls singing;
> gentle and feminine – but cold and so on – and yet such sensational
> applause, as if they were really enthralled, moved and touched.
>
> So one sees with joy how the appearance of sheer talent turns to water
> the ideas of an entire generation, who had become so accustomed to
> suspending the natural.[1]
>
> Carl Friedrich Zelter, to Goethe, in 1815

Madame Milder was Pauline Anna Milder (1785–1838), in 1815 one of the
most celebrated singers in German lands, courted by Spontini for Paris,
and well on the way to securing an advantageous appointment in Berlin.
Madame Milder (sometimes Milder-Hauptmann) was also, most famously,
the first Fidelio, or rather, the first three Fidelios, persistently premiering
the cross-dressing, pistol-toting, husband-devoted Leonore to the Viennese
in 1805, 1806 and 1814.[2] In what follows, I shall pursue the ways in which
her cross-dressing in a range of repertoire, together with the gendered

---

[1] Letter no. 180, Zelter to Goethe, Berlin, 10–17 June 1815; Lorraine Byrne Bodley (trans. and ed.),
Goethe and Zelter: Musical Dialogues (Farnham, 2009), pp. 191–2.
[2] She left her previous post at the Wiener Hofoper in May 1815, a move apparently prompted by
unfavourable economic circumstances in Vienna after the Congress: see J. P. Schmidt,

receptions of her physique and vocal production, contributed to the 'confusion and conflict' expressed in so genteel a fashion by Zelter; and the ways in which this category confusion enabled the discursive construction of a national singing style, which 'turn[ed] to water the ideas of an entire generation'.

For the purposes of this volume, this chapter may also serve to shed new light on a specifically Beethovenian question: how might we understand the contemporary resonances of the cross-dressing in *Fidelio*? This question has been pursued less than one might expect. Despite a measurable spike in female cross-dressing in German stage works during this period, *Fidelio* is one of the few canonical to *music* history, and thus Leonore has rarely been viewed as part of a broader German phenomenon.[3] This is perhaps linked to a historic hesitation, with a few notable exceptions, to bring the fields of gender studies and Beethoven studies together, an approach exemplified by Paul Robinson in his 1996 Cambridge Handbook on the opera:

The most important thing about Leonore's transvestism is that it interests Beethoven not in the slightest. It is for him nothing more than a necessity of the plot ... His art was desexualised on principle, the purest instance of sublimation, uncompromisingly spiritual and disembodied ... In every meaningful musical and dramatic sense, Beethoven treats her exactly as if she were a man.[4]

I am not the first to challenge such a reading: two decades after the handbook's appearance, this supposed transcendence of gender was brilliantly recast by Matthew Head as nothing *less* than a necessity of plot: that it was actually highly significant for Beethoven that Fidelio was female. Heroic action from a woman was all the more heroic (and exceptional), in Beethoven's eyes, because women had to transcend the greater limits of their gender. At the same time, Head argues, identification with women gave access to those 'feminine' qualities prized by Beethoven and the German Romantics, and indeed by the wider Christian culture, in the internalization of heroism via resignation and patient suffering. Both of

---

'Nekrolog', *AmZ*, 40/28 (1838), cols. 449–52, at col. 451. She became Milder-Hauptmann in 1810, when she married the court jeweller Peter Hauptmann (1763–1858); they later separated.

[3] See, for example, Michael L. Griffel and John Potter, 'Transcending Gender and Cross-Dressing: Leonore as Romantic Revolutionary', *The Beethoven Journal*, 11/1 (1996), pp. 9–11; Silke Leopold, 'Frauen in Männerkleidern oder: Versuch einer Antwort auf die scheinbar sinnlose Frage, warum Marzelline Leonore nicht erkennt', in *Von der Leonore zum Fidelio: Vorträge und Referate des Bonner Symposions 1997*, eds. Helga Lühning and Wolfram Steinbeck (Frankfurt am Main, 2000), pp. 147–58.

[4] Paul Robinson, *Ludwig van Beethoven: Fidelio* (Cambridge, 1996), pp. 68–110, at pp. 96–7.

these strands can be seen in Beethoven's affinity with Joan of Arc, whose lines from Schiller's play he quoted in relation to his own situation in letters to Bettina Brentano in 1811.[5]

What if, though, we were to pursue the meaning(s) of cross-dressing not through Beethoven – or Schiller, for that matter – but through its history as staged performance? Through movements, bodies and voices as perceived by audiences and critics? Even when the aim of cross-dressing was not to 'pass' as a man on stage but to express androgyneity (as in the case of Schiller's Joan of Arc who, styled on Minerva, wore a helmet and breast-plate, but not trousers), some at the time seem to have struggled with the qualities that so appealed to Beethoven's imagination.[6] A Berlin reviewer in 1805, for example, lamented the ultimate limits of Luise Fleck's perform-ance of Joan, concluding that 'verisimilitude in this role can only be increased to the extent that the [female] actor's figure is more masculine'. In his view, a 'female role with unfemininity', such as the 'unnaturalness' of a girl's hand grasping a sword, would always resist performance, being convincing only to the intellect, but not to feeling.[7] Cross-dressing on the operatic stage posed similar *and* additional – vocal – challenges for audi-ences in this period. In addressing the relative scholarly neglect of these issues in a German context, I shall focus on the extensive reception discourse that gathers around Milder in the years leading up to 1814, in a range of roles, performed and discussed across German lands.

While my conclusions can be read onto the particular Beethovenian case within a specifically Viennese context, I will ultimately cast the singer in a larger role here. What emerges from descriptions of Milder's perform-ances, as can be seen in Zelter's letter, is that her disruption of increasingly binary gender categories had consequences for other binary oppositions in operatic discourse, in particular those of national singing styles. This period has typically been cast in German operatic history as that of the hunt for a national opera, via Weber and *Der Freischütz*, Hoffmann and *Undine* and so on, in opposition to the dominance of the Italian tradition; and the construction of the German–Italian binary eventually known as the 'twin styles'. Beethoven's opera has always been somewhat offset from

---

[5] Matthew Head, *Sovereign Feminine: Music and Gender in Eighteenth-Century Germany* (Berkeley, 2013), pp. 190–232.

[6] On Schiller's cross-dressing of Joan see Helen Watanabe-O'Kelly, 'Wearing the Trousers: The Woman Warrior as Cross-Dresser in German Literature', in *Women and Death 2: Warlike Women in the German Literary and Cultural Imagination since 1500*, eds. Sarah Colvin and Helen Watanabe-O'Kelly (Rochester, NY, 2009), pp. 28–44, at pp. 35–6.

[7] *Haude und Spenersche Zeitung* (hereafter *HSZ*), no. 49 (23 April 1805).

histories of this discourse, not least because of the emblematic status of his symphonic works. But I would suggest that *Fidelio* can be resituated within it indirectly by pursuing the role that singers – rather than composers and works – played in its construction; and specifically, the role of Milder and her reviewers in this process. Milder's category-crossing voice and figure destabilized pre-existing associations between gender, singing style and nation, and enabled new ones. This space of possibility, I will argue, allowed for the emergence of a newly conceived category of German operatic vocality. For many critics in the first few decades of the nineteenth century, the idea of the 'German voice' was embodied by Milder.

Cross-Dressing on the German (Operatic) Stage

In both operatic and spoken theatre genres, high and low, cross-dressed women were a pronounced feature on the German stage around 1800. In recent literary scholarship this has been attributed to a set of interlocking developments. Firstly, the high profile examples of female heroism and cross-dressed military service in the Revolutionary and Napoleonic wars are thought to have provoked a desire to celebrate or contain the phenomenon.[8] Secondly, as Thomas Laqueur has shown, where previously women were thought to have inverted versions of male genitalia, and gender characteristics thus to exist on a spectrum of greater or lesser masculinity, by the late eighteenth century the emerging 'two-sex', or 'Geschlechtscharakter', model located the differences between men and women in their entirely different bodies, and with fundamental (and 'natural') differences in kind. The qualities of masculine and feminine were thus associated increasingly rigidly with biological sex.[9] At the same time, German Romantic writers such as Novalis, Friedrich Schlegel, Schleiermacher and Jean Paul celebrated androgyny as an ideal of wholeness via a synthesis of polar opposites.[10] These new conceptualizations of gender had their theatrical consequences: the familiar figure of Joan of Arc was accompanied on

---

[8] See, for example, Elisabeth Krimmer, *In the Company of Men: Cross-Dressed Women Around 1800* (Detroit, 2004); Colvin and Watanabe-O'Kelly, *Women and Death 2*; Wendy C. Nielsen, *Women Warriors in Romantic Drama* (Newark, 2013).

[9] Wilhelm von Humboldt's 1795 essays 'Über den Geschlechtsunterschied und dessen Einfluß auf die organische Natur' and 'Über die männliche und weibliche Form' are widely cited examples of this new position. See Thomas Laqueur's *Making Sex: Body and Gender from the Greeks to Freud* (Cambridge, 1990).

[10] Jean Paul called Novalis a 'Mannweib', for example. See Catriona MacLeod, *Embodying Ambiguity: Androgyny and Aesthetics from Winckelmann to Keller* (Detroit, 1998), p. 49, fn. 58; and Christine Battersby, *Gender and Genius: Towards a Feminist Aesthetics* (London, 1989).

stage by women in various states of cross-dress (and musicalization): Klärchen in Goethe's *Egmont* (1788); Zacharias Werner's *Wanda, Königin der Sarmaten* (Weimar, 1808; Vienna, 1810, with Milder as Wanda); Heinrich von Kleist's Amazon *Penthesilea* (not performed, 1808); Piwald's *Das Mädchen von Potsdam* (Vienna, 1814); Friedrich Duncker's *Leonore Prohaska* (Vienna, 1815, with Beethoven's music, but apparently not performed); Johann Gottlieb Naumann's *La Dama soldato/ Das weibliche Soldat* (Dresden, 1791); Adalbert Gyrowetz's *Mirina, Königin der Amazonen* (Vienna, 1806); Johann Friedrich Reichardt's *Bradamante* (Vienna, 1809, with Milder as Bradamante); and Ferdinand Kauer's *Die Amazonen in Böhmen* (Vienna, 1815), to name but a few.

Situations of cross-dressing where women appear temporarily in male disguise, or as androgynous or war-like characters, differ somewhat from the familiar scholarly narratives on operatic (and usually Italian operatic) cross-dressing in this period. Musicological accounts tend to trace the decline of the castrato[11] and his replacement in male soprano roles by cross-dressed women, whether in roles originally written for castrati (such as Zingarelli's *Giulietta e Romeo*, 1796 – created by Girolamo Crescentini but perpetuated by Guiditta Pasta and Maria Malibran), or male roles written for women, continuing the tradition of the heroic soprano pitch (such as the title role in Rossini's *Tancredi*, 1813, created by Adelaide Malanotte).[12] Gradually, solidifying conventions of gender difference produce the rise of the heroic tenor and the decline of cross-dressing women in general, except for particular roles: the youth (such as Romeo in Bellini's *I Capuleti ed i Montecchi*, 1830) or the occasional disguise role (Gilda in Verdi's *Rigoletto*, 1851). During the first few decades of the nineteenth century when women commonly replaced castrati, meanwhile, they have been interpreted as 'haunted' by the 'hidden aesthetic' of the castrato tradition of bel canto,[13] and as summoning nostalgia for the castrato.[14]

---

[11] Meyerbeer's *Il Crociato in Egitto* (1824), for Giovanna Battista Velluti, is thought to be the last castrato role. See Martha Feldman, *The Castrato: Reflections on Natures and Kinds* (Berkeley, 2015); James Q. Davies, *Romantic Anatomies of Performance* (Berkeley, 2014), pp. 13–40.

[12] See, for example, Naomi André's *Voicing Gender: Castrati, Travesti, and the Second Woman in Early-Nineteenth-Century Italian Opera* (Bloomington, 2006); and Heather Hadlock, 'Women Playing Men in Italian Opera', in *Women's Voices across Musical Worlds*, ed. Jane A. Bernstein (Boston, 2004), pp. 285–304; Heather Hadlock, 'On the Cusp between Past and Future: The Mezzo-Soprano Romeo of Bellini's *I Capuleti*', *Opera Quarterly*, 17/3 (2001), pp. 299–322.

[13] See André, *Voicing Gender*, pp. 12, 16–50; and Davies, *Romantic Anatomies of Performance*, p. 17.

[14] Feldman cites Stendhal framing Pasta as part of the 'bonne école' of Crescentini and Velluti, for example: *The Castrato*, pp. 234–7, 239.

Such interpretative frameworks are not easily transferable to the German context: not only were many of the cross-dressed roles disguised or warrior women rather than male soprano roles, but castrati had also long been triply foreign to the discourse of the German music profession, as aristocratic, Italian and, of course, castrated.[15] And although Italian operas were performed in German lands with castrato roles replaced by women, by far the more common instance of cross-dressed women singing male roles hitting the headlines in the first few decades of the nineteenth century was women taking on tenor roles. This was presented as a musical necessity, whether due to the lack of tenors[16] or the lack of good contralto roles to provide a vehicle for stars such as Marianne Schönberger-Marconi (1785–1882).[17] Moreover, while both soprano and alto cross-dressed operatic performance was condemned by some commentators as a perversion of nature, as sexual titillation, or as a musical distortion of the original work (responses also found in Italian discourse), it was the cross-dressing altos that were subject to the most pronounced criticism from the perspective of what we would now call gender performance.[18] Schönberger's appearance in Munich in 1812 as Belmonte in *Die Entführung aus dem Serail*, and then as the lead in Paer's *Sargines*, provoked 'a certain enthusiasm, spread by the novelty of a female man', but led one reviewer to issue a reproof:

The large crowd may well admire the rare and adventurous, but it must also return to the natural and the true. An alto voice can no more replace the tenor, than the male dress or the painted moustache lend male strength. And who [amongst us] who respects the dignity of women would like to see such attempts multiplied?[19]

The deepness of the alto voice (the possibility of equivalence) seems to account for the greater discomfort elicited by alto cross-dressing. The

[15] See Elisabeth Krimmer, '"Evviva il coltello?": The Castrato Singer in Eighteenth-Century German Literature and Culture', *PMLA*, 120/5 (2005), pp. 1543–59; and Sophie Bertone, '"Benedetto il coltello?": Wilhelm Heinse und die Kastraten', in *Musikalisches Denken im Labyrinth der Aufklärung: Wilhelm Heinses Hildegard von Hohenthal*, eds. Thomas Irvine, Wiebke Thormählen and Oliver Wiener (Mainz, 2015), pp. 145–62.

[16] See *AmZ*, 16/19 (1814), col. 317; *AmZ*, 17/11 (1815), col. 186.

[17] *Morgenblatt für gebildete Stände* (hereafter *MfgS*), 5/274 (1811), p. 1096. The contralto Friederike Ellmenreich (1775–1845) was also well known for her tenor roles.

[18] On the first two objections, see Freyherr von Seckendorff's preface to his *Vorlesungen über Deklamation und Mimik* (Braunschweig, 1816), vol. 1, pp. 5–6. Complaints about the distortion of the original composition can be seen in criticism of Milder as Tamino in *MfgS*, 6/166 (1812), p. 664; *AmZ*, 14/34 (1812), col. 559; *AmZ*, 14/41 (1812), col. 668; *AmZ*, 16/10 (1814), col. 163; and of Schönberger at tenor pitch in *MfgS*, 5/142 (1811), p. 568; *MfgS*, 5/274 (1811), p. 1095.

[19] *AmZ*, 14/8 (1812), col. 122.

unpopularity of Marianne Sehring's performance in Königsberg, for example, was attributed to her 'somewhat masculine organ (like [that of] every alto)'.[20] Schönberger's performance in Vienna as Titus in Mozart's opera drew praise for her artistry in song and acting, but prompted the reflection that 'one leaves the theatre with a certain coldness, which, however, may also be explained by the fact that a masculine quality found in a lady excludes both sexes too sharply, and for psychological reasons, cannot arouse lively interest on any side'.[21] Likewise, in his 1816 acting treatise *Vorlesungen über Deklamation und Mimik*, Freyherr von Seckendorff argued that when Schönberger sings at tenor pitch, neither 'unfemininity [nor] unmanliness' are detectable, the curious expression suggesting a specific discomfort with the androgyny of the alto voice in this range, which lacks definite markers of either sex.[22]

The tenorial alto in male clothing was all too ambiguous for these critics, despite the long operatic traditions of cross-dressing and castrati, and their rejection of this androgyny most likely reflects the increasing polarization of gender binaries discussed above. Indeed, Catriona MacLeod has argued that the earlier 'polymorphous, hermaphroditic ideal of androgyny proposed by Winckelmann', which was based on genders existing on a spectrum, gave way to a 'model grounded in heterosexual complementarity' in the theories of Humboldt, Schiller and Schlegel (presupposing the opposition of the two sexes in the first place). This led, she argues, to 'the uncanny doubleness that will mark the androgyne's future: monstrosity in the real world versus perfection in the aesthetic realm'.[23] Any operatic cross-dressing performed – in the real world – a potential disruption of those emerging binaries, and the tenorial alto more than most.

But it was not merely the (re)assertion of those 'natural' binaries that was provoked in response: operatic cross-dressing in this period had a productive destabilizing impact on categories of national style of the kind suggested by Marjorie Garber in her classic formulation of the cause and impact of transvestism:

one of the most consistent and effective functions of the transvestite in culture is to indicate the place of what I call 'category crisis', disrupting and calling attention to cultural, social, or aesthetic dissonances … The binarism male/female, one

---

[20] *AmZ*, 11/40 (1809), col. 638.   [21] *MfgS*, 7/81 (1813), p. 324.

[22] Seckendorff, *Vorlesungen über Deklamation und Mimik*, vol. 1, p. 211. See Marco Beghelli and Raffaele Talmelli, *Ermafrodite armoniche: Il contralto nel'Ottocento* (Varese, 2011) for similar Italian responses to the contralto voice.

[23] MacLeod, *Embodying Ambiguity*, pp. 23, 32.

apparent ground of distinction (in contemporary eyes, at least) between 'this' and 'that', 'him' and 'me' is itself put in question or under erasure in transvestism, and a transvestite figure, or a transvestite mode, will always function as a sign of over-determination – a mechanism of displacement from one blurred boundary to another. [24]

The transvestite produces a 'third' to those binary divisions, 'a mode of articulation, a way of describing a space of possibility' in response to, or inducing, a crisis in category.[25]

Garber's theory can be productively applied here, though its applicability is more suggestive than exact. In fact, precisely because the cross-dressed tenorial alto was so acutely destabilizing, the space it may have opened up for imagining 'thirds' in operatic performance seems to have been shut down discursively – as far as possible – by critics. The less radical but still destabilizing soprano cross-dresser, however, *does* seem to have functioned as a space for the negotiation of categories of national operatic difference in a German context. Because the 'natural' sex of the cross-dressed soprano singer remained recognisably (vocally) female even if hybrid gender characteristics were displayed, a 'masculinized soprano' such as Milder both left the binary categories intact *and* enabled German critics to position their responses to her within the emerging opposition of Italian and German styles ('them' and 'us') in nineteenth-century opera criticism. Here, I would argue, is a new framework through which we can appreciate the distinctiveness of German responses to operatic cross-dressing, understand the cultural work done by Milder's cross-dressing as Wanda, Bradamante, Fidelio et al., and gain new purchase on the transformations in German discourses of national operatic style in this period.

These discursive developments are part of a larger and longer story, of course. If in the eighteenth century the most prominent binary categories of musical nationhood had been the opposition of French and Italian operatic styles (as demonstrated most famously in the Querelle des Bouffons), the international dominance of Italian opera, particularly in German lands, was long established. Effeminacy, moreover, had been attributed by some German writers to Italian music since the mid-eighteenth century, above all to elite opera, above all to the castrato, leading to a common association in German music criticism between vocality itself, Italy and

---

[24] Marjorie Garber, *Vested Interests: Cross-Dressing and Cultural Anxiety* (London, 1993), p. 16.
[25] Ibid., p. 11. See Naomi André's different use of Garber in *Voicing Gender*, pp. 48–50.

effeminacy.[26] The gendered, devalorizing rhetoric surrounding Italian opera contributed to the establishment of masculine instrumental music as the German national musical product, in a way that could be mapped onto other binaries, whether melody versus harmony/counterpoint, or fashion versus profundity.[27] This model of overlapping binaries involved the subsumption of the French, as we shall see, as well as the discursive construction of a distinctively German musical category (partly through mere opposition with its Italian counterpart), where previously the German had been portrayed as a 'mix' of other national styles.[28] But the overlapping binaries created a particularly problematic ground for establishing a German national category in the field of opera, both in theory and practice. With operatic vocality itself associated with Italianness and effeminacy, and the world of opera in German lands dominated by French and Italian composers, genres and Italian performers, the very art of singing required rhetorical transformation for the category of 'German opera' to succeed.

Madame Milder as German Voice

After arriving in Vienna as a young girl, Milder first took music lessons with the village schoolmaster in Hütteldorf, before studying with Sigismund Neukomm and Antonio Salieri. Her vocal persona, as discursively constructed by the press, is at least in part a product of her early role choices and vocal technique. As Andreas Mayer has pointed out, she made her debut in 1803 at the Theater an der Wien as Juno in Franz Süssmayr's heroic-comic opera *Der Spiegel von Arkadien* with a simple rather than a bravura aria.[29] Later the same year, she played the cross-dressed role of

---

[26] See Krimmer, '"Evviva il coltello?"', p. 1543; Mary Sue Morrow shows how these binaries inflected the German reception of Italian instrumental music in *German Music Criticism in the Late Eighteenth Century* (Cambridge, 1997), pp. 46–65.

[27] The twin styles (*Stildualismus*) framework was influentially propagated by Carl Dahlhaus in *Nineteenth-Century Music*, trans. J. Bradford Robinson (Berkeley, 1989). More recently, it has been subject to extensive deconstruction: see Nicholas Mathew and Benjamin Walton (eds.), *The Invention of Beethoven and Rossini: Historiography, Analysis, Criticism* (Cambridge, 2013).

[28] See Bernd Sponheuer, 'Reconstructing Ideal Types of the "German" in Music', in *Music and German National Identity*, eds. Celia Applegate and Pamela Potter (Chicago, 2002), pp. 36–58.

[29] Andreas Mayer, '"Gluck'sches Gestöhn" und "welsches Larifari": Anna Milder, Franz Schubert und der deutsch-italienische Opernkrieg', *Archiv für Musikwissenschaft*, 52/3 (1995), pp. 171–204, at pp. 175–6. The aria comes in Act 2, scene 3: 'Juno wird dich stets umschweben'. There is not the space here to pursue Milder's investment (or not) in a 'German' ideal. Certainly she continued to sing Italian arias in concerts despite her technical limitations, and even, in the

Cambyses in Ignaz von Seyfried's heroic opera *Cyrus in Persien*. Georg August Griesinger, reporting on the performance for the *Allgemeine musikalische Zeitung*, wrote that 'her voice sounds as the purest metal, as is seldom the case, and, since her teacher Neukomm is from the Haydn school, she gives long strong notes without frills and overloaded ornaments'.[30]

Mayer underlines the usefulness of Milder's voice to the supporters of German opera in Vienna, of whom Ignaz von Mosel was the high priest.[31] But her significance was in fact far wider on account of her tours in this period: in 1810, to Frankfurt, Stuttgart und Ludwigsburg; 1811, Linz, Munich, Stuttgart and Darmstadt; 1812, Breslau and Berlin; 1813, Karlsruhe, Linz, Darmstadt and Frankfurt; 1814, Mannheim and Karlsruhe; and 1815, Berlin (twice) and Hamburg. Her performances and voice were therefore discussed in a reading community that stretched across German lands, in journals and in publications such as Reichardt's *Vertraute Briefe geschrieben auf einer Reise nach Wien und den Oesterreichischen Staaten zu Ende des Jahres 1808 und zu Anfang 1809* (itself reviewed in the same journals), where the author stated that hers 'is outright the most beautiful, fullest, purest voice I have ever heard in my life in Italy, Germany, France and England'.[32] As such, she was measured against her reputation in print on arrival in a new city, and offered a shared point of reference for reviewers and correspondents thereafter.[33] The correspondent from Stuttgart in 1810, for example, reported that the 'star of the first greatness on our dramatic horizons' had perfectly satisfied their high expectations;[34] a month later in Frankfurt, on the other hand, 'as a singer who was so

---

1820s, repeatedly (and ill-advisedly) attempted Rossini in order to compete with other prima donnas such as Henriette Sontag. See her letter to Ignaz von Mosel from 1828, cited in Mayer, '"Gluck'sche Gestöhn"', p. 187, fn. 50.

[30] *AmZ*, 6/2 (1803), col. 180. Although the review is anonymous, Griesinger can be identified as its author by the appearance of this passage in his correspondence with Breitkopf and Härtel: Otto Biba (ed.), '*Eben komme ich von Haydn. . .*': *Georg August Griesingers Korrespondenz mit Joseph Haydns Verleger Breitkopf & Härtel 1799–1819* (Zürich, 1987), pp. 212–13.

[31] Mayer, '"Gluck'sche Gestöhn"', pp. 175–6.

[32] Johann Friedrich Reichardt, *Vertraute Briefe: geschrieben auf einer Reise nach Wien und den Österreichischen Staaten zu Ende des Jahres 1808 und zu Anfang 1809*, 2 vols. (Amsterdam, 1810), vol. 1, p. 156.

[33] For examples of Milder used as the point of comparison for other singers, see *Musikalische Zeitung für die oesterreichischen Staaten*, 1/4 (1812), p. 27 (Munich); *MfgS*, 6/289 (1812), p. 1156 (Stuttgart); *MfgS*, 9/50 (1815), p. 300 (Karlsruhe); *MfgS*, 6/210 (1815), p. 840 (Munich).

[34] *MfgS*, 4/209 (1810), p. 835.

popular in the newspapers, in Reichardt's *Briefen* etc., she did not live up to our expectations';[35] while in 1812, the Berlin correspondent warned that '*praesentia minuit famam* [presence diminishes fame]'.[36]

Within this community of critics pronouncing on Milder's voice, there was consensus about its beauty and power, but her technique and singing style was celebrated by some as simple and natural (that is, embodying potentially strong 'German' qualities) and decried by others as lacking the flexibility and polish associated with Italian singing, depending on the affinities of the commentator. As early as 1808, Mosel styled her as the choice of the connoisseurs, with her 'powerful, expressive, deeply thought-out performance' and her 'resurrection of the simple, natural song, which alone corresponds to the true taste'.[37] In 1810, a Stuttgart critic made explicit her national significance:

The impact her singing made on audiences accustomed to the more decorated Italian school was unique. No coloratura, no trills, no mordents, none of all that, by which otherwise the ear can be bribed, but the simplest, most soulful, one would like to say most genuine German song of a 'harmonica voice', which gives the smallest note its full due . . .[38]

Two years later a reporter from Breslau described a continued division in the audience between those with a taste for 'flourishes and fioritura [roulades], leaps and other such arts' and those who appreciated 'the metal of her splendid organ, the evenness of the tones, both in strength and in sound, to an extent of two octaves, the purity'.[39]

There were plenty of critics, however, who remained committed to the art of flourishes and fioritura; for whom Italian models were the benchmark of operatic singing, even for a German singer. One Frankfurter in 1810 doubted that Milder should really be classified as a singer at all (a question raised by Zelter too, in a less pejorative way), on account of the simplicity of her roles (her standard touring repertoire consisted of Emmeline in Weigl's *Die Schweizerfamilie*, the title roles in Gluck's *Iphigenia in Tauris* and Paer's *Sargines*, Therese in Weigl's *Das Waisenhaus* and Tamino in *Die Zauberflöte*) and the absence of all that 'can be expected of a well-trained singer: no growth and disappearance of the sound, not a mordent, even fewer trills and roulades'.[40] During her 1811 visit to Munich, the *AmZ*, while commending Milder for 'striving to restore the rights of

---

[35] *AmZ*, 12/49 (1810), cols. 790–1.   [36] *AmZ*, 14/41 (1812), col. 670.

[37] *Vaterländische Blätter für den österreichischen Kaiserstaat*, no. 7 (31 May 1808), p. 49.

[38] *MfgS*, 4/209 (1810), p. 835.   [39] *AmZ*, 14/41 (1812), col. 668.

[40] *AmZ*, 12/49 (1810), cols. 790–1.

reason and good taste' in theatrical singing, nonetheless remarked that a 'dry song cannot be the height of art', finding her lacking relative to 'Farinelli, David, and Crescentini ... Grassini, Todi and Banti'.[41] A year later, the *AmZ* concluded not only that 'her song is only ever beautiful declamation, [it] never overflows into the actual art of singing', but also that her acting 'portrays nature rather too stark-nakedly [splitternackt]'.[42]

Milder's best and worst vocal qualities were therefore one and the same, and she was presented as incompatible with established Italianate models of singing. The terms of her reviews built on and expanded binary oppositions of vocality: whether 'genuine German song' versus the 'decorated' Italian school; 'Grösse' and 'Ernst' versus 'Galanterie' and 'Scherz';[43] or deficient technique (mere declamation) versus art, or nature versus artifice. These oppositions dominated the reception of Milder's visit to Berlin in 1812 in particular, not least through the rivalry with local, conventionally 'kunstreich' ('artful') singer Auguste Schmalz, against whom Milder's virtues were measured.[44] Reviewers accorded both artists their 'own crowns': Milder 'freshness of voice and ... noble naturalness'; Schmalz 'the art of prodigious skill and precision'.[45] One journalist even dramatized their joint concert as a 'competition' in which audience members shrieked a number of well-constructed soundbites: 'It is the battle of nature with art, but nature will be victorious!'; 'Dem. Schmalz has her voice much more in her power ... but Mad. Milder has much more power in her voice'; 'I dedicate to Dlle. Schmalz my ears, Mad. Milder my heart'.[46]

The familiar elements of this reception (the characterization of virtuosity as empty effect, for example) should not obscure the light it can shed on operatic twin styles rhetoric, in particular the transferral of characteristics between nations and genres relative to eighteenth-century discourses. I have already suggested that German *opera*, as a vocal genre, could not easily fit into the overlapping binaries of the twin styles. Where Italian opera was opposed to German instrumental music, its associated qualities of effeminacy, simplicity/superficiality and melody could be positioned against masculinity, complexity and harmony/counterpoint. German opera could not do without melody, however; nor could it be effeminate. In an attempt to create a distinct – and positive – category for German vocality, genuine, simple and natural German song was opposed to Italian

---

[41] *AmZ*, 13/37 (1811), col. 625.   [42] *AmZ*, 14/18 (1812), col. 304.
[43] *AmZ*, 15/522 (1813), col. 846.   [44] *AmZ*, 15/41 (1812), col. 669.
[45] *AmZ*, 14/41 (1812), col. 669; *MfgS*, 6/250 (1812), p. 1000.
[46] 'Der Wettkampf im Konzerte des Hrn. Sidoni', *MfgS*, 6/261 (1812), p. 1043.

opera's insincerity, *over*-complexity and/or artifice. The opposition of nature and art, which across the course of the eighteenth century had been used to valorize (Italian) vocal simplicity against (often German) instrumental complexity in the form of the galant; Italian vocal naturalness against French operatic formality in the Querelle des Bouffons; and then later, French 'naturalness' against Italian artifice in the operatic reforms of Gluck etc., is here re-employed to elevate the German operatic voice over the Italian.

Such a rhetorical twist was possible in part through an established association of German vocality with simplicity and naturalness in the shape of the Lied and the Singspiel.[47] Both genres had been presented as an indigenous alternative to Italian opera since the eighteenth century, though the very source of their simplicity and 'authenticity' – as products 'im Volkston' – gave them an ambiguous aesthetic status relative to tragic opera. The elevation of the German 'natural' relies, I argue, on the incorporation of 'French' values associated with Gluck's tragic operas into the idea of German opera, at a time when Gluck himself was also being redefined as German.[48] This can be seen in descriptions of Milder's '*noble naturalness*', as above, and in the attention given to her supposedly natural acting, declamation, and general adherence to the score (where celebrated rather than bemoaned, that is). One Stuttgart reviewer suggested that Milder unusually combined the roles of singer and actor;[49] Reichardt highlighted her 'heroic figure and movement' as Iphigenia, 'without the affected operatic comings and goings and distortions of the body and neck', observations that Zelter then echoes in his letter to Goethe: she 'doesn't come and go and stand as if an audience were present'.[50] A Munich correspondent in 1811 rejoiced that in avoiding ornamentation in Gluck's *Iphigenia in Tauris*, Milder 'remains faithful to the serious

---

[47] See Estelle Joubert, 'Songs to Shape a German Nation: Hiller's Comic Operas and the Public Sphere', *Eighteenth-Century Music*, 3/2 (2006), pp. 213–30; and Jennifer Ronyak, 'Anna Milder-Hauptmann's "Favourite Lied": The Domestic Side of a Monumental Simplicity' in *Liedersingen: Studien zur Aufführungsgeschichte des Liedes im 18. und 19. Jahrhundert*, ed. Katharina Hottmann, *Jahrbuch Musik und Gender* (Hildesheim: Georg Olms Verlag, 2013), pp. 93–108.

[48] Gundula Kreuzer has pursued this move in the context of later historiography in '*Heilige Trias, Stildualismus, Beethoven*: On the Limits of Nineteenth-Century Germanic Music Historiography', in *The Invention of Beethoven and Rossini*, pp. 66–95. On the Frenchness of German opera, see John Warrack, *German Opera: From the Beginnings to Wagner* (Cambridge, 2001); on the 'Germanness' of Gluck, see Katherine Hambridge, 'Catching Up and Getting Ahead', *The Oxford Handbook to the Operatic Canon*, eds. Cormac Newark and William Weber (New York, forthcoming).

[49] *MfgS*, 4/209 (1810), p. 835.   [50] Reichardt, *Vertraute Briefe*, vol. 1, p. 157.

character of the composition';[51] reviews from Berlin in 1812 and 1815 likewise celebrated that she did 'nothing other than what the composer wanted'.[52] Her performance in Breslau in 1812, moreover, highlighted her 'proper declamation in the designation of musical and rhetorical accents'.[53] In fact, the adoption of Gluckian reform opera as the model for German opera was explicit in von Mosel's *Versuch einer Aesthetik des dramatischen Tonsatzes* (1812), in which Gluck and Salieri are the primary reference points, and literature from the Imperial French conservatoire is actually quoted in order to describe the art of dramatic song: 'The singer should be the true organ of the poet and composer.'[54]

Even Milder's (probably necessary) alterations to the score could be cast as a kind of operatic reform. Her performance of the title role in Paer's *Sargines* in Vienna in 1808 involved cutting out almost all of the melismatic passages – of which there were a significant number – but 'what remained for us was sung by Dem. Milder all the more beautifully, with such power and purity, that one gladly forgot all passages'.[55] Zelter, in the continuation of his reflections on Milder's performance of Armida in 1815, remarked that 'a true work is clearly recognized by a true performance. This honest Pallas drops what does not impose itself and rises to the heavens with that which suits her. Gluck has clearly paid too much attention to minutiae.' Milder out-Glucked Gluck.

If the emergence of a German (Gluckian) operatic identity against an Italian one represents a vocal complication of the binaries nested within twin styles discourse, this extends to the gendering of those categories. Fashionable Italian virtuosity had long been designated and devalued as effeminate, but its emerging German *vocal* antagonist is not as obviously gendered as German instrumental music. With Italian art(ifice) opposed by German nature, (over-) complexity and technical skill by simplicity, German vocality is in danger of becoming feminine, even with its Gluckian nobility: indeed both types of vocality could oppose the 'masculinity' of German instrumental music. But the masculinized voice, persona and figure of Milder, who in 1816 would be declared by the *Hamburgisches Morgenblatt* both the 'genuine German voice' *and* the 'best German voice',

---

[51] *MfgS*, 5/202 (1811), p. 808.   [52] *MfgS*, 6/239 (1812), p. 956; *MfgS*, 9/163 (1815), p. 652.

[53] *AmZ*, 14/41 (1812), col. 668. See also commendation of her declamation in *AmZ*, 13/37 (1811), col. 625; and *AmZ*, 14/9 (1812), col. 140.

[54] Ignaz Franz von Mosel, *Versuch einer Aesthetik des dramatischen Tonsatzes* (Vienna, 1813), p. 69.

[55] *AmZ*, 11/1 (1808), col. 11.

associated these potentially feminine qualities of simplicity and naturalness with more masculine ones, allowing German critics to accord the emerging category the requisite national prestige.[56]

Madame Milder as Masculinized Voice

The masculinity of Milder's public persona – according to the gender binaries emerging at the time – brings us back, in the first place, to her cross-dressing. The tenor roles of Sargines and Tamino formed part of her regular repertoire not only at home in Vienna but on tour, suggesting not merely the necessities of staffing but rather a palpable vocal or dramatic identification with these roles. At the same time, Milder was employed in one-off male roles in Vienna for the now forgotten *Cyrus in Persien* mentioned above, for Friedrich August Kanne's opera *Orpheus* (1807) and Giovanni Liverati's Biblical opera *David, oder Goliaths Tod* (1813).[57]

And then there were her partially or temporarily cross-dressed bellicose women: the Polish ruling warrior Wanda in Werner's 'Schauspiel mit Gesang'; Reichardt's female knight Bradamante, a part written with Milder in mind but which only received private performance;[58] and of course, Fidelio. Moreover, many of the French roles that were central to Milder's repertoire and acclaim were women who step outside the bounds of idealized middle-class femininity, to put it mildly: Medea (Cherubini), Alceste, Armida, Clytemnestra (Gluck), Semiramis (Catel).[59] This is paradoxically apparent in a strained description of Milder's performance of Clytemnestra in 1809 as having an 'indescribable majesty and grandeur that nevertheless never transgressed the sweet lines of femininity'.[60]

Milder did also play roles that portrayed more conventional ideas of femininity in Emmeline and Therese, though the contrast to Gluck's heroines had as much to do with class as concepts of gender. Having premiered Emmeline in Vienna in 1809, she remained *the* interpreter of the role for many years on account of the simplicity and naturalness of her singing and acting, bringing, as one Berlin reviewer put it, 'deeply-felt expression, high innocence, and moving warmth' to the role of the 'naïve'

---

[56] This was in comparison to Catalani, who was declared the 'best Italian voice'. *Hamburgisches Morgenblatt*, no. 99 (17 August 1816), pp. 799–800.

[57] *AmZ*, 15/23 (1813), cols. 382–3.　　[58] Reichardt, *Vertraute Briefe*, vol. 1, p. 439.

[59] *AmZ*, 9/8 (1806), cols. 121–3.　　[60] *MfgS*, 3/73 (1809), p. 284.

Swiss maid.[61] The intimacy and naturalness of her Emmeline was a trope of her reception,[62] but so too was its seeming contradiction with her other heroic characters. The same Berlin critic found her Emmeline all the more praiseworthy for her Medea, in which her 'play and her posture are everywhere noble and imposing'.[63] A Munich reporter in 1811 had likewise juxtaposed her nobility and heroism with her simplicity; while a critic in Breslau in 1812 identified both the sublime and the cosy ('gemüthlich') in her performances.[64]

For some the notable contrast between Milder's roles was a function of her physical presence: she was, by most accounts, statuesque. One reviewer of her Berlin performances in 1812 compared Emmeline to Iphigenia, noting that 'the noisy part of the theatre audience first turned its attention to the appearance of the foreign artist, and of course found without reservation that a figure of excellent size and fullness [Fülle] was good for Iphigenia, but never for Emmeline'.[65] In 1811 Johann Carl Friedrich Rellstab had described her as 'large and imposing' (terms often repeated, along with noble), 'a head above the other Priestesses' and, for this reason, unsuited to the sweet lovesickness of Emmeline.[66] Jennifer Ronyak has suggested that her stature may have been exaggerated to fit with her vocal image,[67] and a Viennese portrait of her as Alceste, in which her head almost touches the ceiling, would certainly suggest that (see Figure 6.1), but there is a symbiotic relationship between her cross-dressing, masculinized persona and perceived height, whatever her actual measurements. In Vienna as Tamino she was praised for 'masculine bearing',[68] while in the droll dramatization of her 'competition' with Schmalz, where art competed with nature, the Berliners' interest in her height and masculinity was highlighted:

The men thought she was beautiful, the ladies had a lot to complain about; masculinity especially was the reproach against the high figure and the

---

[61] *AmZ*, 14/42 (1812), cols. 691–2.

[62] See, for example, the Munich report: *MfgS*, 5/202 (1811), p. 808; and Letter 147, Zelter to Goethe, Berlin 30 May–13 September 1812, *Goethe and Zelter*, p. 158.

[63] *AmZ*, 14/42 (1812), cols. 691–2.

[64] See *MfgS*, 5/202 (1811), p. 808; *AmZ*, 14/41 (1812), col. 668.   [65] *MfgS*, 6/239 (1812), p. 956.

[66] Rellstab, 'Über die Stimme der Madame Hauptmann-Milder zu Wien', *Thalia, ein Abendblatt; den Freunden der dramatischen Muse geweiht*, 2/95 (27 November 1811), p. 379.

[67] Jennifer Ronyak, 'Performing the Lied, Performing the Self: Singing Subjectivity in Germany, 1790–1832' (PhD thesis, University of Rochester, 2010), p. 242. Heather Hadlock has suggested similar exaggerations in descriptions of the cross-dressing contralto Rosmunda Pisaroni's ugliness in 'Women Playing Men', pp. 292–4.

[68] *AmZ*, 14/34 (1812), col. 55.

Figure 6.1 Pauline Anna Milder as Alceste
Reproduced by permission of Wien Museum, Vienna

determinedness in appearance. 'She should not be called Milder Hauptmann, she should be called Hauptmann [Captain] Milder!' joked a Jewish lady.[69]

The masculinity of her persona also emerges from the evocation of the size and strength of her voice. The anecdote of Joseph Haydn exclaiming to a young Milder, 'dear child, you have the voice of a house'[70] is accompanied by many iterations of 'groß', 'voll' and 'stark' in other descriptions of it. Reichardt pronounced it in his *Vertraute Briefe* to be the 'largest' and the 'fullest' voice he'd heard;[71] and reviewers in the *AmZ* repeatedly extolled her power ['Kraft'] and amplitude ['Fülle']:[72] in *Fidelio* in 1814, it was Milder's melodiousness and *power* that delighted the Viennese.[73] These qualities also emerge from the recurrent themes of Milder's metallic or

[69] *MfgS*, 6/261 (1812), p. 1043.
[70] Reported in C. F. v. Ledebur's *Tonkünstler-Lexicon Berlins von den ältesten Zeiten bis auf die Gegenwart* (Berlin, 1861), p. 375.
[71] Reichardt, *Vertraute Briefe*, vol. 1, pp. 143, 156. See also *AmZ*, 7/22 (1805), col. 351.
[72] *AmZ*, 14/42 (1812), col. 691; *AmZ*, 9/21 (1807), cols. 335–6.   [73] *MfgS*, 6/232 (1814), p. 928.

bell-like 'Klang'. 'Klang' could simply refer to tone or sound, but its use alongside metal and bells suggests rather its figurative meaning of 'sonorousness' and 'ring' (and thereby size, too). As Tamino in Mannheim in 1814, Milder sang the aria 'Pamina retten ist mir Pflicht' with 'the whole force [Gewalt] and bell-sonority [Glockenklang] of her mighty voice';[74] E. T. A. Hoffmann praised her 'enormous [gewaltig], pure silver bell tones' in *Die Vestalin* in 1816.[75] As already cited, Griesinger described her voice in 1803 as 'the purest metal', while in 1806, in Handel's *Messiah*, she displayed a 'full, pure, clear, metal-voice [Metallstimme]'.[76] Establishing the historical resonance of these terms is difficult: Milder is not the only woman to whom 'Klang' or 'Metall' is attributed;[77] nor are they commonly ascribed to men in this period.[78] But Zelter's styling of Milder as a blacksmith suggests the masculinity of metal as material through the strength and stature of those who wield it. In combination with Milder's figure and cross-dressing roles, this projection of vocal size and power, whether explicit or via metallic metaphors, contributes to the accumulation of masculine tropes and to the reinforcing circularity of their use.

Perhaps the invocations of metal and bell-clangs can most usefully be seen as part of an attempt by critics to create a distinctive metaphorical vocabulary for Milder's voice – an impulse that resulted in some slightly bizarre comparisons. The *MfgS* correspondent from Stuttgart in 1810, for example, stated that 'unforgettable to all is the sound which Mad. Milder sustained with the full force of her voice in harmonica vibrations', while earlier in the article, as stated above, hers was the 'harmonica-voice' that produces 'genuine German song'.[79] This analogy lived on in Stuttgart, with a letter from Georg Reinbeck in 1820 reporting a visit from Milder, who had delighted with her 'harmonica-voice': 'there we heard for once genuine German heartfelt song [literally, heart-song]'.[80] In 1812, on the other hand, Mosel cited a description, in the journal *Paris und Wien*, of Milder's voice

---

[74] *AmZ*, 16/19 (1814), col. 164.   [75] *Dramaturgisches Wochenblatt*, no. 3 (20 July 1816), p. 19.
[76] See also *AmZ*, 8/29 (1806), col. 461; *AmZ*, 14/41 (1812), col. 668.
[77] To Catalani is also attributed Klang and Wohlklang: *Hamburgisches Morgenblatt*, no. 99 (17 August 1816), p. 799.
[78] In fact, in his *Vorlesungen über Deklamation und Mimik*, Seckendorff distinguished between 'hard, male metal' and 'strong, feminine metal': see his *Vorlesungen*, vol. 1, pp. 292–3.
[79] *MfgS*, 4/209 (1810), p. 835.
[80] Georg Reinbeck to Friedrich von Matthisson, from Stuttgart, 18 August 1820, in *Friedrich von Matthisson's Literarischer Nachlaß: nebst einer Auswahl von Briefen seiner Freunde* (Berlin, August Mylius, 1832), vol. 4, p. 158.

as 'beautiful, rich in metal and similar to a clarinet';[81] and the *MfgS* the same year used the same adjective ('klarinettähnlich') to describe Milder's romance in Boieldieu's *Johanna von Paris*.[82]

In fact, the self-conscious pursuit of a vocabulary for Milder's voice is both recognized and more explicitly demonstrated by Rellstab in 1811.[83] The critic begins by expressing concern about the language solidifying around the singer, noting that the descriptions of Reichardt and other commentators made one think of her voice as 'a beautiful, full organ stop, but also just as flat, just as unfavourable, and just as monotonous as that [implies]'. He chose instead to compare her tone to violins of the school of the seventeenth-century Tyrolean maker Jakob Steiner, which, he makes clear, he prefers to those of the celebrated Cremona school. Rellstab's distinction between the (Germanic) Steiner and (Italian) Cremona violins reveals that the clarinet and harmonica comparisons and the metal references represent nothing so much as a desire to distance Milder's singing from the selection of trilling birds typically used to compliment (or insult) Italian virtuosity. They are, I would argue, another symptom of the early stages of creation of the rhetorical category of the German voice. Certainly this is suggested by a review of Milder in *Fidelio* in 1814:

It is a great pleasure to hear Milder singing, for, though she possesses none of the methods customary here, and she constitutes, as it were, a new school, she attracts admiration by the rare clarinet-like tone of her voice.[84]

This necessarily brief archaeology of vocal metaphor opens up new ways of thinking about the much-noted instrumental nature of the vocal lines in Beethoven's *Fidelio* as a function of the original Leonore's particular vocal qualities.[85] But my argument here concerns rather the 'new school' that Milder projected through *Fidelio*, through the accumulation of roles, performances and critical discourse, and through her non-conformance (intentional or otherwise) to existing categories in operatic reception. This is the productive 'conflict and confusion' identified by Zelter in his letter to Goethe with which this essay began. Rather like the reviewer keen to assure

---

[81] *Der Sammler*, 4/148 (1812), p. 594.   [82] *MfgS*, 7/4 (1813), p. 16.
[83] *Thalia*, 2/95 (27 November 1811), p. 379.   [84] *Der Sammler*, 6/118 (1814), p. 471.
[85] This is often via brief references to fanfare figures, or sustained and repeated notes: see, for example, Carolyn Abbate and Roger Parker, *A History of Opera: The Last Four Hundred Years* (London, 2012), p. 170; Daniel Chua, *Beethoven and Freedom* (New York, 2017), p. 159; Robinson, 'Fidelio', pp. 93–9.

readers that Milder's Klytemnestra never 'trangressed the sweet lines of femininity', Zelter attempted to reassert the singer's gender identity ('Imagine a calm, really feminine form') in the face of the disorientating androgyny and/or masculinity he identifies: by comparing her to the Pallas of Velletri, a huge, three-metre tall statue of Athena, goddess of war, wearing a helmet and breastplate (to which the head of the Gorgon Medusa is fixed); by comparing her to a blacksmith at the forge; and by commenting on her 'colossal' stature. Precisely the same impulse seems at play in the Stuttgart report that opposed the 'most genuine German song of a "harmonica voice"' to the decorated Italian school:

> She is about twenty-eight at the present time, tall and full in figure, and features, which close up are lovely, have in the distance, something austere, masculine, as well as her whole appearance on stage something determined. But in company she is simple and truly childlike, just like her enchanting song. She bears the stamp of the true genius, well aware of its power, but not showing it because it is natural to it, not acquired. He who learns to know her better will certainly be very fond of her, and is glad to see how the homage that she received on a daily basis has not affected the true femininity in her.[86]

Just as in Zelter's letter, her female – even, here, childlike – simplicity or naivety, as in Emmeline, is important in establishing the natural as a force to counteract the acquired, the artificial. And yet the masculinity of her stage persona and vocal qualities – the height, the strength, power, the heroicness – was equally important to the vindication of German opera: the monumental, masculinized soprano counteracts the effeminate castrato that gendered singing itself feminine. The rhetorical strain is evident in Zelter's negotiation of these contradictions (the broken syntax of 'buts' and 'and yets') and reveals more than ever the processes of category-crossing that Milder enabled:[87] she was sufficiently hybrid, while not too disturbingly androgynous, to provide Garber's 'third'. Little matter that this 'new school' of German singing was dependent on older constructs of Gluckian reform opera.

Inconsistent, irreconcilable binaries continued to haunt those invested in German opera and the German voice, not least because of the larger oppositions of harmony versus melody/instruments versus voices, the dearth of German operatic hits, and the persistent supply and popularity of French and Italian opera. But I would argue that it was through singers and discourse about singers, and specifically through Milder's category-

---

[86] *MfgS*, 4/209 (1810), p. 836.   [87] See too *AmZ*, 14/42 (1812), col. 691.

crossing, that the new national category began to gain traction; it was through her masculinized soprano that German vocality could be imagined and articulated.

Madame Milder as Musical Germania

These male fantasies of the German as a heroic, masculine woman are not limited to the operatic sphere. While the representation of Amazons and cross-dressers peaked in the early decades of Milder's career, the use of women as political symbols continued through the nineteenth century: Marianne, Germania, Joan of Arc etc.[88] In Heinrich von Kleist's ode 'Germania an ihre Kinder' (1809), for example, the nation is imagined not as the body of the monarch, but as an avenging mother, rallying her children with the power of nature (the ocean, thunder); Germania is often represented with Athena's costume of breastplate, helmet and skirt.[89] The increasing importance of the masculinized woman at the symbolic level occurred alongside the increasing binary divisions between genders, just as, as Marina Warner has argued, the feminine allegory of nation relies on the exclusion of women from public life:

Often the recognition of a difference between the symbolic order inhabited by ideal, allegorical figures, and the actual order, of judges, statesmen, soldiers, philosophers, inventors, depends on the unlikelihood of women practising the concepts they represent.[90]

This provides a different answer to the question of why the German voice should be a masculine female voice: the power of the symbol increases with its distance from the everyday.

But perhaps these resonances with broader narratives miss the specificity – and specific challenges – of German operatic discourse. While a focused case study – just under fifteen years, one singer – has some obvious limitations in scope, there are clear long-term ramifications of the tropes developed for and by Milder's performances. In the first place, the

---

[88] See Ute Frevert on the afterlife of the women soldiers on stage in 'German Conceptions of War, Masculinity and Femininity in the Long Nineteenth Century', in Colvin and Watanabe-O'Kelly (eds.), *Women and Death 2*, pp. 169–85.

[89] See Bettina Brandt, 'Germania in Armor: The Female Representation of an Endangered German Nation', in Colvin and Watanabe-O'Kelly (eds.), *Women and Death 2*, pp. 86–126, at pp. 93–5.

[90] Marina Warner, *Monuments and Maidens: The Allegory of the Female Form* (London, 1985), pp. xix–xx.

discourse surrounding Milder has a direct impact on the idea of German operatic vocality and the *Fach* of the German dramatic soprano (Wagner's woman-in-waiting) as it developed across the nineteenth century. In so far as this has been attributed to particular singers, it is Wilhelmine Schröder-Devrient who has caught scholarly attention, not least because of Wagner's most likely apocryphal account of his conversion experience during her performance as Fidelio.[91] To David Trippett, she was 'a mighty hinge for the German discourse on vocal melody' on account of the critical attention to her emphasis on declamation,[92] the deficiencies of her voice and technique (particularly coloratura), the soul and naturalness in her performance that made up for them, and her acting ability. For Stephen Meyer, her role as a national symbol extended directly to political life, her category-crossing in the decades leading up to 1848 embodying an '"aesthetics of liberation" within the German public mind'.[93]

Milder provides an early focal point for this discourse. Her voice, her physique, her person afforded the rhetorical somersaults required of critics to construct German vocality, its combination of the natural and the heroic, its accommodation of male and female characteristics. Her role in this history has been little acknowledged. When Meyer locates Schröder-Devrient's reception in a tradition of German–Italian oppositions, he notably traces them to commentary on compositions or composers: to E. T. A. Hoffmann in 'The Poet and the Composer', or C. M. von Weber's review of Hoffmann's opera *Undine*.[94] Thus the reinsertion of Milder into the history of German national opera and of the twin styles continues a process of increasing attendance to performers and performances alongside works and composers. At the same time, Milder's reception can inform our understanding of *Fidelio*, which has always occupied an uneasy position in histories of German opera: the one operatic output of the totemic composer, which was neither recognized as 'national' at the time, nor conformant to later concepts of German opera. With its French plot, mixed registers and national styles, it has been characterized as a 'craggy

---

[91] Susan Rutherford evaluates the evidence for and against Wagner's encounter, and Schröder-Devrient's role as muse, in 'Wilhelmine Schröder-Devrient: Wagner's Theatrical Muse', in *Women, Theatre and Performance: New Histories, New Historiographies*, eds. Maggie B. Gale and Viv Gardner (Manchester, 2000), pp. 60–80.

[92] David Trippett, *Wagner's Melodies: Aesthetics and Materialism in German Music Identity* (Cambridge, 2013), p. 205.

[93] Stephen Meyer, 'Das wilde Herz: Interpreting Wilhelmine Schröder-Devrient', *The Opera Quarterly*, 14/2 (1997), pp. 23–40, at p. 36.

[94] Ibid., p. 27.

monument to the confused state of German opera at a moment of transition'.[95] Perhaps, however, *Fidelio* can also be seen as a more straightforward monument to emerging German operatic vocality; and the role of Fidelio, described by Michael Steinberg as 'a manly woman ... the most austere of bourgeois, Protestant goddesses ... Athena',[96] as a monument to Milder herself. Perhaps then, we can begin to hear the historical resonances of Fidelio's cross-dressing: as a vehicle for Milder's performance as masculinized soprano, and, above all, for the production of critical tropes of the German operatic voice.

---

[95] Abbate and Parker, *A History of Opera*, p. 170.
[96] Michael Steinberg, *Listening to Reason* (Princeton, 2004), p. 83.

7 | Beethoven and Tonal Prototypes: An Inherited and Developing Relationship

The idea that the most original, individual and organicist composer of all time used some pre-composed materials and formulae might strike some Beethoven admirers as an abomination. Yet, recent scholarly works have evinced the presence of those materials in some of Beethoven's most revered masterworks, including those of his last creative period. Vasili Byros explores Beethoven's network of tonal prototypes in a number of writings, focusing on Beethoven's middle period and in particular on the *Eroica* symphony: the identification of a schema, the *Le–Sol–Fi–Sol*, allows Byros to draw fascinating insights on the relationship between tonal prototypes and musical meaning (more on this later).[1] Job Ijzerman focuses on the contrapuntal and harmonic properties of a selected group of schemata and their modifications in works by Beethoven, Schubert and Schumann.[2] Folker Froebe examines the schemata in Beethoven's Piano Sonata Op. 10 No. 1, and their function in the large-scale tonal context.[3] Analyses of Beethoven's music according to contrapuntal models are also found in Johannes Menke's study of the history and theory of sequences.[4] Felix Diergarten and Ludwig Holtmeier survey Beethoven's connection with thoroughbass theory and practice, with an analysis of the E major piano sonata, Op. 109 (also discussed below).[5]

Galant schemata, contrapuntal techniques, certain thoroughbass procedures, partimento patterns and *Satzmodelle* appear in the music of

---

[1] Vasili Byros, 'Topics and Harmonic Schemata: A Case from Beethoven', in *The Oxford Handbook of Topic Theory*, ed. Danuta Mirka (New York, 2014), pp. 381–414; Byros, 'Foundations of Tonality as Situated Cognition, 1730–1830: An Enquiry into the Culture and Cognition of Eighteenth-Century Tonality with Beethoven's *Eroica* Symphony as a Case Study' (PhD thesis, Yale University, 2009); Byros, 'Meyer's Anvil: Revisiting the Schema Concept', *Music Analysis*, 31/3 (2012), pp. 273–346.

[2] Job Ijzerman, 'Schemata in Beethoven, Schubert, and Schumann: A Pattern-Based Approach to Early Nineteenth-Century Harmony', *Music Theory & Analysis*, 4/1 (2017), pp. 3–39.

[3] Folker Froebe, 'Schema and Function', *Music Theory & Analysis*, 1/1–2 (2014), pp. 121–39.

[4] Johannes Menke, 'Historisch-systematische Überlegungen zur Sequenz seit 1600', in *Passagen: Theorien des Übergangs in Musik und anderen Kunstformen*, ed. Christian Utz (Saarbrücken, 2009), pp. 87–111.

[5] Felix Diergarten and Ludwig Holtmeier, 'Nicht zu disputieren. Beethoven, der Generalbass und die Sonate op. 109', *Musiktheorie*, 26/2 (2011), pp. 123–46.

Beethoven as they do in the music of any other composer educated in the eighteenth-century system of training: therefore, a mere quest for those patterns in his music makes little sense unless one askes some questions regarding their presence, such as the connection between Beethoven's studies in thoroughbass and his practice of extemporization.[6] And again: does Beethoven's usage of particular patterns correlate with certain genres? Did Beethoven use them throughout his career, or only in certain periods? What is the relationship between schemata and topics in Beethoven's music?

In these opening paragraphs I have used different terms for a number of musical constructs that have one thing in common: they pre-exist the act of composition of individual works. Those constructs include galant schemata, many sorts of cadences, the stylized bass motions taught by Italian partimento masters (called *moti del basso* in Italian, *marches d'harmonie* in French), sequential techniques (such as 5–6 or 7–6 sequences) that originated in counterpoint and later found their way into thoroughbass theory, modulatory patterns, the Rule of the Octave and the imitation of models handed down through works that gained the status of exemplars.[7] Since the study of those constructs has been conducted in the last twenty-five years or so by scholars in different countries with different cultural traditions and who mostly worked independently of each other, different names have been devised; schemata, *Satzmodelle*, partimento patterns are commonly encountered. We must also keep in mind that the terms are not exactly interchangeable, but that there exist subtle but significant differences in meaning, arising from different cultural traditions.[8]

A general term covering all the above-mentioned does not yet exist, so I suggest using 'tonal prototype'. By 'tonal prototype' I designate a set of pre-composed materials shared by composers through different generations, handed down by means of imitation and teaching.[9] Most tonal prototypes are contrapuntal in nature, with harmony playing a secondary role: for example, galant schemata are defined by the relationship between bass and melody, whereas the chords are often interchangeable. For few of

---

[6] The reference monograph on galant schemata is Robert O. Gjerdingen, *Music in the Galant Style* (New York, 2007).

[7] For a survey of partimento patterns, see the author's *The Art of Partimento* (New York, 2012).

[8] For a history of the recent success of what he calls 'pragmatic theories of music analysis', see Felix Diergarten, 'Editorial', *Eighteenth-Century Music*, 14/1 (2017), pp. 5–11.

[9] On the subtleties of terminological problems, see Jan Philipp Sprick, 'Schema, Satzmodell and Topos: Reflections on Terminology', *Music Theory & Analysis* 1/1–2 (2014), pp. 101–6.

them, such as modulatory models, the harmony is more fixed, and consequently has greater significance.

The majority of tonal prototypes originated as early as the sixteenth century, some of them even earlier.[10] Some very early patterns, such as the 5–6 ascending and 7–6 descending sequences, originated in the fourteenth century, entered late sixteenth-century polyphony, were incorporated into the thoroughbass tradition, passed through the Classical period and were very much alive in late Romantic music. This impressive lifespan is shared by some other prototypes, such as the Romanesca, which travelled across centuries from its origins in the sixteenth century to late twentieth-century popular music.

Tonal prototypes are conceptually distinct from topics, even though they may occasionally overlap; they are also more precise and more general.[11] Their grammar can be described with remarkable precision: for example, we know exactly how a Prinner is made, including the scale degrees in the melody and in the bass, the metric position on which the four stages are expected to appear, the chords used and their possible substitutes. However, we can hardly attach to a Prinner a specific meaning: a Prinner (as well as a fragment of a Rule of the Octave, or a sequence) is in itself semantically neutral.[12] On the other hand, we have a fairly accurate idea about the meaning of an *Ombra*, but in no way can we specify how exactly an *Ombra* is made.[13]

Tonal prototypes could not have enjoyed such a long life without a manner of transmitting them through generations. Thanks to a recent surge of interest in compositional pedagogy through the ages, we know that the main venue of transmission occurred through imitation of works

---

[10] Johannes Menke, 'Die Familie der *cadenza doppia*', *Zeitschrift der Gesellschaft für Musiktheorie*, 8/3 (2011), pp. 389–405.

[11] The *Le-Sol-Fi-Sol* is one of the rare cases of a schemata that may assume the significance of a topic; see Byros, 'Topics and Harmonic Schemata'. Also Hans Aerts, '"Modell" und "Topos" in der deutschsprachigen Musiktheorie seit Riemann', *Zeitschrift der Gesellschaft für Musiktheorie*, 4/1–2 (2007), pp. 143–58.

[12] On the interactions between schemata, topics and form, see William E. Caplin, 'Topics and Formal Functions: The Case of the Lament' in *The Oxford Handbook of Topic Theory*, pp. 415–52.

[13] In order to define the *Ombra* topic Clive McClelland lists no fewer than ten parameters, with several possibilities for each (for example, the parameter 'Melody' lists the following possible characteristics, 'exclamatory, often fragmented, sometimes augmented/diminished leaps, occasionally narrow intervals contrasting with wide leaps, monotones/triadic lines for oracles and invocations'). Clive McClelland, 'Ombra and Tempesta', in *The Oxford Handbook of Topic Theory*, pp. 279–300, at p. 282. See also McClelland's *Ombra: Supernatural Music in the Eighteenth Century* (Lanham, 2012).

that gained the status of 'exemplars' and through the practice of specifically designed exercises such as partimenti and solfeggi.[14] Since tonal prototypes did not change much between the seventeenth and the nineteenth centuries, their uninterrupted transmission ensured a remarkable continuity in musical language. In Italy, tonal prototypes were at the core of teaching in the Neapolitan conservatories from at least the mid-seventeenth century, so it is hardly surprising that they are easily detected in the music of Italian-trained composers, especially in the eighteenth century. But tonal prototypes were not confined to Italy: they were at the core of the musical language of non-Italian composers too. The works of composers such as Archangelo Corelli – where so many tonal prototypes are exposed with admirable clarity – were considered models for imitation all over Europe until the nineteenth century.[15]

Partimenti and solfeggi travelled through Europe following the large-scale emigration of Italian musicians that took place in the eighteenth century.[16] An impressive number of Italian musicians and poets lived and worked in Vienna, with one modern scholar describing Austria as 'a promised land for Italian music'.[17] According to George Buelow the 'Italian domination of the Viennese court was virtually complete by the end of the [seventeenth] century. The Italian language had largely replaced German at court and among the educated classes.'[18] A famous case is that of the Roman Pietro Metastasio, who in the middle of the following century spent forty years in Vienna as court poet and never felt the need to learn German.[19] As well as the Italian tradition partimenti existed also in Austrian and German versions: in Austria the Partitura tradition lasted

---

[14] On exemplars in composed works, see Elisabetta Pasquini, *L'Esemplare, o sia saggio fondamentale pratico di contrappunto. Padre Martini teorico e didatta della musica* (Florence, 2004), in particular pp. 59–102.

[15] See Nicola Cumer, '"Se il divin Corelli imparerai": Didaktische Anregungen zum Partimento-Studium', in *Corelli als Modell: Studien zum 300. Todestag von Archangelo Corelli (1653–1713)*, ed. Pedro Memelsdorff, *Basler Jahrbuch für historische Musikpraxis*, 37 (2015); Kenneth Nott, 'Corelli's op. 5, no. 8. Sarabanda as a compositional model for Handel and his contemporaries', *Göttinger Händel-Beiträge*, 7 (1998), pp. 182–207; Eugenia Angelucci, 'Il modello Corelliano in area germanica', *Studi Corelliani V: Atti del quinto congresso internazionale (9–11 settembre 1994)*, ed. S. La Via (Florence, 1996), pp. 393–439.

[16] Reinhard Strohm (ed.), *The Eighteenth-Century Diaspora of Italian Music and Musicians* (Turnhout, 2001).

[17] Theophil Antonicek, 'Österreich: Ein gelobtes Land der italienischen Musik', in *The Eighteenth-Century Diaspora of Italian Music and Musicians*, pp. 121–38.

[18] George J. Buelow, *A History of Baroque Music* (Bloomington, 2004), p. 231.

[19] Gianfranco Folena, *L'italiano in Europa. Esperienze linguistiche del Settecento* (Turin, 1983), p. 437.

until the nineteenth century and German partimenti existed within the Generalbass tradition.[20] In France, tonal models were widely used and taught well into the nineteenth century. A work such as Luigi Cherubini's *Marches d'harmonie* (posthumous published in 1847) is a collection of partimento patterns contrapuntally elaborated, clearly inspired by Fenaroli and Sala but larger and more systematic.[21]

As was generally the case at the time Beethoven was educated in thoroughbass and counterpoint.[22] According to Ludwig Holtmeier, while Nottebohm had proposed that Neefe made Beethoven familiar with fundamental bass theory, 'it is much more likely that Beethoven's understanding of harmonic theory was characterized by a symbiotic coexistence of Italian partimento tradition (Rule of the Octave) and French fundamental bass theory, a combination that is particularly characteristic of Viennese thoroughbass teaching'.[23] Holtmeier lists a number of German thoroughbass treatises that Beethoven owned and used for his own teaching: they include C. P. E Bach, *Versuch über die wahre Art das Clavier zu spielen* (second edition, 1797); D. G. Türk, *Kurze Anweisung zum Generalbaßspielen* (first edition, 1791); J. G. Albrechtsberger, *Gründliche Anweisung zur Composition* (first edition, 1790); and J. P. Kirnberger, *Kunst des reinen Satzes* (Viennese edition, 1793). To further corroborate Beethoven's involvement with thoroughbass theory we might add his acquaintance with other authors of thoroughbass treatises, such as Emanuel Aloys Förster[24] and Joseph Drechsler,[25] as well as the collection compiled by Ignaz von Seyfried of materials found after the composer's death and published as *Beethovens Studien im Generalbasse, Contrapuncte und in der Compositions-Lehre*.[26]

---

[20] Felix Diergarten, '"The True Fundamentals of Composition": Haydn's Partimento Counterpoint', *Eighteenth-Century Music*, 8/1 (2011), pp. 53–75.

[21] Luigi Cherubini, *Marches d'harmonie pratiquées dans la composition produisant des suites reguliéres de consonnances et de dissonances* (Paris, 1847).

[22] On Beethoven and thoroughbass, see Diergarten and Holtmeier, 'Nicht zu disputieren'.

[23] Ludwig Holtmeier, 'Generalbaß', in *Beethoven-Lexikon*, eds. Heinz von Loesch and Claus Raab (Laaber, 2015), p. 285.

[24] Emanuel Aloys Förster, *Anleitung zum General-Bass* (Leipzig, 1805); *Praktische Beispiele als Fortsetzung zu seiner Anleitung* (Leipzig, 1818).

[25] Joseph Drechsler, *Harmonie und Generalbass-Lehre* (Vienna, 1816).

[26] *Beethovens Studien im Generalbasse, Contrapuncte und in der Compositions-Lehre, aus dessen handschriftlichen Nachlass ges. und herg. v. Ignaz Ritter von Seyfried* (Wien, 1832; Leipzig, 1853); (reprint Hildesheim, 1967). Beethoven's studies have recently been published in a critical edition: Julia Ronge (ed.) *Ludwig van Beethoven, Kompositionsstudien bei Joseph Haydn, Johann Georg Albrechtsberger und Antonio Salieri*, Ludwig van Beethoven: Werke: Neue Ausgabe Sämtlicher Werke, XIII/2 (Munich, 2014). See also Ronge, 'Beethoven's Apprenticeship: Studies

Evidence of contact between Beethoven and the Italian partimento is largely circumstantial. The Bonn Kapellmeister Andrea Luchesi, under whom the young Beethoven worked as a member of the court chapel, was a student of Giuseppe Saratelli, maestro di cappella at St Mark's in Venice, who left a fine collection of northern Italian partimenti.[27] Two of Beethoven's teachers in Vienna, Haydn and Salieri, used partimenti in their learning or teaching. In his youth Haydn had studied with Nicola Porpora, a student of Gaetano Greco (one of the most distinguished Neapolitan teachers) and the author of a manuscript partimenti collection,[28] while Salieri compiled for his students a *Libro di partimenti di varia specie per profitto della gioventù*, now lost. Intriguingly, Beethoven's name appears among the subscribers of the largest Italian partimenti collection ever published, Alexandre-Étienne Choron's *Principes de composition des Écoles d'Italie* (Paris, 1808), a monument of exhausting erudition. Book 1 is a thoroughly revised version of his *Principes d'accompagnement des Écoles d'Italie* (Paris, 1804), written in collaboration with Vincenzo Fiocchi (1767–1843), a pupil of Fenaroli and Padre Martini. In this work Choron attempted to rationalize the principles underlying the Italian partimento tradition and included his own treatise on harmony together with an appendix of partimenti by Fenaroli, Durante, Sala and others, realized by Fiocchi for a variety of settings. Choron's theory of harmony still shows some obvious influence of Rameau (such as the *basse fondamentale*), but the main conceptual frame comes from the northern Italian school of Padua, in particular from Luigi Antonio Sabbatini's *La vera idea delle musicali numeriche segnature*.[29]

A key characteristic of Choron's *Principes de composition* is the presence of a series of *modèles* for each of the six books. For Book 1 (the treatise of harmony) the models are a collection of 210 partimenti, each with the name of its author, crowned by Leo's triple fugue in F minor (a work that, given the large number of manuscripts copies in which it is found, must

---

with Haydn, Albrechtsberger, and Salieri', *Journal of Musicological Research*, 32/2–3 (2013), pp. 73–82.

[27] Irene Maria Caraba, 'I bassi per esercizio d'accompagnamento all'antico: Giuseppe Giacomo Saratelli e la tradizione del partimento in area veneta', *Rivista Italiana di Musicologia*, 53 (2018), pp. 57–72.

[28] Nicola Porpora, *Partimenti*, I-Mc Ms. Nc. 176. On Haydn's engagement with the partimento tradition see Diergarten, '"The True Fundamentals of Composition"'.

[29] Luigi Antonio Sabbatini, *La vera idea delle musicali numeriche segnature diretta al giovane studioso dell'armonia* (Venice, 1799).

have been considered a model of fugue writing).[30] Book 2 is a partial reprint of the *Regole del contrappunto pratico* by Nicola Sala, supplemented by a translation of Marpurg's *Handbuch bey dem Generalbasse*. In the *modèles* part Choron added to Sala's examples a series of sixteen trios on regular bass progressions composed by Cristoforo Caresana, organist of the Royal Chapel of Naples, dated 1681. Book 3 is based on Marpurg's *Abhandlung von der Fuge*. In the preface Choron explains that although Marpurg's treatise is so good that even Padre Martini recommended it, it suffers from poor organization. For that reason, Choron revised Marpurg, put the content in a different order and added models drawn from Nicola Sala's *Regole del contrappunto pratico*. Books 4 (fugue) and 5 (canon) have the same pairing of Marpurg and Sala. Under the rubric 'Musical rhetoric' Book 6 deals with the 'non-scholastic' parts of music – phrases, form, styles and genres – and is, apparently, original. The volume is completed by a 380-page anthology of examples of all kinds of music described in the text, almost exclusively by Italian composers.

One of the most striking aspects of Choron's *Principes de composition* is that three out of six books of a compendium devoted to the Italian 'school' of composition are actually the work of German authors. In the preface to his and François Fayolle's *Dictionnaire historique des musiciens* Choron states that Italian and German 'schools' share the same principles, and that they are basically the same.[31] Unfortunately, Italians were great for models, but not so for theorizing, for which Germans were better: so Choron decided to compile the best of both.

The publication of this huge work almost drained the financial resources of its author. Therefore, Choron made recourse to a subscription system, publishing the names of the subscribers at the beginning of the first volume. The list of 'Compositeurs, Professeurs, Editeurs et Marchands de Musique' opens with the name of Joseph Haydn, followed (among others) by Paisiello, Fenaroli, Sabbatini, Spontini, Albrechtsberger and Asioli. The name of Beethoven is in eleventh position, followed by Cimarosa, Clementi and Forkel.

---

[30] Using the same copper plates, Choron also published the collection as *Régles de Contrepoint pratique contenant une série de modéles sur toutes les partes de l'art du counterpoint par Nicolas Sala, maitre de chapelle, Napolitain, Nouvelle èdition, mise en ordre et augmentée de la collection complete des partimenti ou leçons de basse chiffrée du même auteur par M. A. Choron* (Paris, preface dated 1808).

[31] Alexandre-Étienne Choron and François-Joseph-Marie Fayolle, *Dictionnaire historique des musiciens, Tome premier* (Paris, 1817), p. lxxvii.

The presence of Beethoven among the subscribers is something of a mystery; Choron's volume is not included in documents related to the composer's estate. It is similarly absent from Haydn's estate.[32] The fact that one apparent subscriber, Cimarosa, was no longer alive, raises questions about the nature of the subscription list. Nathalie Meidhof has suggested some of the names on it do not represent individuals who actually paid for, and came to own, the book.[33] Perhaps Beethoven's name, as well as that of Haydn and others, was added for prestige and the composer may never have come to know of it. Certainly no record has been found.

Tonal Prototypes and Improvisation

It is generally assumed that free-form pieces such as variations and cadenzas, or those bearing titles such as 'fantasia', reflect the improvisational practice of their author better than compositions such as sonatas or fugues. Indeed, works such as Beethoven's Fantasia, Op. 77, seem to originate from actual improvisation (in this case, during an academy held in December 1808). However, confining improvisation to a few peripheral genres downgrades its importance in Beethoven's compositional practice. Relying on coeval critics, Angela Carone makes the point that 'for an improvisation to be positively evaluated ... it had to be provided with a well-defined form, which therefore represented an aspect of the musical performance that was anything but negligible. In particular, in order to make a positive impression, the improvisation had to present a treatment of the musical material that was similar to the one found in a sonata or a strict contrapuntal construction.'[34] According to Carl Czerny, Beethoven's improvisation could belong to three 'forms': (1) the form of the first movement or the final rondo of a sonata; (2) free variation; or (3) a 'mixed genre' or a potpourri, as in the Fantasia, Op. 77. In addition, like many other composers of his time who had trained as organists, Beethoven used

[32] See documents transcribed in Elliot Forbes (rev. and ed.), *Thayer's Life of Beethoven* (Princeton, 1967), pp. 1061–76; and H. C. Robbins Landon, *Haydn: Chronicle and Works. Haydn; the Late Years 1801–1809* (London, 1977), pp. 392–403.

[33] Nathalie Meidhof, *Alexandre Étienne Choron Akkordenlehre. Konzepte, Quellen, Verbreitung* (Hildesheim, 2016), p. 56.

[34] Angela Carone, 'Formal Elements of Instrumental Improvisation: Evidence from Written Documentation, 1770–1840', in *Musical Improvisation and Open Forms in the Age of Beethoven*, eds. Gianmario Borio and Angela Carone (London, 2018), pp. 7–18, at p. 7.

to improvise fugues in public.[35] Therefore, fantasia was only one of the three 'forms' of improvisation practised by Beethoven. This leads us to distinguish between improvisation as extemporized composition and improvisation as rhetoric (as Marco Targa called it). In the first kind, all musical genres can be present, included the strictest ones, such as the fugue: and, the closer to a written composition the result, the better. In the second kind, the music consists of a free flowing of ideas, characterized by open form, tonal instability and brilliant style. This latter kind of music must give the impression of being improvised, but does not necessarily have to be improvised: indeed, many of these pieces (usually titled 'fantasia') have been preserved in written form.[36]

The illusion of freedom often concealed the fact that the use of models was standard practice. As Jan Philipp Sprick put it, 'many improvisation treatises from the mid-eighteenth century onwards, such as the prominent chapter on free improvisation in C. P. E. Bach's *Versuch über die wahre Art das Clavier zu spielen* (1753–62), focus mostly on harmonic schemata, ornamentation or the efficient use of special chromatic chords'.[37] Those 'formulas, tricks and models', as Dahlhaus called them, were an essential toolbox for improvisation in many different styles.[38] A compelling example of Beethoven's use of 'tricks' and 'formulas' – what I would prefer to call tonal prototypes – is the first movement of the Piano Sonata, Op. 27 No. 2, the so-called 'Moonlight' sonata; like its companion, Op. 27 No. 2, it was given the suggestive title of 'Sonata quasi una Fantasia'.[39]

The Adagio sostenuto opens with a descending tetrachord in the bass from C sharp to G sharp (the A is decorated by a consonant skip to F sharp; Example 7.1). On the second bass note, B, the chord remains the same as in the previous bar, thus producing a dissonant 6-4-2 chord that moves on a 5-3 chord on VI. This procedure corresponds to a variant of the Romanesca that became popular in northern Italy about 1760, thanks to Giovanni Battista Sammartini, which Gjerdingen accordingly calls 'Romanesca à la Sammartini'.[40] The short Romanesca leads to cadence on G sharp lasting a

---

[35] Carone, 'Formal Elements', pp. 9–10.

[36] Marco Targa, 'Improvisation Practices in Beethoven's Kleinere Stücke', in *Musical Improvisation and Open Forms in the Age of Beethoven*, pp. 178–92.

[37] Jan Philipp Sprick, 'Musical Form in Improvisation Treatises in the Age of Beethoven', in *Musical Improvisation and Open Forms in the Age of Beethoven*, pp. 19–29, at p. 20.

[38] Quoted in ibid., p. 20.

[39] The outer bifolio of the autograph of Op. 27 No. 2 is lost, and we cannot know whether the title was given by Beethoven or by his publisher, Cappi.

[40] Gjerdingen, *Music in the Galant Style*, p. 43.

Example 7.1 Beethoven, Piano Sonata in C sharp Minor, Op. 27 No. 2, 1st movement, bars 1–5

full bar, with the harmonic progression 7-5-3 / 6-4 / 5-4 / 5-3. This cadence is known as Cadenza doppia and, according to Johannes Menke, it was first described by Nicola Vicentino in *L'antica musica ridotta alla moderna prattica* (1555), who characterized it as 'all'antica' (old fashioned).[41] The variant used by Beethoven was called by Francesco Gasparini a 'major compound cadence with suspended seventh'.[42] The Cadenza doppia was one of the three principal cadences in the Neapolitan partimento tradition, and continued to be taught and practised in the eighteenth century, its 'all'antica' nature emphasized by its use in sacred music extensively.[43] The Cadenza doppia appears again in Op. 27 No. 2 in a version called by Gasparini 'cadenza maggiore diminuita' (bars 40–41, with a double neighbour figure in the bass). A shorter kind of archaic cadence is used more frequently, the Cadenza composta (compound cadence) with its characteristic 4–3 suspension (bars 8, 14, 22, 45 and 59).

Altogether the first movement of the 'Moonlight' sonata is remarkable for its usage of archaic cadences (in particular the Cadenza doppia), a characteristic highlighted by their absence in similarly titled works such as the companion sonata, Op. 27 No. 1 and the Op. 77 Fantasia; indeed, apart from the Rule of the Octave, these latter two works do not use any standard

---

[41] Menke, 'Die Familie der cadenza doppia'.
[42] Francesco Gasparini, *L'armonico pratico al cimbalo* (Venice 1708), pp. 46–7.
[43] A beautiful instance of a Cadenza doppia is the closing Adagio of the Kyrie in Mozart's Requiem (K. 626).

patterns to a significant degree. In general, it seems to me that there is no real difference between improvisation-related pieces and fully worked compositions in the employment of tonal models. There are differences, however, between genres, and from one creative period to another.

Tonal Prototypes and Genre

Within musical works composed in the second half of the eighteenth century, schemata, *Satzmodelle* and other patterns are more apparent in those genres where there is a focus on the performer before a listening public, such as the concerto. A comparison between the opening ritornellos of three concertos, all of them in C major, by three different composers, Haydn, Mozart and Beethoven, illustrates the conspicuous function of tonal models in this genre between 1760 and 1800. The three concertos are Haydn's Cello Concerto in C (Hob. VIIb:1) from c. 1763, Mozart's Piano Concerto in C, K. 415 (1783) and Beethoven's Piano Concerto in C major, Op. 15 (1793–1800).

The opening ritornello of Haydn's cello concerto is composed almost entirely of tonal prototypes (see Table 7.1). It begins with a variant of the classic opening move, the Do–Re–Mi (here, Do–Fa–Mi) followed by a short Cadenza lunga ④⑤① and a Cadenza semplice; the repetition of the Do–Fa–Mi brings to a half cadence that opens the space for the transition, beginning with a Sol–Fa–Mi, followed by a modulating Prinner and a twofold Sol–Fa–Mi that leads to a Cadenza lunga. After a filled-in

Table 7.1 Haydn, Cello Concerto in C Major, 1st movement: tonal prototypes and formal functions in the opening ritornello

Bars	Tonal model	Formal function
1–5	Do–Fa–Mi/Cadenza lunga	Main theme
6–8	Sol–Fa–Mi	Transition
8–9	Prinner	"
9–10	Sol–Fa–Mi	"
10–11	Cadenza lunga	PAC (MC)
12–15	*Contrappunto alla scala* descending/Indugio	Subordinate theme group
15–17	Fenaroli	"
18	Cadenza lunga	PAC (EEC)
19	Heartz	Post-cadential section
20–21	*Basso che cala di terza*/cadenza lunga	Post-cadential – PAC

(medial?) caesura there comes a new theme based on a descending scale (from g^2) in the upper voice accompanied by a counterpoint in the middle voice/bass (*contrappunto alla scala*) that includes an Indugio in bar 13. Another theme begins on the third beat of bar 15 based on the Fenaroli that is closed by a Cadenza lunga. Bar 19 has a Heartz followed by a 'bass descending by thirds' leading to a Cadenza lunga.

The substantial usage of tonal models in many classical concertos may be related to social and musical expectations: though a very familiar and very popular genre it lacked the prestige that late-eighteenth century writers accorded to the symphony as a genre. The entry 'Concert' in Sulzer's *Allgemeine Theorie der schöne Künste* (1771–74) is quite dismissive in this regard, asserting that as a genre the concerto 'has no fixed character' and that 'no one can say what it is supposed to represent'; it is nothing more than 'a practice session for composers and players, and a totally indeterminate aural amusement, aimed at nothing more'.[44] Extensive usage of tonal prototypes allowed the composer to make his music more accessible and to focus on the skills of the soloist. Listeners, however, could include connoisseurs; for their enjoyment a resourceful composer would make sure that the tonal models were cleverly elaborated and combined with ingenuity. I think that this is what Mozart meant in an often-quoted passage in a letter to his father dated 28 December 1782 concerning the three piano concertos, K. 413, 414 and 415:

These concertos are a happy medium between what is too easy and too difficult; they are very brilliant, pleasing to the ear, and natural, without being vapid. There are passages here and there from which the connoisseurs alone can derive satisfaction; but these passages are written in such a way that the less learned cannot fail to be pleased, though without knowing why.[45]

As Haydn did twenty years earlier, Mozart made extensive use of tonal prototypes in the opening ritornello of his piano concerto K. 415 (summarized in Table 7.2). The movement opens with a Do–Re–Mi played by the first violin, and followed in canon by the second violin. The third entry

---

[44] Simon P. Keefe, 'Koch's Commentary on the Late Eighteenth-Century Concerto: Dialogue, Drama and Solo/Orchestra Relations', *Music & Letters*, 79/3 (1998), pp. 368–85. The translation of Sulzer is taken from Keefe's article.

[45] Emily Anderson (trans. and ed.), *The Letters of Mozart and His Family*, 3rd ed. (London, 1985), p. 1242; Wilhelm A. Bauer, Otto Erich Deutsch and Joseph Heinz Eibl (eds.), *Mozart: Briefe und Aufzeichnungen, Gesamtausgabe* (Kassel, 1975), vol. 3, p. 245. This passage has been discussed by, among others, Leonard Ratner, *Classical Style: Expression, Form, and Style* (New York, 1980), p. 3; and Joseph Kerman, 'Critics and the Classics' in *Write All These Down* (Berkeley, 1994), pp. 51–72, at p. 65.

Table 7.2 Mozart, Piano Concerto in C Major, K. 415, 1st movement: tonal prototypes and formal functions in the opening ritornello

Bars	Tonal model	Formal function
1–4	Canon on Do–Re–Mi	Main theme
5–10	7–6 sequence ascending	"
10–18	*Contrappunto alla scala* ascending	Transition
18–20	Bass falling by thirds	"
20–24	Indugio	HC (MC)
25–35	Bass rising by step and falling by thirds	Caesura fill
36–46	Prinner by canon; cadenza lunga	Closing theme I
47–52	Cadenza lunga	Closing theme II
52–59	Cadenza lunga	Closing theme III

of the canon, in the bass, starts an ascending scale through an octave accompanied by the partimento scheme 8-7-6. In bars 10–18 the ascending scale moves up to the first violin accompanied with a *contrappunto alla scala* played by the viola and the second violin on a pedal point. The bass skips down by consecutive thirds (bars 18–20, another partimento pattern) leading to an Indugio (bars 20–21) and a half cadence. The extended passage between bar 26 and bar 34 is based on the partimento pattern 'ascending by step and descending by thirds' accompanied by alternating 6-5 and 5-3 chords (the true bass is the viola), and accelerated from bar 32. The first perfect authentic cadence is reached at bar 41 through a Prinner in canon.[46]

Beethoven followed Haydn and Mozart's approach in his early piano concertos. Like the earlier composers, Beethoven sought to make his early concertos appeal through easily comprehensible tonal prototypes. The opening ritornello of the C major concerto is entirely composed from standard eighteenth-century patterns, but presented on a broader scale (summarized in Table 7.3). The opening ritornello of the Haydn cello concerto has twenty-one bars; that of the Mozart concerto fifty-nine bars; but Beethoven's has 105 bars.[47] The tonal prototypes are correspondingly

---

[46] On the Heartz, see John A. Rice, 'The Heartz: A Galant Schema from Corelli to Mozart', *Music Theory Spectrum*, 36/2 (2014), pp. 333–9.

[47] However, given the tempo indication in the Haydn (Moderato) and the length of the thematic units, we can reasonably assume that a notated bar is twice the length of the real (or experienced) bar. The first tutti of the Haydn thus approximates in length the first tutti of the Mozart (forty-two and fifty-nine bars respectively). On notated versus real bars, see Caplin, *Classical Form*, p. 35.

Table 7.3 Beethoven, Piano Concerto No. 1 in C Major, Op. 15, 1st movement: tonal prototypes and formal functions in the opening ritornello

Bars	Tonal model	Formal function
1–8	Do–Re–Mi	Main theme
9–12	Prinner	"
13–15	Passo indietro/cadenza lunga	"
16–23	Do–Re–Mi	Transition
24–31	Prinner	"
32–38	Prinner/scale mutation	"
38–45	Ponte	Leads to MC
46–66	Fifth up, fourth down	Subordinate theme
66–69	Fenaroli	"
72–75	Fonte	Subordinate theme II
75–79	Syncopation in the bass	"
79–81	Rule of the Octave	"
81–85	Passo indietro/cadenza lunga	EEC
85–105	Cadences	Post-cadential section

expanded: the Prinner in the transition of the Haydn concerto takes one-and-a half notated bars, while the same schema in the exposition of the Beethoven concerto takes seven bars, and is followed by another modulating Prinner of the same length.[48] The sequence 'fifth up, fourth down' has no fewer than twenty-one bars. The opening theme is a sixteen-bar sentence that is entirely made of galant schemata: a Do–Re–Mi, a Prinner, a Passo indietro and a Cadenza lunga. This passage, however short, highlights an interesting point: here Beethoven uses tonal prototypes to generate thematic function, something that he would avoid in other genres and styles.

The solo sections of the movement are also largely composed with tonal prototypes. For instance, the first solo opens with an Aprile, followed by a ③④⑤① cadenza lunga repeated twice. Afterwards, the main theme Do–Re–Mi is followed by a Fonte, both greatly enlarged by the soloist's passagework, before a major/minor Fenaroli opens the path to the modulation to V, reached through a Phrygian cadence.

---

[48] The Prinner in Beethoven is coupled with a Heartz (see the pedal point in the bass): only at the third stage do we realize that the melodic line descends further onto the third degree of the scale.

Beethoven and Tonal Prototypes: An Attempt at Periodization

Around the turn of the century, Beethoven used tonal prototypes also in music written for private enjoyment, such as solo piano music. The main theme of the Rondo in G, Op. 51 No. 2, written in 1800, features no fewer than four Fonti, all of them with a thematic function.[49] The Fonte is also discernible in other works composed at the turn of the century: in the Cello Sonata in G Minor, Op. 5 No. 2, the main theme of the Rondo (in G major) has a ternary structure in which the contrasting middle section consists entirely of a Fonte.[50] In the second movement of the Piano Sonata in C Minor, Op. 10 No. 1, the transition is composed of a Fonte, a Phrygian cadence and a Ponte leading to a subordinate theme beginning with a Fenaroli.[51]

If one had to choose one work that showed the changing nature of Beethoven's relationship with tonal models, that would probably be the substitution of the original middle movement of the 'Waldstein' sonata, Op. 53 (subsequently published separately as *Andante favori*, WoO 57), by an *Introduzione* (marked Adagio molto). Alan Gosman suggests that Beethoven may have replaced the *Andante favori* because the Andante's theme originated from the same descending octave line that also underlies the first movement's second theme, and that he wanted to avoid too close an affinity.[52] I agree with Gosman, but from a slightly different angle: not only is the melody similar, but the two themes share, too, the same prototype, as Example 7.2 shows.

As Job Ijzerman convincingly argued, the first movement of Op. 53 is largely based on elaborated variants of the Romanesca prototype: a stepwise Romanesca with passing 6-4-2 chords underlies the main theme and its transformations, while the subordinate theme is based on a modified leaping version.[53] Now, the main theme of the Andante is based on a variant of the leaping Romanesca with 6-3 chords at the second stage, that is the simplest and most regular version of this prototype (the differences from the standard schema are the inverted metrical placement and the use

---

[49] Bars 5–6; 21–22; 25–26; 27–28.   [50] Bars 8–12.

[51] Gjerdingen, *Music in the Galant Style*, p. 238.

[52] Alan Gosman, 'From Melodic Patterns to Themes: The Sketches for the Original Version of Beethoven's 'Waldstein' Sonata, Op. 53' in *Genetic Criticism and the Creative Process: Essays from Music, Literature, and Theater* (Rochester, 2009), pp. 95–107, at pp. 105–6.

[53] The stepwise Romanesca with passing 4-2 is coupled with a chromatic descending tetrachord in the main theme, and with a Monte in the development. The leaping version features seventh chords in place of the standard 6-3 on the weak beat. Job Ijzerman, 'Schemata in Beethoven, Schubert and Schumann', *Music Theory and Analysis*, 4/1 (2017), pp. 3–39.

(a)

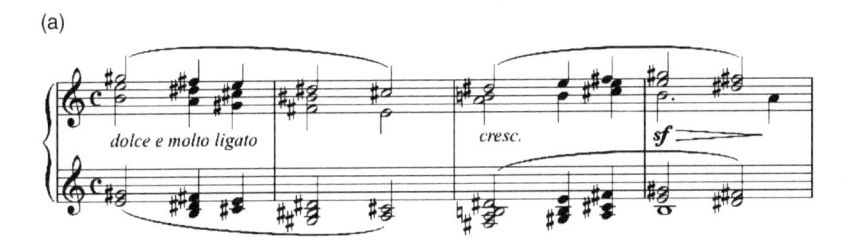

(b)

Example 7.2 (a) Beethoven, Piano Sonata in C Major, Op. 53, 1st movement, bars 35–38; (b) Beethoven, *Andante favori* (WoO 57), bars 1–4

of a 6-3 chord at its beginning). It is possible that Beethoven realized that this display of a bare prototype was incongruous after a first movement in which the existing prototypes are elaborated in a very complex and individual fashion. In fact, the new *Introduzione* is based on a radical transformation – almost beyond perception – of the descending 5–6 pattern (also known as galant Romanesca) with passing 4-2 chord that is the foundation of the first movement's main theme (see Example 7.3).[54]

As a bold generalization, I would venture to say that Beethoven's 'heroic style' tended to eschew tonal prototypes because they do not sit easily with two of the major hallmarks of that style: the motivic and thematic individuality of each work and what has been summarized as the general tendency of Beethoven's heroic-style music towards 'the monumentalization of tonics, subdominants, and dominants'.[55] Consequently, tonal prototypes are either transformed almost beyond recognition (as in the 'Waldstein' sonata) or are excluded from thematic units and confined to formal sections such as the transition or the development. But they do not completely disappear. A telling case is a passage in the first movement of the Fifth Symphony. Often regarded as the epitome of the heroic style ('a drama of tonic and dominant' in Burnham's words) and of totalizing

---

[54] For the diatonic version with interpolated augmented fourth, see Sanguinetti, *The Art of Partimento*, p. 140. In the Largo of Op. 53 the succession of 5-3 – 4#-2 – 6-3 is clearly recognizable only in bars 3–4.

[55] Scott Burnham, *Beethoven Hero* (Princeton, 1995), p. 83.

(a)

(b)

Example 7.3 Beethoven, Piano Sonata in C Major, Op. 53: (a) 1st movement, opening bars; (b) 2nd movement, opening bars

motivic unity, the Fifth Symphony does make use of tonal prototypes.[56] One of the most extraordinary passages in the first movement, the huge intensification and prolongation of the tonic harmony in bars 33–43 leading to the onset of the tutti in bar 44, is entirely dependent on the same partimento pattern noted in Mozart's Piano Concerto in C (K. 415): the ascending 8–7–6. This prototype is one of the main sequential accompaniments for the ascending scale, together with the 5–6 and the 9–8: all three were taught as alternatives to the Rule of the Octave. Example 7.4 shows the ascending 7–6 in the version given by Fenaroli, alongside the passage in the Fifth Symphony (strings only). In Beethoven the sequence is part of the transition passage, but its characteristic shape also matches the main theme's motive.

Tonal Prototypes and Musical Meaning in Beethoven

When the heroic style gave way to different, sometimes strikingly new, modes of expression the old stock phrases surfaced again, often in a thematically exposed function. The main theme of the rondo of the Sonatine in G, Op. 79 (1809), a plain galant Romanesca moving stepwise

---

[56] Ibid., p. 39.

Example 7.4 (a) Fenaroli, bass ascending stepwise with 8–7–6; (b) Beethoven, Symphony No. 5, Op. 67, 1st movement, bars 33–44, strings

through a sixth, from 1 to 3, is an early example of Beethoven's renewed interest in tonal prototypes. Ten years later, the same tonal prototype through the same span of a descending scale became the main theme of the first movement of the Piano Sonata in E, Op. 109 (1820), the fifth of the Six Bagatelles, Op. 126 (1824) and the *Neue Kraft fühlend* of the third movement of the Quartet in A minor, Op. 132 (1825; this passage is discussed later). Not only did Beethoven use the stepwise Romanesca in three major works in five years, but the tonal prototype is plainly exposed on the surface of the music.

The stepwise Romanesca is not an isolated case of Beethoven's interest in tonal prototypes in his late style. The Allegro of the first movement of the Quartet in E flat, Op. 127 (1825), is based on a Prinner repeated twice, and the main theme of the Andante ma non troppo e molto cantabile from the C sharp minor Quartet, Op. 131 (1826), is an obvious, unadorned Meyer. Also formulaic is the subject of the fugue in the Sonata in A flat, Op. 110 (1821); the subject is based on a sequence of rising fourths and falling thirds.[57]

This return to bare, unelaborated tonal material caught the attention of no less a critic than Theodor W. Adorno, who, prompted by Op. 127, wrote the following:

> The late Beethoven *covers its traces.* But which? That is no doubt the riddle. For, on the other hand, the musical language is displayed here nakedly and – as compared to the middle style – *directly.* Does he, in order to enable tonality, and so on, to emerge in this way, obliterate the traces of *composition*? Is this supposed to sound as if it had not been composed? Has the subject passed over into the production, so that it is *eliminated* as the producer? An image of *autonomous motion*?[58]

Adorno's idea is that Beethoven withdraws from the compositional process, leaving the musical language and its conventions to speak for themselves. Adorno uses here the term composition not in the etymological sense of assembling objects (from the Latin *cum-ponere*); rather, he means the process of forcing conventional language into expressing the individuality of the author. As a result the metaphor of organicism is not relevant anymore; instead '[t]he bareness of the very late Beethoven's music is connected to the inorganic element. What does not grow, does not luxuriate. Unadornedness and death. – Allegorical rather than symbolic.'[59] Michael Spitzer, in his book on Adorno and Beethoven's late style, argues that Adorno points 'to the possibility of a tonal semiosis based on the concept of allegorical harmony'; by 'allegorical' he means a musical language that is neither organic nor individual but rather literal, that is plain and unadorned.[60] There could be no greater contrast with the middle style: individuality versus conventionality, organic versus inorganic, and compositional elaboration versus bare language. And yet, Adorno runs into trouble when he tries to identify exactly what these conventions or utterances of bare language are. He writes about 'decorative trills', 'cadences', 'fiorituras',

---

[57] One of the *Trios sur les intervalles de la gamme par Cristoforo Caresana, Organiste de la Chapelle Royale de Naples* (Naples, 1681) published by Choron in the second volume of his *Principes de Composition* is based on the same sequence.

[58] Theodor W. Adorno, *Beethoven: The Philosophy of Music. Fragments and Texts*, ed. Rolf Tiedermann, trans. Edmund Jephcott (Oxford, 1998), p. 154.

[59] Ibid., pp. 154–5.

[60] Michael Spitzer, *Music as Philosophy: Adorno and Beethoven's Late Style* (Bloomington, 2006), pp. 64–5.

'elementary accompaniments' and, very generally, 'formulae'.[61] When describing pieces where tonal models are in full evidence, such as the fifth bagatelle from Op. 126, he observes the effect ('Tender, lyrical polyphony'), but not the prototype that yields that effect. Reading Adorno's prose one almost feels his discomfort at not being able to pinpoint the cause. At the same time, he gives the reader further remarkable insight into the possible meaning of convention in late Beethoven's style: '[t]he compulsion of identity is broken and the conventions are its fragments. The music speaks the language of the archaic, of children, of savages and of God, but not of the individual. All the categories of the late Beethoven are challenges to idealism – almost to "spirit". Autonomy is no more.'[62]

Among the conventions displayed in Beethoven's late style, I believe a notable place is occupied by tonal prototypes. They not only sound again in unadorned fashion as they had done decades earlier, but also convey a special meaning, one that Adorno connects with the 'language of the archaic, of children, of savages and of God'. In other words, they become topics of a primal state of nature, innocence and joy. Nowhere is this meaning clearer than in the contrasting section in the slow movement of Op. 132. After the religious reverence of the *Heiliger Dankgesang eines genesenen in die Gottheit, in der lidischen Tonart* comes a section in D major entitled *Neue Kraft fühlend*. This section opens with a twofold Romanesca galante, whose bass descends stepwise from ① to ③, joined by another stepwise motion by double tenth played by the second violin (bars 31–34) and then by the first violin (bars 35–36). All of Adorno's hallmarks of conventionality are present here, 'decorative trills', 'cadences' and 'fiorituras', but the single most important ingredient is the complex of features that makes the galant Romanesca utterly distinctive: the bass descending stepwise from the tonic to one of the triadic tones (the fifth, the third, or the lower tonic); the alternation of 5-3 and 6-3 chords; the metrical (or hypermetrical) placement, with the 5-3 on the strong and the 6-3 on the weak bar; and the melodic profile of the upper voices, one descending in parallel motion with the bass by tenths, the other alternating fifths and sixths above the bass. All these features are synthesized in Fenaroli's prototype shown in Example 7.5.

There is no doubt about the meaning of this section. In Robert Hatten's words, 'Beethoven expresses new strength and vitality within the context of

---

[61] Trill as convention is also mentioned in Thomas Mann's *Doktor Faustus*; Adorno was the principal advisor to Mann in matters of music analysis. A critique on the nature and function of trills in Op. 111 is offered by Spitzer, *Music as Philosophy*, pp. 165–6.

[62] Adorno, *Beethoven*, p. 157.

(a)

(b)

Example 7.5 (a) Beethoven, Quartet in A Minor, Op. 132, 3rd movement, bars 31–39; (b) Fenaroli, partimento with descending bass, harmony of third and fifth on the first degree, and of third and sixth on the second degree

grateful prayer and the use of a stylized Baroque dance . . . This dance is the perfect blend of energy (trills and melodic figures in a vibrant triple metre) and dignity (stately tempo, with pomp in the alternating forte measures, and a "ceremonial" stepwise descent in the bass.'[63] To quote Adorno, the galant Romanesca becomes the 'language of the archaic, of

---

[63] Robert Hatten, *Musical Meaning in Beethoven: Markedness, Correlation, and Interpretation* (Bloomington, 1994), p. 199.

children, of savages and of God'. This particular tonal prototype seems to have been employed by Beethoven in his late style as a signifier of inno-cence: the withdrawal from individuality, leaving space for a language of nature.

A similar feeling of almost nirvanic contemplation can be heard in the *Cavatina* of the Quartet in B flat, Op. 130. In his extensive analysis of this movement Hatten draws attention to its 'primal' expressivity, notably its 'Chorale-like harmonic progressions and hymnic textures', a high style whose sincerity 'is established by the use of straightforward harmonic progressions at the beginning'. This style stands in striking opposition to the recitative-like section marked 'Beklemmt' (anguished). The 'straight-forward harmonic progressions' are, once more, derived from a tonal prototype, the most general and least individual of them all: the Rule of the Octave. To claim that the Rule of the Octave is a topic would be nonsense: it is a tonal paradigm like a scale; in fact, it *is* a scale. Nonethe-less, the primeval quality of simple tonal prototypes and – to quote Adorno once more – this 'bare language of music, purified of all individual expressions' allows Beethoven to look music 'in the eye'.[64]

---

[64] Adorno, *Beethoven*, p. 154.

8 | Shared Identities and Thwarted Narratives: Beethoven and the Austrian *Allgemeine musikalische Zeitung*, 1817–1824

DAVID WYN JONES

Thayer's biography of Beethoven begins its coverage of 1817 with a brief account of a new music journal in Vienna, the *Allgemeine musikalische Zeitung mit besonderer Rücksicht auf dem österreichischen Kaiserstaat*, a journal that was to run for eight years until December 1824. While the Forbes edition of Thayer notes that its pages provide a valuable corrective to the prevalent nineteenth-century view that Beethoven was not valued in Vienna in this period, none of the various editions of Thayer's biography makes extensive use of the journal.[1] In one sense this is understandable. For the focused biographer there is much to be said about Beethoven in this period: his debilitating near-deafness, his preoccupation with the welfare and education of his nephew, Karl, the role of Anton Schindler in his life, his disconnection from public musical life, and the composition of many totemic works such as the Diabelli Variations, the *Missa solemnis*, the last piano sonatas and Ninth Symphony, as well as the commission for three of the five late quartets. In another sense, however, it is unfortunate. The new journal provided weekly (from 1819, twice-weekly) coverage of musical life in Vienna in a way that is not equalled by any other single printed source during Beethoven's lifetime.

As the title of the journal suggests, it was modelled on the *Allgemeine musikalische Zeitung* established by Breitkopf & Härtel in Leipzig in 1798, a journal that was to report on musical life in German-speaking Europe through to the 1850s. From its earliest issues it had included regular summaries of musical events in Vienna by anonymous correspondents in the city, presented alongside similar summaries of musical life in other German cities such as Berlin, Hanover, Leipzig, Mannheim and Munich. By 1817, while the reports from Vienna continued to be reasonably informative about operatic life, those devoted to concert life increasingly took the form of lists of events with very little commentary. There had,

---

[1] Hermann Deiters and Hugo Riemann, *Ludwig van Beethovens Leben von Alexander Wheelock Thayer* (Leipzig, 1923), vol. 4, pp. 3–6. Elliot Forbes (rev. and ed.), *Thayer's Life of Beethoven*, rev. ed. (Princeton, 1967), pp. 661–2.

meanwhile, been a notable earlier attempt to set up a music journal in Vienna, again modelled on Breitkopf's journal, the *Wiener allgemeine musikalische Zeitung*; the first issue appeared in January 1813 and for the whole of that year provided detailed critical commentary on musical life in the city before ceasing publication at the end of December, the likely victim of the straitened economic and political climate arising from the renewed and, ultimately, decisive war with France.

Austria played a key role in the defeat of Napoleon and an equally central role settling the peace when the imperial capital gained a new European primacy as the host city for the Congress of Vienna. This international presence seemed a long way from the repeated humiliation Austria had suffered at the hands of Napoleon, and under the shrewd and calculating guidance of its foreign minister, Prince Metternich, there was a new post-war self-confidence. It was against this background that the new *Allgemeine musikalische Zeitung* was established in 1817. Its opening editorial refers to Vienna as a city that prided itself on its musical life and states that the journal was fulfilling a long-felt need. While, for many musicians, it was clear that this *Allgemeine musikalische Zeitung* was intended to equal that issued in Leipzig, its wider purpose is evident in the phrase that is added to that title, *mit besonderer Rücksicht auf den österreichischen Kaiserstaat*, 'with particular consideration of the Austrian imperial state'. Even though it was a commercial venture the journal was very much a product of Metternich's Austria, one that had to seek, however nominally, the approval of the censors.[2] In the previous year, 1816, public interest in art, literature, theatre and fashion had been rewarded with a new, mainly twice-weekly journal, the *Wiener-Moden-Zeitung*, while the scholarly debate of literature was stimulated by the founding, also in 1817, of a quarterly publication, the *Jahrbücher der Literatur*.[3] The clear Austrian identity of the music journal also sat along-side that of the official newspaper, the *Oesterreichische Beobachter*, which provided carefully filtered summaries of political developments elsewhere in Europe. Of more significance for musicians was the earlier journal, the *Vaterländische Blätter für den österreichischen Kaiserstaat*, founded in 1808 to foster loyalty to the four-year-old Austrian Empire. Between that

---

[2] For censorship and the wider social and political climate see Pieter M. Judson, *The Habsburg Empire. A New History* (Cambridge, MA, 2016), pp. 103–54; and Alan Sked, *Metternich and Austria. An Evaluation* (Basingstoke, 2008), pp. 139–64.

[3] For the latter see Paula Sutter Fichtner, 'History, Religion, and Politics in the Austrian *Vormärz*', *History and Theory*, 10/1 (1971), pp. 33–48, at pp. 43–6.

year and 1814 it contained several articles on music by Ignaz von Mosel (1772–1844), a government official as well as a composer and conductor, that promoted the idea of Vienna as a musical city and advocated the setting up of new institution to develop and enhance that characteristic. With Mosel playing a key role in private and in public, that institution was formally approved by the emperor in 1814; its official title, like that of the later musical journal, made its Austrian credentials clear, the Gesellschaft der Musikfreunde des österreichischen Kaiserstaates.[4]

The journal went through several phases of development. It was founded by the leading music publisher in Vienna at the time, S. A. Steiner, a firm with a back catalogue of over 2,500 items and an annual output that numbered between 500 and 1,000 items.[5] Its role in Beethoven's career is well understood: the publisher of some sixty works (often in multiple formats) and whose leading figures, Sigmund Anton Steiner and Tobias Haslinger, were also close friends. An editor for the journal was not named until October 1819, when Ignaz von Seyfried (1776–1841) was credited with the role; he may have acted in that capacity before then, either alone or in conjunction with others. The four sides (eight columns) of each issue contained essays and short reports; there was also a monthly musical supplement and an annual engraving of a major composer together with a complementary index. For reviews of recent music publications it was effectively a house journal for Steiner, dominated by works published by the firm. Available on advance subscription only, it was evidently a success and from 1819 appeared twice a week. In 1821 Friedrich August Kanne (1778–1833) took over as editor and is named as the publisher from the beginning of the following year. Under his control the nature of the journal changed markedly; he dispensed with the regular musical supplements and the annual engraving and index, and wrote most of the articles himself, revealing wide intellectual sympathies, aesthetic, analytical, historical and theoretical, all expressed in vivid prose that often moved towards the polemical and the eccentric. At the end of 1823 there was evidently some kind of commercial crisis and publication was suspended until March 1824; there was now a new publisher (the Lithographic Institute), a change of print from roman to gothic and music supplements were again offered.

---

[4] David Wyn Jones, *Music in Vienna 1700, 1800, 1900* (Woodbridge, 2016), pp. 117–19, 143–9. A short-lived music journal published in Linz between April 1812 and March 1813 had also signalled an Austrian identity: the *Musikalische Zeitung für die oesterreichischen Staaten*.

[5] Alexander Weinmann, *Vollständiges Verlagsverzeichnis Senefelder, Steiner, Haslinger*, vol. 1, *Senefelder, Chemische Druckerey, S. A. Steiner, S. A. Steiner & Comp. (Wien 1803–1826)* (Munich, 1979).

Most important, there was a change of title, first to the very clumsy *Wiener allgemeine musikalische Zeitung mit besonderer Rücksicht auf den österreichischen Kaiserstaat*, followed in July by the removal of 'allgemeine', which made it only slightly less clumsy.[6] By autumn 1824 Kanne seems to have lost interest, had difficulty filling two issues a week and often resorted to printing pages of poetic texts in the hope that aspiring composers might set them. There was not the customary call for subscriptions for the following year and the journal ceased publication at the end of the year.

Museum Culture

Beethoven's name first figures prominently in *AmZÖ* in the fourth issue, dated 23 January 1817.[7] It opens with a detailed review of his most popular symphony, No. 7, recently published by Steiner. Next comes a report on a series of subscription concerts given the previous November in a large room in the 'Zum römischen Kaiser', by a quartet led by Joseph Böhm, that featured 'the best compositions of their kind', including three quartets from Beethoven's Op. 18 set, Nos. 1, 3 and 5. An account of operatic life in Milan – from 1814 once more part of Austrian territories in northern Italy – also mentions a private concert series that presented 'the most splendid symphonies' of Haydn, Mozart and Beethoven. Finally, an appended advertisement by Steiner details works available from his shop in the Paternostergasse, off the Graben. Compositions by Beethoven dominate the list: the piano sonata in E minor (Op. 90), *Wellington's Victory* (the 'Battle' Symphony), the Seventh Symphony in score, parts and no fewer than six different arrangements, the F minor quartet (Op. 95), the G major violin sonata (Op. 96), the 'Archduke' trio (Op. 97), *An die ferne Geliebte* and three single songs. Equally eye-catching, the advertisement announces a new venture, a series of single piano works by a variety of composers to be issued under the bilingual title of *Musée musical des clavicinistes, Museum für Klaviermusik*. Its ambition is made clear in the advertisement: 'Only musical products of recognized value will find a place here, ones which through aesthetic purity reveal to an exceptional degree the process of composition with art, feeling and clarity ... By these means we hope not for an ephemeral product, rather to establish a repertory for a

---

[6] This essay uses the abbreviation *AmZÖ* to cover all versions of the title. Online access at www.anno.onb.ac.at.

[7] *AmZÖ*, 1 (1817), cols. 25–32.

longer period that must be of value for the history of our art.' The first number was a new sonata 'by our justly famed Herr Ludwig van Beethoven', Op. 101. Over three years, from 1817 to 1820, a total of seven works by seven different composers was issued in this musical museum, each one followed by a review in the journal (details in Table 8.1). Each number had two title pages, a general one for the series followed by an individual one for the particular work, cultivating the sense that these were collectable items that were to be kept together.[8] After this focused period of publication, the series lost its impetus, though the title was twice revived in later years for single items of piano music by Hummel and Schubert.[9]

This exclusive museum of piano music avoids those composers, such as Czerny, Diabelli and Gelinek, who for years had provided endless sets of variations, dances and simple sonatas for the insatiable amateur market in Vienna. Indeed, three of the composers, Wolfgang Ebner, Eduard von Lannoy and Archduke Rudolph were in different ways little-known as composers at the time of publication, while a fourth, Maximilian Stadler, was strongly associated with Catholic church music, not with piano music. Hummel and Moscheles, in contrast, both enjoyed international careers as pianist-composers. Although no longer resident in Austria they had been raised and educated in the empire and were easily appropriated into a national museum.

How did Beethoven fit into the museum? He was no longer a performer or a teacher of the piano but he had written a considerable corpus of piano music to date. The established view that the A major sonata is one of those works that widens the space between the composer, on the one hand, and the player and listener, on the other, fits well with Steiner's principle that the museum should include works of permanence; Beethoven himself, in a letter concerning the sonata addressed to Steiner, had made a virtue of its difficulty, 'for what is difficult is also beautiful, good, great and so forth'.[10]

---

[8] The general title page is reproduced in BG, vol. 4, p. 23.

[9] Hummel's Fantasy in E flat, Op. 18, was first published in 1805 by the Bureau d'Arts et Industrie; their stock was taken over by Steiner in 1823 when the work was reissued as volume 8 of the series. Four years later, Schubert's Sonata in G (D894) was printed by Haslinger, Steiner's successor, as volume 9 in the series. Alexander Weinmann, 'Vollständiges Verlagsverzeichnis der Musikalien des Kunst- und Industrie Comptoirs in Wien, 1801–1819', *Studien zur Musikwissenschaft*, 22 (1955), p. 238; Weinmann, *Steiner*, pp. 10, 221; Alexander Weinmann, *Vollständiges Verlagsverzeichnis Senefelder, Steiner, Haslinger*, vol. 2, *Tobias Haslinger (Wien 1826–1843)* (Munich, 1980), p. 7.

[10] Letter of 9 January 1817 or later: BG, vol. 4, p. 8; LOB, vol. 3, p. 661.

Table 8.1 *Musée musical des clavicinistes, Museum für Klaviermusik*: vols. 1–7 (Steiner, 1817–20)

Volume/Exemplar	Composer	Work	Dedicatee	Publication date	*AmZÖ* review
1 A-Wn, MS 7648	Ludwig van Beethoven (1770–1827)	Sonata in A, Op. 101	Dorothea Ertmann	March 1817	1 (1817), cols. 65–6
2 A-Wn, MS 7648	Ignaz Moscheles (1794–1870)	Fantasy (in the Italian Style) and Rondo, Op. 38	Eleonore von Hayd	June 1817	1 (1817), cols. 217–18
3 A-Wn, MS 7648	Maximilian Stadler (1748–1833)	Fugue with prelude	Archduke Rudolph	February 1818	2 (1818), cols. 61–3
4 A-Wst, Mc-3967	Wolfgang Ebner (1612–1665)	Aria by his imperial majesty Ferdinand III; arranged thirty-six times	–	October 1818	3 (1819), cols. 38–9
5 A-Wn, MS 7648	Johann Nepomuk Hummel (1778–1837)	Sonata in F sharp Minor, Op. 81	Archduchess Maria von Sachsen Weimar	April 1819	3 (1819), cols. 333–6
6 GB-Lbl, f. 790. c (9)	Eduard von Lannoy (1787–1853)	Sonata in A flat Minor, Op. 9	K. T. von Nittel	May 1819	3 (1819), cols. 459–60
7 A-Wn, MS 7648	'R. E. H'. [Archduke Rudolph] (1788–1831)	An exercise devised by Ludwig van Beethoven, varied forty times, and dedicated to its creator by his pupil R. E. H.	Beethoven	January 1820	4 (1820), cols. 369–73

An observation recorded in the *AmZÖ* by another composer in the series, Eduard von Lannoy, provides a wider perspective on the general standing of Beethoven's piano music in Vienna at the time. Born into an aristocratic family in Brussels he had lived with his family in Styria from 1806, where he was much involved with its musical life, as a composer and as a patron. From 1818 onwards he spent most of the year in Vienna where, as well as a developing a career as a composer, he became a commentator on musical matters and an increasingly influential administrator.[11] At the end of 1818 – that is five months before his own piano sonata appeared in Steiner's series – Lannoy contributed an article to the *AmZÖ*, 'Casual thoughts on the present state of music in Vienna'.[12] Evoking the long-standing division into *Kenner* and *Nichtkenner* he offered the following remarks on Beethoven's piano music. 'Here I found that Beethoven's splendid piano works were not as well known as I had imagined, and this surprised me at first … Beethoven's masterworks enchant the connoisseur ['Kenner'], please even more the more frequently one hears them, and mystify the amateur ['Nichtkenner'] who experiences them a few times.'

There are other telling interrelationships in the series. Archduke Rudolph emerges as a pivotal figure: the dedicatee of Maximilian Stadler's contribution (volume 3) and the composer of a set of variations on a theme provided by his teacher, Beethoven, the composer who had opened the series (volume 7). As well as the being the ultimate *Kenner*, this member of the Habsburg family, the brother of Emperor Franz, imparts a wider sense of historical legacy to Steiner's project. From the age of thirteen he had built up a private library of music, meticulously entering details in his own handwritten catalogues.[13] Housed in his private quarters in the Hofburg, by 1817 it consisted of some 6,000 items. As well as works by living composers, it had a substantial collection of older music from a wide range of national traditions, especially Italian, French and German, and Beethoven is known to have borrowed items from this library. With the *Museum für Klaviermusik* Beethoven and the archduke were now contributing to a public library. Maximilian Stadler shared this sense of historical legacy.

---

[11] Wolfgang Suppan, *Heinrich Eduard Josef von Lannoy (1787–1853). Leben und Werke.* Musik aus der Steiermark. Reihe 4: Beiträge zur steirischen Musikforschung Bd. 2. (Graz, 1960), pp. 7–26.

[12] 'Flüchtige Bemerkungen über den jetzigen Zustand der Musik in Wien', *AmZÖ*, 2 (1818), cols. 473–6.

[13] For an overview of the catalogues see Susan Kagan, *Archduke Rudolph, Beethoven's Patron, Pupil and Friend. His Life and Music* (Stuyvesant, 1988), pp. 263–96. Particular comments drawn from the *Alphabetisches Verzeichnis des Musik-Componisten* in A-Wgm, 1268/33.

Now in his seventieth year, he was almost a historical figure himself, a friend of Haydn and Mozart and an abbot who had been required to oversee the dissolution of several monasteries in the 1780s as part of Joseph II's reforms. From 1815 onwards he began to assemble material for a projected history of music in Austria that would have begun in Gregorian times and concluded with Haydn and Mozart. His research took him to the imperial library and archive, Archduke's Rudolph library and to the equally rich holdings of several monasteries.[14] His musical contribution to Steiner's series, a prelude and fugue, is as much a celebration of the intellectual outlook of a national historian as it is a demonstration of compositional prowess. That historical perspective is even more evident in the next work in the series, volume 4 issued in October 1818.

This was not the work of a living composer, but one that had been written 170 years earlier by Wolfgang Ebner. As the review in *AmZÖ* indicates, Stadler had recommended the work to Steiner, and the journal duly described it as having 'particular interest for our fatherland'. Ebner was one of several organists who had worked in the court of Emperor Ferdinand III, from 1637 to his death in 1665. That emperor was the first in a sequence of four competent Habsburg composers and performers – the others were Leopold I, Joseph I and Karl VI – and Steiner's title page informs the curious reader that Ebner had taken an 'aria' (an eight-bar binary tune in A minor) by Ferdinand as the subject for thirty-six variations. Also recorded on the title page is the year of its original publication, 1648, a date that would have had resonances 170 years later, in 1818: it was the year in which the Peace of Westphalia was signed, ending the most protracted period of warfare in Austrian history, the Thirty Years War, longer even than the recently ended Napoleonic Wars. For Steiner's museum of piano music, it provided, moreover, one of two instances of a link between a capable Habsburg musician and a faithful servant: Emperor Ferdinand and Wolfgang Ebner, Archduke Rudolph and Beethoven.[15]

But there is a very public reversal of traditional roles here: while the emperor had been the dedicatee of a work by a loyal servant, the archduke

---

[14] Karl Wagner (ed.), *Abbe Maximilian Stadler: seine Materialien zur Geschichte der Musik unter den österreichischen Regenten* (Kassel, 1974), pp. X–XIV, XXIII–XXIV.

[15] An article by Barry Cooper and Erica Buurman focuses on the musical links between Ebner's set of variations and works by Archduke Rudolph (his Forty Variations, volume 7 in Steiner's series), Bach (Goldberg Variations), Beethoven (Diabelli Variations), Froberger (Mayerin Variations) and Schubert (Impromptu in C minor, D899): 'The Influence of Wolfgang Ebner's Ferdinand Variations on Bach, Beethoven and Others', *Musical Times*, 153 (Winter 2012), pp. 17–28.

was the composer of a work dedicated to a loyal servant, Beethoven. Steiner's title page, which must have been agreed with the archduke as well as the state censor, includes the composer's name as initials only, 'R. E. H.', that is Rudolph Erzherzog Habsburgensis. While this could be construed as imperial condescension, the title of the composition itself suggests that it was a sincere act of humility, a personality trait that had been very deliberately cultivated by recent generations of the Habsburg family, notably Rudolph's father, Leopold II, and his uncle, Joseph II. It takes the form of a description: 'an exercise devised by Ludwig van Beethoven, varied forty times, and dedicated to its creator by his pupil R. E. H.'

The associated review of each of the seven works in the *AmZÖ* acts as a prospectus for the particular work and, cumulatively, for the distinctive nature of the series, typically combining laudatory evaluations with a running commentary on the music. Since none of the reviews is signed it is difficult to say whether they constitute the views of one person or the shared views of several. Certainly, there are some recurring characteristics, even preoccupations. The first is that these works are to be appreciated for their compositional mastery and emotional reach, not merely as examples of good piano writing. For those two composers, Moscheles and Hummel, who were recognized as leading performers, the reviews are at pains to explain that the undoubted technical challenges of their two works are always at the service of a higher cause, in Moscheles's case the avoidance of musical 'egotism', in Hummel's case the linking 'of inner strength with modern elegance of outer form'. Similarly, for Beethoven's sonata the pianist need not be a 'practical wizard', but 'sense and feeling, head and heart, are indispensable requirements'. 'Fantasy' is a key yardstick. Used in the title of Moscheles's composition it features in all the reviews except that of Ebner's variations; it is never associated with vapid, glossy passage work, rather with heightened emotional states, contrasts and unpredictability, including the choice of unusual keys, F sharp minor by Hummel and, even rarer, A flat minor in the outer movements of Lannoy's sonata. Two particular compositional skills are prized, variation and contrapuntal mastery. For the former, the endless possibilities of the theme – thirty-six in Ebner, forty in Archduke Rudolph – are admired, also the very distinctive alteration of the metrical and rhythmical character of the original theme to promote a broadening of the variation process: in the Ebner the first twelve variations are nearly all in common time (with anacrusis), the second group of twelve are based on a reworking of the theme as a courante in 3/4 (with anacrusis), and the final twelve are based on a sarabande version of the theme in 3/4 (without anacrusis but with the characteristic stress on the second beat); in Archduke Rudolph's work the theme is in common time but for the penultimate variation (no. 39) it switches to a minuet in 3/4. Intricacies of contrapuntal writing that are willingly highlighted in the reviews include the canons in the trio section of the march and the C major section in the finale of Beethoven's sonata, Stadler's four-part fugue and the concluding four-part fugue in Rudolph's work.

Oratorio: Mosel, Kanne and the Artwork of the Future

The very first article in *AmZÖ*, issued on 2 January 1817, is not about private discrimination, but about developing the musical taste of the wider public. A few weeks earlier, on 22 November 1816, the Gesellschaft der Musikfreunde des österreichischen Kaiserstaates had presented a perform-ance of Maximilian Stadler's oratorio, *Die Befreyung von Jerusalem*. Rather than a review of that performance, the journal offers an extended account (across three issues) of the history of the work from its first performance in 1811, followed by a detailed description of each of its twenty musical numbers.[16] The author of the review was the influential figure of Ignaz von Mosel who openly reveals his overriding ambition for musical life in Austria, describing Stadler's work as 'an artistic product of the fatherland' and, even more extravagantly, 'a constantly admirable model that will endure for years to come'. In the first issue of an Austrian musical journal, here is an author long identified with improving the nature of public musical life in Austria reviewing an ambitious work by a composer who was also compiling material for a history of music in Austria. Moreover, oratorio had long been central to Mosel's vision for music in Austria, an outlook that he practised as well as preached.[17]

In November 1812 Mosel had directed the hugely successful performance of Handel's *Alexander's Feast* in the Imperial Riding School that led to the foundation of the Gesellschaft der Musikfreunde; he also prepared the musical text, greatly expanding Mozart's orchestral version to suit the performing forces of 500 plus. As editor and conductor he went on to give

---

[16] *AmZÖ*, 1 (1817), cols. 1–8, 9–12, 17–22.

[17] For accounts of oratorio in Vienna in the first decades of the nineteenth century and Mosel's role see Eduard Hanslick, *Geschichte des Concertwesens in Wien* (Vienna, 1869), pp. 191–201; and David Wyn Jones, '"What Noble Simplicity, What Strength and, Certainly, Melody This Music Has." Handel's reputation in Beethoven's Vienna', *Händel-Jahrbuch*, 63 (2017), pp. 73–86, at pp. 78–86.

the same treatment to four further oratorios by Handel, *Samson*, *Jephtha*, *Solomon* and *Messiah*. For Mosel, this was never an exercise in musical antiquarianism as he sought to wrap the English Handel into an Austrian national tradition that also featured the oratorios of local composers, principally Haydn's *Creation* and *Seasons* and, now, Stadler's *Die Befreyung von Jerusalem*. Accordingly, his review of Stadler's oratorio in the first issue of *AmZÖ* carefully weaves in references to Handel and Haydn. Archangel Gabriel (a soprano role, as in Haydn's *Creation*) is trying to reassure the Christian warrior, Goffredo, of God's power: 'God is Love, Do not deny him, What do you doubt? God is mighty' ('Gott ist die Liebe, Versage nicht, Was zweifelst du? Gott ist die Macht'), exhortations that are immediately followed by a thunderbolt. Mosel tells the reader that in the original version of the oratorio Stadler had evoked the thunderbolt with a *fortissimo* chord, but this had proved to be too reminiscent of 'Es werde Licht, und es ward Licht' from Haydn's *Die Schöpfung*; it was replaced by a lengthy roll on a large drum, which Mosel then neatly proceeds to link with Handel's practice of using extra-large timpani in his oratorio performances.

For Mosel, historical legacy was a recurring way of legitimizing the potency and appeal of oratorio, and articulated an understanding that was not accorded to operatic culture in Vienna. At the same time Mosel seems never to have explained the particulars of this appeal, perhaps because they were self-evident: broadly Christian rather than narrowly Catholic, often at the service of charitable causes, promoted by public institutions (the Tonkünstler-Societät since 1771, now joined by the Gesellschaft der Musikfreunde) and, above all, a public demonstration of the power of a participatory culture, singers and instrumentalists, the professional alongside the amateur. Managed by the people, oratorio had the support of the aristocracy and the Habsburg family too. In Mosel's eyes, oratorio unified Austrian society in a way that no opera, symphony, quartet or sonata could do.

Steiner played a full part in this process. Four years after his new journal had begun with a review of Stadler's *Die Befreyung*, the publisher issued the oratorio in full score.[18] A handsome, elegantly engraved volume of 351 pages, it precedes the music itself with a cast list and the full libretto. The title page is similarly generous, especially in its dedication: 'to Franz I, Emperor of Austria, King of Hungary, and Bohemia, of Lombardy and Venice, Galizia and Lodomeria; Archduke of Austria etc. etc. with deepest

---

[18] Exemplar: A-Wn, S.A.82.D.21.

reverence humbly dedicated by S. A. Steiner and Company, Music Publisher in Vienna'.

Beethoven figured in this local oratorio tradition to a limited extent and
could have been a compelling figure: certainly, in the eyes of many he
should have been. His one completed oratorio, *Christus am Ölberge*, has
never featured centrally in Beethoven's reputation, infrequently performed
and routinely excused by the composer's own remarks that it was written
very quickly for his benefit concert in 1803. It had some currency in
Austria in the years after the end of the Napoleonic Wars as part of Mosel's
agenda: performed in March 1815 during the Congress of Vienna, in
March 1817 by the Tonkünstler-Societät (the customary two performances) and in the Concerts Spirituels in April 1821.[19] Unlike the works
of Handel, Haydn and Stadler it was a short work, no more than fifty-five
minutes, something that may have inhibited further presentations.
A performance by local forces in Linz during Holy Week in 1820 addressed
this issue by dividing the work into two parts: Part 1 ended with the chorus
of warriors in C major, 'Wir haben ihn gesehen'; Part 2 began with a new
substantial orchestral introduction, the 'Marcia funebre' from the *Eroica*
symphony, followed by Jesus's accompanied recitative ('Die mich zu fangen ausgezogen sind') and the remainder of the work.[20]

In 1815 Beethoven had received a commission from the recently
founded Gesellschaft der Musikfreunde to compose a new oratorio, one
that would take its place alongside Stadler's *Die Befreyung* in the continuing enhancement of an Austrian oratorio tradition.[21] Beethoven was keen
on the idea, accepted the commission, but was less keen on the libretto he
was eventually given, *Der Sieg des Kreuzes*, written by Josef Karl Bernard,
editor of the court newspaper the *Wiener Zeitung*. He drew attention to a
fundamental weakness, that the text did not readily suggest musical treatment. Beethoven may have been worried too that the essential subject
matter of the drama as well as details of the unfolding narrative were
similar to those of Stadler's *Die Befreyung*, now well established in the local
repertory: both oratorios tell the story of conflict between Christian and
infidel forces, the first set in Jerusalem, the second in ancient Rome; both

---

[19] Elisabeth Fritz-Hilscher, 'Musik und Musikleben rund um den Wiener Kongress (1814/15) aus
der Sicht einiger Zeitzeugen', *Studien zur Musikwissenschaft*, 57 (2013), pp. 215–39, at p. 238;
AmZÖ, 1 (1817), cols. 118–19; ibid., 5 (1821), cols. 269–70.

[20] *AmZÖ*, 4 (1820), cols. 270–1, 328.

[21] For a detailed history of this commission see Michael Ladenburger, 'Beethoven und die
Gesellschaft der Musikfreunde in Wien. Mitteilungen zum Oratorium: "Der Sieg des Kreuzes"
oder: Das Verdienst der Geduld', *Studien zur Musikwissenschaft*, 49 (2002), pp. 253–97.

have a scene of heavenly apparition, Archangel Gabriel in Stadler, a vision of the Cross (with angels) in Bernard's text; both have battle scenes that graphically juxtapose good and evil; and both conclude with choruses of praise, 'Sein is die Macht und die Kraft, und die Herrlichkeit, von Ewigkeit zu Ewigkeit' in Stadler, 'Hosanna' and 'Ehre sei Gott' in Bernard's libretto.

Beethoven's reluctance to commit to this particular oratorio project did not affect the continuing view that the genre ought to be central to ambitious music making. As a public advocate of this view in the columns of *AmZÖ*, Ignaz von Mosel was succeeded by Kanne, an altogether different personality. While Mosel was certainly enthusiastic, as someone trained in the way of Austrian imperial bureaucracy he was also measured, considered and efficient; Kanne, on the other hand, was not a product of the Austrian establishment; a composer and poet as well as a writer, he was challenging and often disconcerting, someone who was reputed to have died with a bottle of wine in his hand.[22] He had enthusiastically welcomed the publication of Stadler's *Die Befreyung*, complimenting the publisher on the quality of the printing and noting the appropriateness of the dedication to the emperor.[23] In the same year, 1823, he wrote two extended articles on the oratorio as a genre, 'On the marked dearth of new great oratorios', published in five successive issues in January, and 'On the oratorio', across three issues in December.[24] The opening of the first article is typically arresting, greeting the reader with two metaphors about the lamentable absence of new oratorios: Noah looking anxiously from the ark for dry land and an expedition to the North Pole. He then goes though the honourable history of the oratorio, familiar enough to his readers, from England to Haydn, praises Beethoven's *Christus am Ölberge* ('a splendid flowering of his great imagination') and, once more, Stadler's *Die Befreyung*. In his search for reasons why there are no more new works he draws attention to the preference of the public for 'frivolous ostentation' – a constant refrain in Kanne's writings – and recommends that musical institutions should be willing to offer more financial support for the composition and performance of new oratorios.

The second article has a hidden purpose that is only gradually revealed, and explains why Kanne returned to the topic so soon after the first article.

---

[22] Hermann Ullrich, 'Beethovens Freund, Friedrich August Kanne', *Österreichische Musikzeitschrift*, 29 (1974), pp. 75–80.

[23] *AmZÖ*, 7 (1823), cols. 177–8.

[24] 'Über den fühlbaren Mangel an neuen grossen Oratorien', ibid., cols. 1–4, 9–11, 17–21, 25–9, 37–8; 'Über das Oratorium', ibid., cols. 777–81, 785–9, 801–4.

It begins in a similar vein, that composers seem unwilling to contribute to this 'most sublime form of music', casually mentions that Beethoven, 'our great, ever more vigorous master', is composing an oratorio, but follows this with the teasing remark that he will say more about that later. 'Later' turned out to be the eleven days that elapsed between the appearance of the first instalment of the article and the third. Towards the end of that final instalment Kanne reveals what he knows about Beethoven's oratorio: title, dramatis personae and the narrative content of the text that had been prepared by Bernard. 'May Beethoven's genius produce in this work of art its greatest triumph, and the poem its finest transfiguration.'

In modern parlance this was something of a scoop for Kanne and the *AmZÖ*. The completed libretto had been delivered to Beethoven and the Gesellschaft only a couple of months earlier,[25] and Kanne must have been given sight of one of those two manuscripts. Over the next few months, however, he seems to have become less informed, persisting in the view that Beethoven was to set the text, even when the composer himself had informed the Gesellschaft on 23 January that he could not do so.[26] Kanne's apparent ignorance may have been due to other preoccupations, the first performance of his opera, *Lindane oder Die Fee und der Haarbeutelschneider*, in the Leopoldstadt theatre in March and the very future of *AmZÖ* itself; January and February 1824 were the two months when no issues of the journal were published, with publication resuming at the beginning of March. In February thirty leading Viennese figures, prompted by the news that the *Missa solemnis* and the Ninth Symphony might be given their first performances in Berlin, signed a lengthy public letter to the composer,[27] urging him to give public performances of his newest works in Vienna. Quite reasonably, this letter has always been interpreted as a galvanizing moment in the process that led to Beethoven's two benefit concerts in May, featuring first performances of the Ninth Symphony and three movements from the *Missa solemnis*. These two works are, indeed, specifically mentioned in the letter but so, too, is the oratorio commissioned for the Gesellschaft der Musikfreunde. Clearly, the signatories, who included many close acquaintances of the composer, such as Carl Czerny, Diabelli, Steiner, Andreas Streicher, Zmeskall and others, did not know about the recent correspondence between Beethoven and the Gesellschaft. Kanne was not a signatory but that he was equally uninformed is suggested by

[25] Ladenburger, 'Beethoven und die Gesellschaft', pp. 270, 282.
[26] BG, vol. 5, pp. 260–1; LOB, vol. 3, pp. 1104–6.   [27] BG, vol. 5, pp. 273–6; LTB, vol. 3, pp. 4–7.

the subsequent publication of the entire letter in the *AmZÖ* of 21 April,[28] just seventeen days before the first of the two benefit concerts. This was the last time that the journal was to mention an oratorio project by Beethoven and, although the composer was to consider other plans for oratorios in the last three years of his life, the demise of *AmZÖ* in December 1824 removed a potentially influential form of public encouragement.

'From the Heart, May It Again Go to the Heart': Beethoven and the Austrian Catholic Inheritance

Probably the least expected work from the last period of Beethoven's life was the *Missa solemnis*, a work that seems to lack a wider context in comparison with the Ninth Symphony, the last quartets and sonatas, and, certainly, the projected oratorio. Beethoven began serious work on it in April 1819 stimulated by the news that Archduke Rudolph was to be enthroned as Archbishop of Olmütz, became consumed by a project that was to last three years, missed the original intended deadline of March 1820, wrote a work that verged on the impractical, never witnessed a complete performance and resorted to selling the work as an oratorio for concert performance. It is the ultimate late-period work: musically far-reaching, the indulgent product of a solitary individual who had lost contact with his environment. Yet the *Missa solemnis* is not without a context, one that went beyond an enthronement service for an archbishop.

One of the most striking aspects of the *AmZÖ* across the eight years of its existence is how much coverage is given to church music, a natural consequence of the fact that this was a journal for the Austrian Empire, overwhelmingly Catholic in religion and socially conditioned by it, even when, as seems to have been the case in Beethoven, it was not actively practised by all its people. For the best part of two centuries, music for the Catholic liturgy had been fundamental to Habsburg identity, as Holy Roman emperors, leaders of the Counter-Reformation and, now somewhat diminished, emperors of Austria.[29] A few years after the end of the

---

[28] *AmZÖ*, 8 (1824), pp. 87–8.

[29] The following articulates the relationship between the Habsburg dynasty and Catholicism from the seventeenth to the twentieth centuries: Anna Coreth, *Pietas Austriaca*, trans. William D. Bowman and Anna Maria Leitgeb (West Lafayette, 2004). For developments in the early nineteenth century see William D. Bowman, 'Popular Catholicism in *Vormärz* Austria, 1800–48', *Catholicism and Austrian Culture*, eds. Ritchie Robertson and Judith Beniston, *Austrian Studies* 10 (Edinburgh, 1999), pp. 51–64; and Fichtner, 'History, Religion and Politics'.

Napoleonic Wars the *AmZÖ* reveals a reinvigoration of that link between music, religion and Habsburg polity, not as a consequence of a carefully formulated policy that sought to isolate other Christian religions that were now freely tolerated, Protestant and Greek Orthodox, but as a reassuring acknowledgement of a shared inheritance.

S. A. Steiner, the music publisher and, for the first four years the publishers of *AmZÖ*, was at the heart of this activity. In 1817 he had just embarked on two major projects, a subscription series of twenty items of church music by Johann Nepomuk Hummel, six masses, six graduals, six offertories, one litany and one Te Deum, and a very different series aimed at those churches in the country that had more limited musical resources, *Kleinere Kirchen-Musikalien, vorzüglich für das Land geeignet.*[30]

Two masses by Hummel were issued in the first series, Op. 77 in B flat and Op. 80 in E flat, works originally written for the Esterházy court in the early 1800s as a continuation of the Haydn tradition of name day masses for Princess Marie Hermenegild Esterházy, one to which Beethoven had contributed with his Mass in C. Scored for four soloists, chorus and orchestra they are substantial works of the solemnis type, forty-five minutes of music distributed across a liturgical service that would easily amount to ninety or more minutes. Steiner's second series was aimed at those churches in the Austrian Empire that did not have extensive or very skilled musical resources. The title of the series suggests that these works were particularly suited to churches in small villages and towns in the countryside; *Landmesse* soon became a common term, even though the works themselves might well have been performed in major towns and cities too. The first six works in the *Kleinere Kirchen-Musikalien* series were all by Johann Baptist Schiedermayr (1779–1840), cathedral organist in Linz, scored for a basic ensemble of voices, two violins and continuo, allowing performance with forces as small as seven, but with optional parts for other instruments too, especially trumpets and timpani. The series continued with works by Diabelli, Stadler, Vanhal and others, and within ten years had reached forty-six issues.[31]

Some of the works in the *Kleinere Kirchen-Musikalien* were given brief reviews in the *AmZÖ*, but the two masses by Hummel were given particular attention. The first, in B flat, was reviewed in 1818 and gained further notice as the work that was sung, instead of Beethoven's planned mass, at

---

[30] Advertised in *AmZÖ*, 1 (1817), cols. 339–40.
[31] Weinmann, *Steiner*, pp. 155–6, 160, 169, 205, 232, 234, 236–7.

the enthronement of Archduke Rudolph in March 1820.[32] The review of
the E flat mass in October and November of the same year is especially
lavish, eighteen columns across six issues and with eleven musical
examples in short score.[33] As always the review takes the approach of a
commentary for each movement in turn, drawing attention to particularly
effective moments, especially Hummel's mastery of counterpoint. When
this review appeared Beethoven had completed the Kyrie and Gloria of the
Missa solemnis in score, and sketched all the remaining movements with
the exception of the 'Dona nobis pacem'. Although it was already clear that
Beethoven's mass was on an even larger scale than Hummel's mass, some
seventy-five minutes as opposed to forty minutes, its approach to long-
standing generic practices is broadly similar.[34] If Beethoven read this
extended review of Hummel's mass he would have sympathized too with
its concluding observations that this was the kind of work that would
reinvigorate contemporary interest in church music.

The promotion of particular items of Catholic church music in the
columns of the *AmZÖ* sits alongside a clear desire to relate current practice
to the traditions of the past. Forty years earlier, in the 1780s, the reforms of
Joseph II had considerably reduced the role of music in the Catholic liturgy
in general and redefined the role of monasteries in society.[35] Rather than
ignoring that past the *AmZÖ* presents an accommodation with it, promot-
ing a general awareness of the historical legacy of Catholic institutions and
Catholic music. Major articles are devoted to the history of music in four
venerable institutions, the Augustine abbey in St Florian, the Benedictine
abbeys in Kremsmünster and Melk, and the Cistercian abbey in Lilienfeld.[36]
In the case of Melk, the reader is reminded that Albrechtsberger had
worked there, someone who had nurtured the talent of many living
composers, including Beethoven, Eybler and Stadler. As for Lilienfeld,
where Stadler had served as abbot, it now has a flourishing music life,

---

[32] *AmZÖ*, 2 (1818), cols. 329–31; ibid., 4 (1820), cols. 196–7.

[33] Ibid., 4 (1820), cols. 668–72, 686–8, 695–6, 711–12, 719–20, 731–6.

[34] Warren Kirkendale has pointed out that the two masses share one unusual detail. The
traditional threefold repetition of 'Agnus Dei, qui tollis peccata mundi, miserere nobis' has the
complete text each time, whereas most settings omit the final clause on the third iteration: 'New
Roads to Old Ideas in Beethoven's Missa solemnis', *Musical Quarterly*, 56 (1970), pp. 665–701,
at p. 690.

[35] See Derek Beales, *Prosperity and Plunder: European Catholic Monasteries in the Age of
Revolution, 1650–1815* (Cambridge, 2003), pp. 179–228.

[36] St Florian: *AmZÖ*, 1 (1817), cols. 128–31. Kremsmünster: ibid., 1 (1817), cols. 242–5; 4 (1820),
cols. 315–19. Melk: ibid., 2 (1818), cols. 349–52, 357–60, 365–7. Lilienfeld: ibid., 2 (1818), cols.
53–6.

not in the monastery itself but, in accordance with the educational dynamic of Joseph II's reforms, at the associated Gymnasium; there, thrice-weekly concerts of quartets drew on a library that had the complete quartets of Haydn, Mozart and Beethoven, and on Sundays after Holy Mass there were regular performances of symphonies too.

Above the Kyrie of the autograph score of the *Missa solemnis* Beethoven scrawled the annotation 'From the heart, may it again go to the heart' ('Von Herzen – möge es wieder – zu Herzen gehn'). This annotation has always been interpreted as a touching gesture of sincerity by a single creative artist who had laboured for years to produce a work of unparalleled ambition. The reciprocity embedded in the phrase – from one heart to another that is similarly inclined – points to a collective identity between composer, performer and listener, one formed by the religious and social practices of the day. Birgit Lodes has argued that this inscription was a dedicatory comment to Archduke Rudolph;[37] if so, then the word 'heart' embraces the political too, an expression of the indissolubility of church, nation and the Habsburg dynasty.

It is possible to infer from columns of the *AmZÖ* that the quality of liturgical performances in Vienna was variable. In April 1821 Kanne placed an open request in the journal for organists and choirmasters in Vienna to forward details of performing forces and the repertoire for Easter in their churches with a view to writing an article about church music in the imperial capital.[38] Nothing came of this idea, presumably because of the poor response. The Hofkapelle, with a choir of sixteen to eighteen and an orchestra of up to thirty or so, maintained a full calendar of liturgical performances, mainly drawing on the works of its own composers, past and present, from Reutter to Salieri and Eybler, supplemented by acknowledged masters in the genre such as Albrechtsberger, Michael Haydn and Stadler. Beethoven did not belong to that particular institutional tradition and his Mass in C was not to be performed at the Hofkapelle until 1840.[39] By far the most ambitious music making took place in the nearby Augustinerkirche, thanks to the energy of two individuals, Franz Xaver Gebauer (1784–1822) and Ferdinand Piringer (1780–1829).

---

[37] Birgit Lodes, '"Von Herzen – möge es wieder – zu Herzen gehn!" Zur Widmung von Beethovens *Missa solemnis*', *Altes in Neuen, Festschrift Theodor Göllner zum 65. Geburtstag*, eds. Bernd Edelmann and Manfred Hermann Schmid (Tutzing, 1995), pp. 295–306.

[38] *AmZÖ*, 5 (1821), cols. 214–15.

[39] Calendar of performances in Richard Steurer, *Das Repertoire der Wiener Hofmusikkapelle im neunzehnten Jahrhundert* (Tutzing, 1998), pp. 180–639.

Born in Silesia, Gebauer had arrived in Vienna in 1810, first establishing himself as a piano teacher before being appointed Kapellmeister at the Augustinerkirche in 1816, where he was to transform the standard of performance. Within a year the *AmZÖ* reported favourably that liturgical music was now being rehearsed properly and with sizeable forces, all committed to a 'noble purpose'; the report particularly mentions a liturgical performance on 26 October 1817 of Beethoven's Mass in C, described as little-known, in which the orchestra numbered eighty players.[40] By 1819 Gebauer's ambition had led to a series of 'practice concerts' (*Übungs-Konzerte*) in the Mehlgrube (later transferred to the Landständischer Saal in the Herrengasse) throughout the winter season, at which the liturgical items for the following Sunday, in the case of masses often single movements, were rehearsed alongside a run-through of a symphony; singers and instrumentalists were drawn from the city as a whole and paid an annual subscription to participate.[41] Around this time Beethoven briefly contemplated writing a mass for double choir for the Augustinerkirche.[42] In the second season the series acquired the title Concerts Spirituels, a venerable one that was to forge a new identity for Catholic church music within public concert life in Vienna in the 1820s. Following an illness and a period of recuperation in Switzerland – all reported in the *AmZÖ* – Gebauer died in December 1822 at the age of thirty-eight, without being able to plan the 1822–23 season. The concerts were subsequently revived under the joint direction of Ferdinand Piringer, Gebauer's former assistant, and Joseph Geissler, and were to maintain a distinct presence in Viennese musical life through to 1848. Movements from Beethoven's Mass in C were publicly rehearsed on four further occasions up to 1824 in preparation for subsequent liturgical performances of the whole work in the Augustinerkirche.[43] From being a little-known work in 1817 the mass now constituted a distinct strand in Beethoven's reputation in Vienna.

Awareness of these concerts sheds light on the nature of Beethoven's two benefit concerts at the Kärntnertortheater and the Grosser Redoutensaal in May 1824 that included movements from the *Missa solemnis* plus the Ninth Symphony, preceded by the overture *Die Weihe des Hauses*. At the second concert Beethoven's 'Tremate, empi, tremate' and an aria from

---

[40] *AmZÖ*, 1 (1817), cols. 401–2.

[41] David Wyn Jones, *The Symphony in Beethoven's Vienna* (Cambridge, 2006), pp. 184–9.

[42] Julia Ronge, 'Beethoven's Ambitions in Church Music: Plans, Ideas, and Fragments', *The Beethoven Journal*, 30/2 (Winter 2015), pp. 52–61, at p. 55.

[43] *AmZÖ*, 4 (1820), col. 377; ibid., 5 (1821), col. 706; ibid., 8 (1824), p. 399.

Rossini's *Tancredi* were substituted for the Credo and Agnus Dei from the mass, but the first concert – overture, Kyrie, Credo, Agnus Dei, Ninth Symphony – was a concert spirituel in all but name.

Beethoven, 'with Particular Consideration of the Austrian Imperial State'

In March 1819 the *AmZÖ* published a set of six sonnets by Eduard von Lannoy, three on major literary figures, Goethe, Schiller and Jean Paul, balanced by three on major composers, Mozart, Haydn and Beethoven.[44]

Beethoven

Die Urkraft wohnet in des Berges Tiefen	Elemental force dwells in the depth of the mountains
Und fördert nie Geahndetes zum Licht;	And advances without portent to the light;
Sie wecket Stürme, die gefesselt schliefen,	It rouses tempests, that had lain dormant,
Ein feur'ger Strom aus hohem Crater bricht.	A fiery torrent breaks from a high crater.
Doch wo die Glutenbäche tödtend liefen,	Yet, where the fiery streams deadly flow,
Da wächst die Rose bald auf neuer Schicht	There, on a new bed, soon grows the rose
Und wo empört die Winde heulend riefen,	And where the furious winds howled,
Der Edelstein mit Phöbos Glanze ficht.	There with the splendour of Phoebus the precious stone fights.
Du bist der Berg, die Kraft im Busen wohnet,	You are the mountain, strength abides in your breast,
Du strebst hinan zu dem, der straft und lohnet,	You strive upwards to him that punishes and rewards,
Berührst im Fluge alle Seelensaiten.	You set in motion all the strings of the soul.
Es klingt in Dir die Welt mit Lust, mit Schmerzen;	In you the world resounds with joy, with sorrow
Du singst; es dringet jeder Ton zum Herzen;	You sing; each sound penetrates the heart;
Dir horchen alle Menschen, alle Zeiten.	All mankind, in all ages, hears you.

The elemental and impassioned imagery of the Beethoven sonnet conjures up a highly romanticized view of the composer. Poetry celebrating composers and musical creativity was a recurring feature of *AmZÖ*,

---

[44] Ibid., 3 (1819), cols. 161–3; I thank Birgit Lodes for her assistance with the translation. There was an earlier sonnet on Beethoven, by the Tyrolean poet Friedericke Susan (1784–1848): ibid., 1 (1817), col. 340.

particularly during Kanne's stewardship, part of the pervading outlook that music should be something much more than pleasant entertainment. The journal constantly promotes the high-minded and ambitious in piano music, oratorio, church music, quartet and symphony. Concertos, most piano music and song do not feature in this agenda. The attitude to opera is a different one too, regularly reported, including the sensational popularity of Rossini from 1816 to 1824, also of Weber's *Der Freischütz* in 1821, but hardly ever scrutinized in the same way; there is an unspoken acceptance that a flourishing operatic culture is something to cherish, but not necessarily something that needs fostering in the way that certain other genres do.

Part of the reason for this divergence of outlook has to do with the words 'Austrian imperial state' that figure in the title of the journal, a constant element, present even when the word 'Vienna' was added. Seeking an identity for an empire that had been created in a moment of crisis during the Napoleonic Wars and was now confidently projecting itself on the European stage, the journal celebrated an art form that was already widely practised and enjoyed by its people and whose leading figures, Haydn, Mozart and Beethoven, enjoyed European status. In the same way that political authority at home was bolstered by influence abroad, musical pre-eminence was to be claimed on the basis of international distinction. But it needed to project an identity. Rather than being wholly manufactured, as had been the case in Louis XIV's France or Catherine the Great's Russia, that identity carefully built on established traditions, such as Catholic church music, oratorio, quartet and symphony, and sought to create a self-defining space between them and other kinds of music, especially opera.

How does Beethoven fit into this picture? Ambition, discrimination, exclusivity, high-mindedness and other synonyms are routinely associated with third-period Beethoven, but even the most broad-minded of biographers tend to present them as the product of personal circumstances rather than of his environment. In varying degrees and with differing emphases many of these determining attributes were shared by his Austrian contemporaries. Some, such as Archduke Rudolph and Schuppanzigh, are acknowledged by biographers; others, such as Gebauer, Kanne, Lannoy, Mosel, Piringer, Seyfried, Stadler and Steiner, are not. While Beethoven may be described as socially isolated because of deafness, he was not socially unaware, as the conversation books show. These individuals and others, such as Matthäus von Collin (co-author of the text of *Die Befreyung von Jerusalem*) and Joseph Sonnleithner (the organizing force behind the

Gesellschaft der Musikfreunde), represented a wider, active presence in musical society, as administrators, authors, composers, choir masters, civil servants, journalists, performers, publishers, all headed by a musically engaged member of the imperial family, someone who was also a cardinal and an archbishop.

While it would seem entirely reasonable to accept that Beethoven was part of this wider outlook, it has also to be accepted that he did not respond – or felt unable to respond – to all of its characteristics. The *Missa solemnis* is given a new context if Steiner's promotion of church music and the enterprise of the Concerts Spirituels are taken into account alongside the very traditional interests of the Habsburg Archduke Rudolph as a capable musician and a proponent of the Catholic faith. Similarly, the nature of the late piano sonatas and the Diabelli Variations is entirely consonant with the works that were published in Steiner's *Museum für Klaviermusik*, including the probing use of fugue and variation, the use of A flat minor in the slow movement of Op. 110 and the bold use of two metres, 3/4 and 4/4, in the Diabelli Variations. On the other hand, the failure to complete an oratorio for the Gesellschaft der Musikfreunde shows the composer as a reluctant, eventually unproductive participant in the broader narrative in which he was meant to play a pivotal role. Ironically, Beethoven's failure to write an oratorio itself fulfilled a repeated concern in the pages of the *AmZÖ*, the lack of new works that would take their place alongside those of Handel, Haydn and Stadler. Beethoven's decision to write a symphony rather than an oratorio in the 1820s effectively killed off one historical agenda in favour of another.

Finally, reading the 730 issues of the *AmZÖ* printed between 1817 and 1824 invites the question to what extent did Beethoven consider himself a musician who was in sympathy with the Austrian imperial state. Was he Austrian, or just a rootless composer who happened to live in the empire? He was certainly up-to-date in describing himself as Austrian, whereas forty years earlier Mozart would have used the word German. Often the usage is a self-deprecating one, as in 'poor Austrian musical drudge' that appears (with variants) several times in his correspondence.[45] More revealing are Beethoven's occasional comments on Austrian politics and society, though they are often prompted by irritating personal circumstances rather than abstract idealism, as when, in July 1817, he attributes

---

[45] For instance, Beethoven's letter to Nanette Streicher, before 23 August 1817. BG, vol. 4, p. 102; LOB, vol. 2, p. 704.

the difficulty of finding a trustworthy housekeeper to the 'utter moral rottenness of the Austrian state'.[46]

If Beethoven was sometimes critical of contemporary Austrian politics he was at the same time loyal to the Habsburg dynasty itself, a clear and crucial distinction, one that was also innate and genuine rather than concocted and convenient. Until 1792 he had lived and worked in Bonn, part of the electorate that belonged to the Holy Roman Empire and ruled from 1784 onwards by Elector Maximilian Franz, the brother of Joseph II. This formative attachment never weakened: only the unexpected death of Maximilian Franz prevented Beethoven from dedicating his First Symphony to him; the Septet (Op. 20) was dedicated to Empress Marie Therese; he wrote two military marches for Archduke Anton; one of his most enduring personal friendships was with Archduke Rudolph, the recipient of fourteen dedicated works; he openly canvassed for a position at the imperial court in 1809 when faced with the prospect of moving to Kassel; and he was the willing composer of several patriotic works in 1814–15, including 'Es ist vollbracht', a chorus that culminates in a quotation from the national anthem, 'Gott erhalte Franz den Kaiser'.

On 15 February 1823 the *AmZÖ* published a tribute to Anton Teyber (1756–1822), a composer at the imperial court who had died the previous November.[47] Outlining a dutiful career that had lasted nearly thirty years, the article records that Teyber had taught five archdukes (Anton, Johann, Rainer, Ludwig and Rudolph), draws attention to his commitment to church music at court and mentions the notable performance the previous Easter in Olmütz of a new mass in B flat at a service led by Archduke Rudolph. Beethoven had already expressed an interest in succeeding Teyber as a court composer and had borrowed a mass by Reutter from the imperial library to familiarize himself with the musical preferences of the Hofkapelle,[48] which he knew to be rather different from those at the Augustinerkirche. Had this Habsburg loyalist succeeded it would have brought him into the centre of the *Kaiserstaat*. This was another narrative that remained unfulfilled. The court had decided that the post should be abolished.

---

[46] Letter to Nanette Streicher, 7 July 1819, BG, vol. 4, p. 77; LOB, vol. 2, p. 686.

[47] *AmZÖ*, 7 (1823), cols. 111–12.

[48] As related in two letters. Beethoven to Count Moriz von Dietrichstein (between 18 November 1822 and 30 January 1823): BG, vol. 4, pp. 548–9; LOB, vol. 3, p. 987. Dietrichstein's letter to Count Moritz von Lichnowsky (23 February 1823); BG, vol. 5, pp. 55–6; Theodore Albrecht (ed. and trans.), *Letters to Beethoven and Other Correspondence*, vol. 2, pp. 245–7.

9 | Composing with a Dictionary: Sounding the Word in Beethoven's *Missa solemnis*

BIRGIT LODES
Translated by HELEN CONWAY*

When three movements from the *Missa solemnis* sounded through the Kärntnertortheater on the 7 May 1824 for the first time in Vienna, in a concert that also included the premiere of the Ninth Symphony, the press reported as follows:

> The treatment of the Credo is truly unusual and exceptionally original; the main key, B flat major, as well as the tempo, are frequently – perhaps rather too frequently – changed, and the ear is hardly capable of keeping up with the pace of such changes; ... one feels peculiarly surprised, that 'et vitam venturi saeculi' is intoned as a slow fugue; ... and the whole thing ends quietly, with a similarly long, fading postlude by the orchestra ... [It] is also undeniable that this hesitant, nervously awaited ending weakens those earlier effects, since there can be no logical reason for this, other than a determination to follow an individual path. In many places it would be more appropriate to adhere to traditional conventions. Who does not find himself in a state of euphoria when listening to a fiery, magnificent fugue by Naumann, Haydn and Mozart, as if soaring heavenwards borne on seraphic wings?[1]

Today the *Missa solemnis* has an undisputed place on the concert stage alongside the Ninth Symphony as the only other fully symphonic work from Beethoven's late period – the work is hardly ever heard in the context of a church service. Interrupted only by time spent on, among other works, three piano sonatas (Op. 109, Op. 110 and Op. 111) and the Diabelli Variations (Op. 120), Beethoven worked for a good three years on the mass, a composition he described as his greatest and for which he charged the publisher a higher fee than for his Ninth Symphony.[2] Musicology, however, has had a hard time with the mass: Theodor W. Adorno, for instance, struggled so unsuccessfully with the idiosyncrasies of a work he

---

* Revised and translated for publication, this essay was first presented by the author as an inaugural lecture at the University of Vienna, 16 December 2004.

[1] Josef Karl Bernard reporting on the first performance of the Kyrie, Credo and Agnus Dei from the *Missa solemnis*, AmZ, 26 (1824), col. 439; Stefan Kunze et al. (eds.), *Ludwig van Beethoven. Die Werke im Spiegel seiner Zeit. Gesammelte Konzertberichte und Rezensionen bis 1830* (Laaber, 1987), pp. 471–2.

[2] Sven Hiemke, *Ludwig van Beethoven. Missa solemnis* (Kassel, 2003), pp. 45–9, 130–7.

described as an 'alienated masterpiece', that he could not complete his book on Beethoven.[3] He and many musicologists after him were concerned by the paradox as to why Beethoven, the creator of formally coherent and motivically integrated instrumental music, presented in the *Missa solemnis* a work that barely acknowledged those qualities.

A document that belongs to the earliest stages of the creative process that informed the *Missa solemnis* has been mentioned only in passing in previous studies: a six-page transcript of the text of the Ordinary of the mass, with accompanying notes, all in Beethoven's handwriting.[4] Its significance has never been thoroughly explored. It not only provides fascinating and unusual insight into Beethoven's compositional workings, but also sheds light on some of the hitherto unexplained idiosyncrasies of the *Missa solemnis*.

Seeking the Word: Beethoven's Notes on the Text of the Mass

Let us proceed step by step, layer upon layer, and start with the first page of the manuscript. There is a short description in ink by Anton Schindler at the top of Beethoven's manuscript: 'Before Beethoven started on the composition of his second Mass in D in 1818, he had the text translated into German and also had the syllabic metre of the Latin verified, as presented here. This is the Credo in his own hand.' Schindler's description, as will become clear, is only partly accurate. First, Beethoven's notes are probably not from 1818, rather from 1819 onwards; Beethoven became fully engaged in the composition of the mass from, at the latest, March 1819, when it is mentioned in a letter to Archduke Rudolph congratulating him on his appointment as Archbishop of Olmütz and expressing the hope that the mass might be performed at the installation service.[5] The variety of ink used together with the differing layout of the text for each portion of the mass suggest that Beethoven did not write this document at one sitting,

---

[3] Theodor W. Adorno, 'Verfremdetes Hauptwerk. Zur Missa Solemnis (1959/1964)', reprinted in *Ludwig van Beethoven*, ed. Ludwig Finscher (Darmstadt, 1983), pp. 98–112; English translation in Adorno, *Beethoven: The Philosophy of Music*, ed. Rolf Tiedemann, trans. Edmund Jephcott (Oxford, 1998), pp. 138–53. For discussion of Adorno's views see Michael Spitzer, *Music as Philosophy: Adorno and Beethoven's Late Style* (Bloomington, 2006), pp. 66–8; and Daniel K. L. Chua, *Beethoven & Freedom* (Oxford, 2017), pp. 189–98, 238–42.

[4] D-B, Mus. ms. autogr. Beethoven 35,25; https://digital.staatsbibliothek-berlin.de/werkansicht? PPN=PPN726600091&PHYSID=PHYS_0001&DMDID=DMDLOG_0001. A critical edition of the document is in preparation by the author.

[5] BG, no. 1292

rather in instalments over a period of time, and that he had already done a similar exercise for the Kyrie and Gloria, material that has not survived.[6] The notes for the Credo are written on a large bifolio (39.7 cm × 25.5 cm). Notes for the Sanctus and Agnus Dei also survive, written on a narrower single sheet (39.7 cm × 24.2 cm).

How did Beethoven go about making his notes? First, on the left half of the page he wrote the Latin text of the Credo in large letters. When he had done this he noted a German-language version of the text on the right-hand side of the page. This is noteworthy because translations of the Ordinary into German are found only rarely in prayer books of this period;[7] more common are the so-called 'Mass prayers' (*Messgebete*), complementary prayers that believers could utter while the priest or choir recited the obligatory Latin mass. The fact that the few located literal translations that have survived all differ from Beethoven's German text would seem to confirm Schindler's comment that the composer himself had instigated the translation. However, it is clear that Beethoven did, indeed, use an existing translation, albeit a rather unusual one. As indicated in the inventory of his possessions, he owned Ignatius Aurelis Feßler's *Ansichten von Religion und Kirchentum* (2 vols., Berlin, 1805), a work listed in the index of prohibited books issued by the Viennese church authorities.[8] At the end of the second volume (pp. 409–49) Feßler included a 'Supplement. The Mass of the Catholic Church for the Feast of St John the Baptist, 24 June' ('Beylage. Die Messe der katholischen Kirche am Feste Johannis des Täufers, den 24. Junius') with a full translation of the Ordinary and Proper for that feast day, with observations on the origins and use of the texts.

The differences between Feßler's German Credo and Beethoven's handwritten text are negligible; apart from orthographic details (such as the use of upper case and lower case, and personal idiosyncrasies such as the spelling of 'gebohren' with an 'h'), there are hardly any discrepancies, not even in the punctuation, and those that exist (such as the omitted words indicated by [missing] in Figure 9.1) can reasonably be attributed to scribal casualness.

Interestingly, Beethoven took over one of Feßler's most original translations. Instead of rendering the words 'Deum verum de Deo vero' with

---

[6] Birgit Lodes, *Das Gloria in Beethovens Missa solemnis* (Tutzing, 1997), pp. 19–22.

[7] For example, Johann Aloysius Schneider, *Gebeth und Erbauungsbuch für katholische Christen* [Vienna, 1805]; the translation of the Credo (pp. 27–8) differs from that copied by Beethoven.

[8] The one-time Capuchin and priest – also a Jansenist and an Enlightenment author – converted to Lutheranism in 1791. Concerning the religious books in Beethoven's possession, see Alexander Wolfshohl, 'Beethoven liest Autoren und Texte mit Bezug zu Religion und Theologie', *Beethoven liest*, eds. Bernhard R. Appel and Julia Ronge (Bonn, 2016), pp. 105–42.

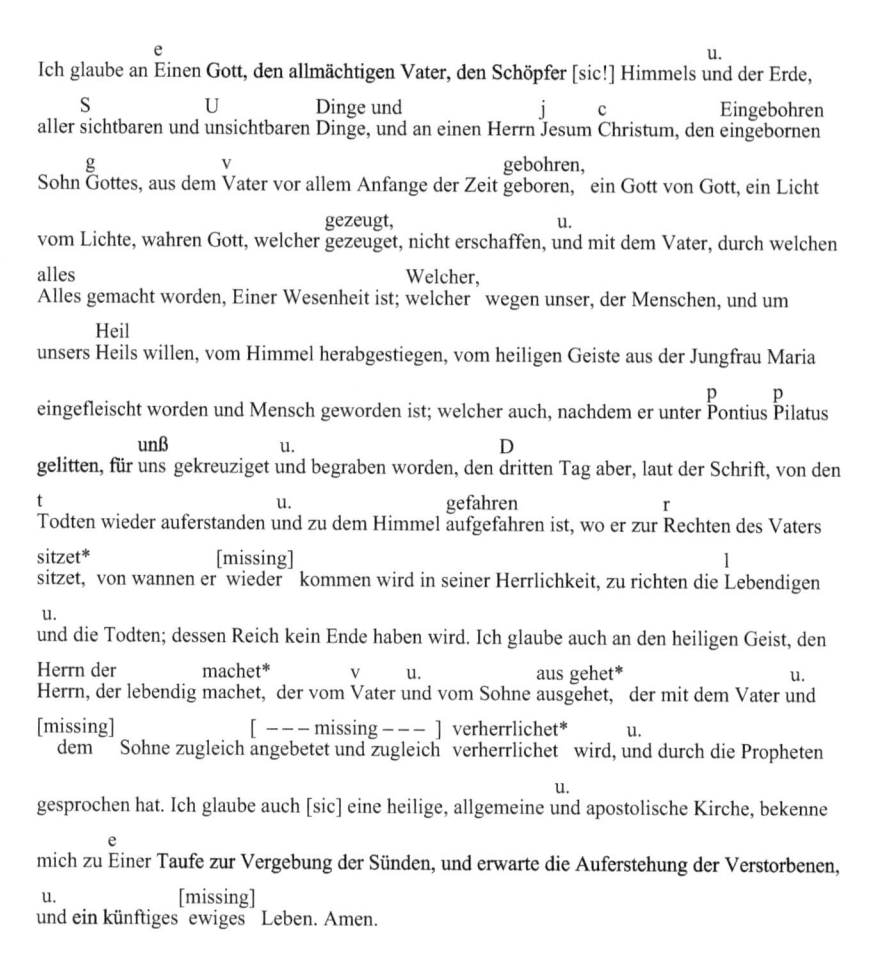

Ich glaube an Einen Gott, den allmächtigen Vater, den Schöpfer [sic!] Himmels und der Erde, (with superscript 'e' over Einen, 'u.' over und)

aller sichtbaren und unsichtbaren Dinge, und an einen Herrn Jesum Christum, den eingebornen (with superscript 'S' over aller, 'U' over unsichtbaren, 'Dinge und' over Dinge, 'j' 'c' over Jesum Christum, 'Eingebohren' over eingebornen)

Sohn Gottes, aus dem Vater vor allem Anfange der Zeit geboren, ein Gott von Gott, ein Licht (with 'g' over Gottes, 'v' over Vater, 'gebohren,' over geboren)

vom Lichte, wahren Gott, welcher gezeuget, nicht erschaffen, und mit dem Vater, durch welchen (with 'gezeugt,' over gezeuget, 'u.' over und)

Alles gemacht worden, Einer Wesenheit ist; welcher wegen unser, der Menschen, und um (with 'alles' over Alles, 'Welcher,' over welcher)

unsers Heils willen, vom Himmel herabgestiegen, vom heiligen Geiste aus der Jungfrau Maria (with 'Heil' over Heils)

eingefleischt worden und Mensch geworden ist; welcher auch, nachdem er unter Pontius Pilatus (with 'p' 'p' over Pontius Pilatus)

gelitten, für uns gekreuziget und begraben worden, den dritten Tag aber, laut der Schrift, von den (with 'unß' over uns, 'u.' over und, 'D' over dritten)

Todten wieder auferstanden und zu dem Himmel aufgefahren ist, wo er zur Rechten des Vaters (with 't' over Todten, 'u.' over und, 'gefahren' over aufgefahren, 'r' over Rechten)

sitzet, von wannen er wieder kommen wird in seiner Herrlichkeit, zu richten die Lebendigen (with 'sitzet*' over sitzet, '[missing]' over wannen, 'l' over Lebendigen)

und die Todten; dessen Reich kein Ende haben wird. Ich glaube auch an den heiligen Geist, den (with 'u.' over und)

Herrn, der lebendig machet, der vom Vater und vom Sohne ausgehet, der mit dem Vater und (with 'Herrn der' over Herrn, der; 'machet*' over machet; 'v' 'u.' over vom Sohne; 'aus gehet*' over ausgehet; 'u.' over und)

dem Sohne zugleich angebetet und zugleich verherrlichet wird, und durch die Propheten (with '[missing]' over dem; '[– – – missing – – –]' over angebetet und zugleich; 'verherrlichet*' over verherrlichet; 'u.' over und)

gesprochen hat. Ich glaube auch [sic] eine heilige, allgemeine und apostolische Kirche, bekenne (with 'u.' over und)

mich zu Einer Taufe zur Vergebung der Sünden, und erwarte die Auferstehung der Verstorbenen, (with 'e' over Einer)

und ein künftiges ewiges Leben. Amen. (with 'u.' over und, '[missing]' over ewiges)

Figure 9.1 Comparison of German Credo text in I. A. Feßler's *Ansichten von Religion und Kirchentum* (Berlin, 1805) with Beethoven's transcription
* 'e' added later according to Feßler, also in following 'machet' 'gehet' and 'verherrlichet'.
D-B, Mus. ms. autogr. Beethoven 35, 25, p. 5 (upper line, when different from Feßler)

'wahrer Gott vom wahren Gott' ('very God of very God'), or something similar, Feßler wrote just 'wahren Gott' ('very God');[9] this formulation is not to be found in any other known translation and its presence in Beethoven's hand provides compelling evidence that he was copying the text from Feßler's book rather than relying on his memory of some other translation.

His engagement with Feßler's German text even led him to alter the authorized Latin. The repeated use of 'Et' ('And') in the Credo, as in 'Et in spiritum sanctum' and 'Et in unam sanctam catholicam', is not rendered in

[9] I thank Marianne Schlosser for her theological and linguistic expertise.

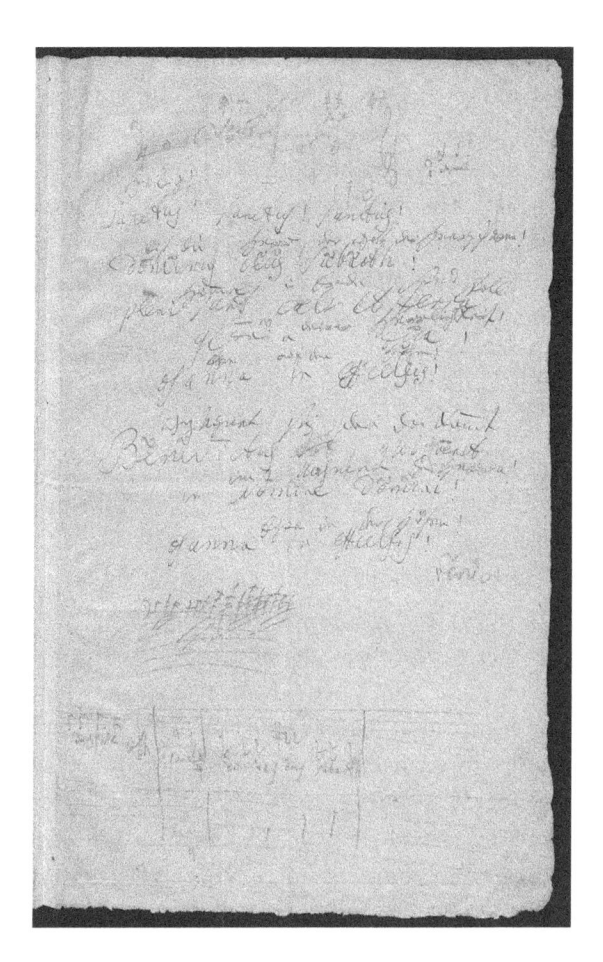

Figure 9.2 Text of the Sanctus and Benedictus in Beethoven's hand
D-B, Mus. ms. autogr. Beethoven 35, 25, p. 5. Reproduced by permission of the Staatsbibliothek
zu Berlin – Preußischer Kulturbesitz

German with 'und' ('and') or even 'und auch' ('and also'); Feßler has 'Ich
glaube auch' ('I also believe') which, in turn, prompted Beethoven to replace
the conjunction ('Et') of the Latin text with the verb 'Credo'.[10]

Beethoven's close engagement with the text, whether the original Latin
or the parallel German,[11] has a further layer of detail. As a separate and
later exercise he also annotated the Latin text (inked) with pencil markings
to show the proper declamation (see Figure 9.2).

---

[10] D-B, Mus. ms. autogr. Beethoven 35, 25, p. 3.
[11] The text of the Sanctus and the Agnus Dei is not presented in parallel columns; instead the
Latin is written across the width of the page, with the German translation interspersed between
the lines.

One might assume that Beethoven would have taken these markings from any readily available missal.[12] This, however, was not the case: contemporary printed liturgy books show stressed syllables only, that is the accentuation, whereas Beethoven consistently marked quantities, that is long and short syllables. He could not have gleaned this level of philological detail from a printed liturgy. Instead he turned to a three-volume Latin school dictionary that he owned: Imm. Joh. Gerh. Scheller, *Lateinisch-deutsches und deutsch-lateinisches Handlexicon, vornehmlich für Schulen. Von neuem durchgesehen, verbessert und vermehrt durch G. H. Lünemann* (Vienna: B. Ph. Bauer and Anton Strauß, [1806, 1807]); the title page is given in Figure 9.3. Beethoven's copy has survived.[13] He painstakingly looked up almost every word of the mass in this dictionary and copied out the given symbols for long and short syllables, respectively strokes and ticks. Those words in Beethoven's handwriting that do not have an annotation are not to be found in the dictionary.

This comprehensive interest in prosodic long and short syllables, a rather unorthodox approach to a non-poetic text, reflects a wider interest that Beethoven had recorded in his Tagebuch in 1818: 'In order to write true church music go through all the Gregorian chants of the monks etc. Also look there for the segments in the most correct translations along with the most perfect prosody of all Christian-Catholic psalms and hymns in general'.[14] In some instances, such as 'Deum' or 'Dei' words are marked in the text not only for their long and short syllables but also – probably somewhat later – for their stress pattern, a distinction that evidently confused the composer.[15] A few years later, in 1823, after the completion of the *Missa solemnis*, this uncertainty was the subject of a conversation with his nephew Karl. Beethoven had asked him to mark up a set of Latin Proper texts, with a view to setting some of them to music; the subject of appropriate stress patterns came up. Karl wrote in a conversation book: 'There is a great difference, however, between verse scansion and prose scansion. I know both equally well. I would note the prose one only, because it's prose.' Beethoven's response was not recorded. That he was still unsure is

---

[12] Such as the *Missale Romanum* (Venice, 1770) listed in Beethoven's estate; it has not survived.

[13] D-B, Mus. mus. autogr. Beethoven 40,8.

[14] Maynard Solomon, 'Beethoven's Tagebuch of 1812–1818', in *Beethoven Studies 3*, ed. Alan Tyson (Cambridge, 1982), pp. 283–4 (translation amended).

[15] Accents and length are marked with the same symbol (-).

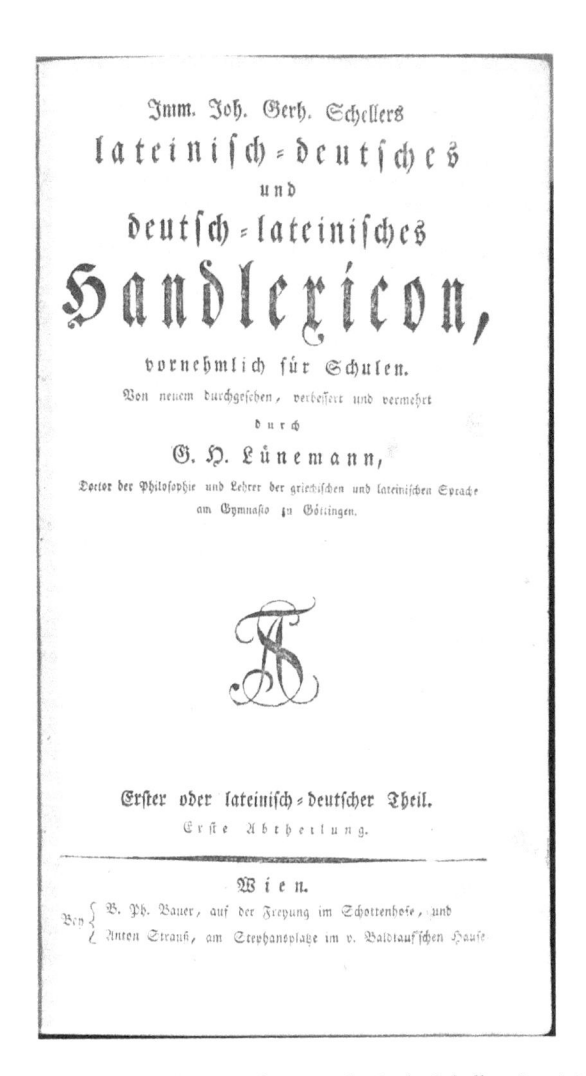

Figure 9.3 Title page of Imm. Joh. Gerh. Scheller, *Lateinisch-deutsches und deutsch-lateinisches Handlexicon, vornehmlich für Schülen. Von neuem durchgesehen, verbessert und vermehrt durch G. H. Lünemann (Vienna, [1806, 1807])*; private exemplar, not Beethoven's copy

evident from Karl's next written comment: 'I think you should stick to prose pronunciation, because it's not Roman verse.'[16]

---

[16] BK, vol. 3, pp. 315–16, 478. Count Moritz von Dietrichstein had sent three Gradual and Offertory texts to Beethoven (see BG, no. 1609), which Karl annotated with accent marks (D-B, Mus. ms. autogr. Beethoven 37,15). Karl then wrote out the texts again and went through it twice, noting it according to verse scansion and then prose scansion (D-B, Mus. ms. autogr. Beethoven 38,22).

In the course of their discussion, Karl later very correctly points out that the literary genre (prose or poetry) dictates whether accents or quantities are to be used, a distinction that Beethoven had not understood in his study of the (prose) text of the *Missa solemnis*. But Beethoven's particular approach to syllable quantities grew from a combination of curiosity and attentional to detail: in a text that was comparatively familiar – perhaps too familiar[17] – he sought to uncover new possibilities for the setting of particular words and phrases, and it was this individual, sometimes haphazard, outlook that characterized the exercise. Though fuelled by his much-documented interest in traditions of antiquity, it was not the careful approach of a rigorous scholar.

One more layer of the document remains to be unpacked. Mixed in with the Latin of the Ordinary and the German translation are some remarks on the wider meaning of the text, even of individual words. Difficult to decipher, they have customarily been viewed as spontaneous comments by Beethoven himself. However, close reading reveals, once more, an indebtedness to Scheller's dictionary. Beethoven did not restrict himself to copying the marks for long and short syllables but went on to explore the full range of meaning of particular words as given in that dictionary. Sometimes he copied the main meaning only, at others he selected a specific meaning from a whole range or jotted down one of the quoted classical phrases that featured the word in question.

Here are a few examples (see Figure 9.4). I will follow the Latin text of the mass, written in large letters in the left column, from top to bottom.

Above the words 'in remissionem' Beethoven copied both the nominative and genitive cases from the dictionary and, underneath, a translation, 'Nachlassung' ('remission'). Above the word 'peccatorum' he again records the nominative and genitive forms, followed by a Nota bene that has further information from the dictionary (right column, marked as a box). At the very top a musical idea appears, notable for its elongation of the prosodic long second syllable. Similar comments are linked to 'et exspecto' and 'resurrectionem'. Occasionally Beethoven's curiosity led him astray. For 'mortuorum' he looked up the verb, 'morior, mortuus [sum]', read on and,

---

[17] Beethoven's duties as organist in the Bonn court would have made him familiar with the text of the Ordinary at an early age. See the following research project: https://musikwissenschaft .univie.ac.at/maxfranz; and John D. Wilson, Elisabeth Reisinger in collaboration with Birgit Lodes, *The Sacred Music Collection of the Bonn Electorial Court* (Bonn, forthcoming). Also, throughout his life Beethoven had a number of unfulfilled plans to compose masses and other items of liturgical music; see Julia Ronge, 'Beethoven's Ambitions in Church Music: Plans, Ideas, and Fragments', *The Beethoven Journal*, 30/2 (Winter 2015), pp. 52–61.

Figure 9.4 Beethoven's autograph copy of a portion of the Credo text with annotations. Diplomatic transcription.

D-B, Mus. ms. autogr. Beethoven 35, 25, p. 4

five columns later, found the adjective 'mortuosus' ('death-like'), which he then noted. Whether he mistakenly assumed he had found the closest possible word to 'mortuorum' or whether he was simply intrigued by a related word is not clear. Alongside 'vitam' Beethoven typically noted the prosodic pattern followed by the primary meaning in Scheller's dictionary, 'das Leben' ('life'). Then he read on in the dictionary as far as the sixth meaning (p. 1712), 'Seele oder Schatten in der Unterwelt' ('soul or shadows in the underworld') with the associated reference to Virgil's *Aeneid* (VI, 292), 'tenues sine corpore vitae' ('the semblance of life without a body') – a peculiar choice but one that reflected his wider interest in the afterlife. Against 'venturi' Beethoven adds a small cross, a cue to the lower left portion of the document. If one looks up 'venio' in Scheller's dictionary, 'Věnĭo, vēni, ventum' appears exactly as Beethoven has noted it here. He also seems to have worked his way through the lengthy entry looking for the correct grammatical form amongst the many quotations from Classical literature that are given. Near the end of the entry Beethoven came across 'ventum est' ('one has come'), having overlooked the earlier, more appropriate 'venturum' ('the future'). Finally, against the word 'saeculi', Beethoven wrote one of several definitions given in the dictionary: 'die Zeit im biblischen Verstande' ('time in the Biblical sense'). The translation of the phrase 'et vitam venturi saeculi' as 'und das Leben künftiger Jahrhunderte' ('and the life of centuries to come') is unusual in that it seems not to have been taken from Scheller's dictionary; it might be Beethoven's own translation (or that of an acquaintance), a more literal one than he had copied from Feßler's book where it is rendered as 'u. ein künftiges Leben' ('and a future life'). Exploring associative, resonant meanings of certain words was clearly more important to Beethoven than literal translation. This is especially evident in the following example, from the notes he made to the text of the Agnus Dei (see facsimile in Figure 9.5, diplomatic transcription in Figure 9.6).

Beethoven first copied out the Latin text, then Feßler's translation above it, 'O, du lamm Gottes welches du hinwegnimmst die Sünden der Welt: erbarme dich unser!' ('O, Lamb of God who takest away the sins of the world: have mercy upon us!'). Sparing himself the routine task of writing the sentence twice Beethoven instead focused his curiosity on one word, 'mundi' ('of the world'). Looking it up in the Latin–German portion of his dictionary he found 'mundus' with its translation, 'Welt' ('world'). He then became curious about 'Welt' as a word and concept and looked it up in the German–Latin portion of the dictionary, from where he copied the definition 'Himmel u. Erde u. alles, was Gott geschaffen hat' ('Heaven and Earth and everything that God has created'), a clear allusion to the story of the Creation as recounted in the first

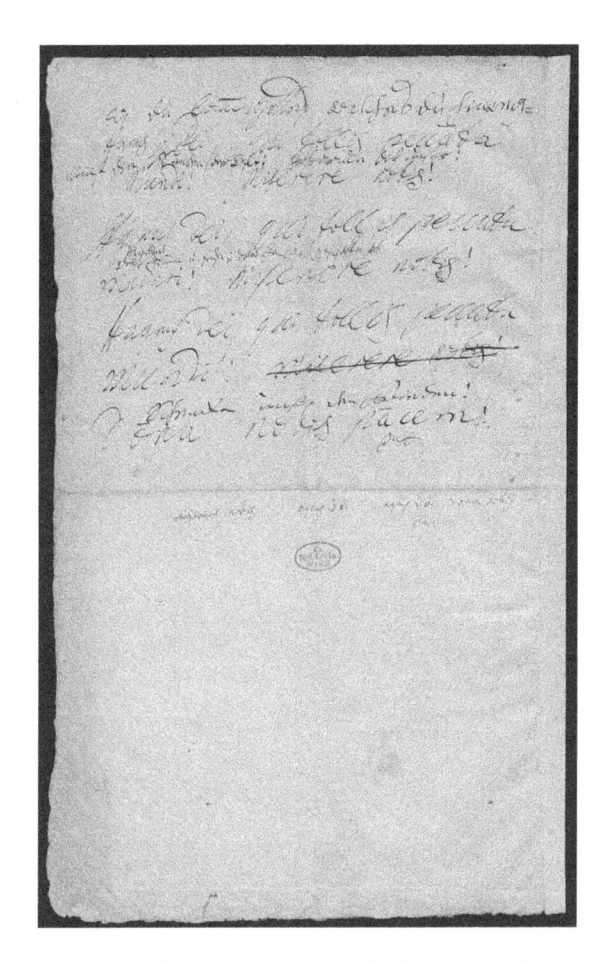

Figure 9.5 The Agnus Dei text in Beethoven's hand
D-B, Mus. ms. autogr. Beethoven 35, 25, p. 6. Reproduced by permission of the Staatsbibliothek
zu Berlin – Preußischer Kulturbesitz

chapter of Genesis, 'In the beginning God created Heaven and Earth'. This
text would have been particularly familiar to Beethoven from its use right at
the beginning of Haydn's *Creation*: Beethoven seems to be evolving an
understanding that all Creation was capable of sinning.

Beethoven's close interrogation of the mass text for its meanings and
associations followed the ideas of a contemporary theologian whom he
highly respected, Johann Michael Sailer, to whom he wanted to send his
nephew, Karl, for instruction.[18] According to Sailer, believers should not

[18] Arnold Schmitz, 'Beethovens Religiosität', *Bericht über den I. musikwissenschaftlichen Kongreß
der deutschen Musikgesellschaft in Leipzig* (Leipzig, 1926), pp. 274–9, at p. 278; Schmitz, *Das
romantische Beethovenbild* (Berlin, 1927), p. 95; Birgit Lodes, 'Probing the Sacred Genres:

O, du lam Gottes, welches du hinweg-
Agnus Dei,   qui tollis peccāta
nimst die Sünden der Welt: erbarme dich unser!
Mundi!   Miserere   nobis!

Agnus dei,   qui tollis peccata
    Mundus[a]
Welt himel u. Erde u. alles was Gott geschaffen hat
mundi!   mĩsẽrẽre nobis!

Aagnus [sic] dei, qui tollis peccata
mundi!   ~~miserere nobis!~~
    Schenke unß den Frieden!
dōna   nobis   pācem!
         pax

—   —   —   —   —   —   —   — [fold]
miserere nobis   agnus dei   agnus dei   dona nobis
                                    pacem

[a] First in lower case letter, then changed to upper case.

Figure 9.6 Diplomatic transcription of Beethoven's autograph copy of the Agnus Dei text

unthinkingly repeat liturgical prayers parrot-fashion; rather they should uncover the spiritual meaning through their own discernment; Feßler, the author of Beethoven's translation, had made a very similar point in his *Ansichten von Religion und Kirchentum*. Although Beethoven occasionally poked fun at Catholic devotional practices,[19] there is ample evidence from c. 1800 onwards of an intense intellectual and spiritual engagement with

Beethoven's Religious Songs, Oratorio, and Masses', *The Cambridge Companion to Beethoven*, ed. Glenn Stanley (Cambridge, 2000), pp. 218–36, at pp. 234–5; for a fuller discussion of Beethoven's interest in Sailer's theological writings and its influence on the *Missa solemnis* see Nicholas J. Chong, 'Beethoven's Catholicism: A Reconsideration' (PhD thesis, Columbia University, 2016), esp. chapters 1, 4 and 5.

[19] For an instance from his final years in Bonn see Jens Duffner, 'Eine Anleitung zum Improvisieren – Ludwig van Beethovens Begleitungen zu den Lamentationen des Propheten Jeremia', *Kirchenmusikalisches Jahrbuch*, 99 (2015), pp. 81–96.

God, the godly and the transcendental, one that was not limited to Christian understanding.[20] His detailed and multifaceted scrutiny of the text of the mass is most appropriately viewed in this broader religious context.

Sounding the Word

To what extent did Beethoven's detailed engagement with the text of the Ordinary shape his compositional decisions and live on in the final work? Three overlapping areas are identified: the influence of Feßler's German text; the perceived prosody of the Latin; and the horizons of meaning behind specific words.

As we have seen, Beethoven developed the idea of having the additional affirmative statements of 'Credo' from Feßler's German translation of the text. This finding should modify the widely held view that these repetitions came from the so-called 'Credo mass' tradition.[21] The number of repeated statements is less than is typically encountered in that tradition and, crucially, occurs only when it makes semantic sense, not when it is musically opportune.[22] While for many composers of Credo masses this kind of repetition was essentially a musically unifying device, for Beethoven it enhances textual meaning.[23]

Beethoven's interest in prosodic long and short syllables also left its mark on the *Missa solemnis*, notably those occasions when his musical

---

[20] Maynard Solomon, 'The Quest for Faith', *Beethoven Jahrbuch,* 10 (1978/1981), pp. 101–19; Birgit Lodes, '"so träumte mir, ich reiste [. . .] nach Indien". Temporality and Mythology in Opus 127/I', *The String Quartets of Beethoven*, ed. William Kinderman (Urbana and Chicago, 2006), pp. 168–213; Wolfgang Rathert, 'Beethovens Kirchenmusik im geistesgeschichtlichen Kontext', *Beethovens Vokalmusik und Bühnenwerke*, eds. Birgit Lodes and Armin Raab (Laaber, 2014), pp. 155–72; Charles Witcombe, 'Beethoven's Markings in Christoph Christian Sturm's *Reflections on the Works of God in the Realm of Nature and Providence for Every Day of the Year*', *The Beethoven Journal*, 18/1 (Winter 2003), pp. 10–17; and Ernst Herttrich, 'Beethoven und die Religion', *Spiritualität der Musik: Religion im Werk von Beethoven und Schumann*, ed. Gotthard Fermor (Rheinbach, 2006), pp. 25–44.

[21] For instance Carl Dahlhaus, *Ludwig van Beethoven und seine Zeit* (Laaber, 1987), pp. 239–40.

[22] Birgit Lodes, 'Messen-Kompositionen im Ausgang der Wiener Klassik: Konnte Beethoven von Cherubini lernen?', *Anton Bruckner – Tradition und Fortschritt in der Kirchenmusik des 19. Jahrhunderts*, ed. Friedrich Wilhelm Riedel (Sinzig, 2001), pp. 207–36, at pp. 225–34.

[23] As Figure 9.4 (p. 197) shows, Beethoven analysed and marked the text with a view to its musical setting even at this early stage. He groups a few words together to form a musical section that ends in *piano*, marks parallel beginnings to sentences ('qui, qui, qui') with an underline plus supplementary marks in the margin, and indicates dynamics (*piano*) and structural features ('ritornell').

Example 9.1 Declamation of 'peccatorum', choral parts: (a) *Missa solemnis*, Credo, bars 287–9; (b) Mass in C, Credo, bars 267–8

realization of a single syllable is an unusually lengthy one, reflecting an unaccented, but prosodic long syllable. Two instances will make this highly individualized response clear.

Beethoven's setting of the single word 'peccatorum' ('of sins') is appropriately ear-catching: homophonic declamation by the choir, *sforzando* markings that pierce the *piano* and tortuous chromatic harmony (see Example 9.1a). The rhythms and *sforzando* accents draw attention to the prosodic long second and third syllables, as Beethoven had encountered in Scheller's dictionary, 'pe-ccaaaaa-toooooo-rum'. If Beethoven had wanted to reflect the more direct accent structure he would have used the simpler 'peeee-cca-tóooo-rum', with an accent on the penultimate syllable and a secondary accent on the first, precisely his approach in the earlier Mass in C (see Example 9.1b).

The 'Crucifixus' sections in the C major Mass and the *Missa solemnis* have so much in common that the former must have acted as a model for the latter.[24] In one respect, however, they are very different: the setting of the central word 'crucifixus' ('was crucified').

In the earlier mass Beethoven sets it according to its natural accentuation, 'crúcifixus' (see Example 9.2a); in the *Missa solemnis* the setting once more reflects the prosodic length as indicated in Scheller's dictionary, with an exaggerated long third syllable, 'crucifiiiiiiixus' (see Example 9.2b).

[24] See Andreas Friesenhagen, *Die Messen Ludwig van Beethovens. Studien zur Vertonung des liturgischen Textes zwischen Rhetorik und Dramatisierung* (Köln, 1996), pp. 284–97.

Example 9.2 Declamation of 'crucifixus', choral parts: (a) Mass in C, Credo, bars 147–148; (b) *Missa solemnis*, Credo, bars 157–158

As these two instances show, thematic material in both masses is consistently drawn from a rhythmic reading of the text, rather than fitted to an independently conceived musical theme or motif. However, Beethoven follows different principles in the two works. In the C major mass he translates the accent structure of the Latin text very sensitively (more sensitively than many of his contemporaries), leading him to claim that he had 'treated the text in a manner in which it has rarely been treated'.[25] In the *Missa solemnis* he went a step further and created his motifs from the accentuation and the prosody of the Latin words in a highly distinctive manner. I know of nothing comparable in any other Mass setting. But this was not an indulgent, rarefied approach, rather one that linked naturally with wider compositional issues.

For 'et exspecto' Beethoven surprisingly jotted down only the literal meaning given at the beginning of the relevant entry in the dictionary (see Figure 9.7): 'hinaus od. hinauf sehen' ('to look out or to look up'), not the common translations of 'neugierig seyn' ('to be curious') or 'warten, erwarten' ('to await, expect'). On the same page he transposed this primary meaning of looking upwards into an ascending musical motif (see Figure 9.4 (p. 197), middle of right column); in the finished work this is intensified by a sweeping line in the strings that culminates in a rapidly rising tremolo scale.

In Beethoven's Mass in C, the word 'descendit' ('came down') is presented three times with a natural accent on the second syllable, lengthened on the third iteration (see Example 9.3a). In the *Missa solemnis*, however, 'descendit' is set in a notably unorthodox manner, verging on the eccentric (see Example 9.3b). The three-syllable motif here is marked by a sudden *forte* and *sforzato* and an (unvocal) octave leap, while the elongated setting of the first, unaccented syllable is even more unusual: 'deeeeeee-scén-dit'. The prosodic length of that first syllable had been marked as such in Beethoven's notes on the text. This particular moment in the *Missa solemnis* caught the attention of Friedrich August Kanne who, in his review

---

[25] Letter to Breitkopf & Härtel, 8 June 1808; BG, no. 327.

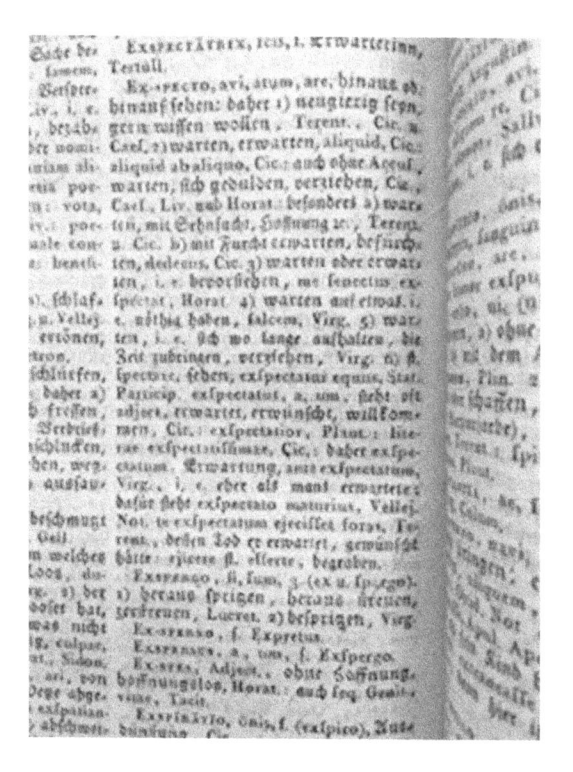

Figure 9.7 Entry for the word 'Exspecto' in Scheller's *Handlexicon*, p. 488

of the concert of 7 May 1824, wrote the following: 'Beethoven has placed special emphasis on the word "descendit", giving the impression that the initial syllable "de" is the longest and strongest and the following pair of syllables, "scendit", less so.'[26] Though prosodically correct this particularly vivid setting of one word has almost an alienating effect, similar in its effect, if not in scale, to the sound world of earlier periods that is invoked elsewhere in the mass, such as the Gregorian chant, vocal polyphony and *falsobordone* of the 'Et incarnatus' and the modal harmony and *a cappella* section at 'Et resurrexit'.[27] These evocations of different sound worlds first attract and then channel the attention of the listener.

[26] Friedrich August Kanne, 'Academie des Hrn. Ludwig van Beethoven', *Allgemeine musikalische Zeitung mit besonderer Rücksicht auf den österreichischen Kaiserstaat*, 8 (1824), pp. 149–51, 157–60, 173–4.

[27] On the historical reach of the mass see Warren Kirkendale, 'New Roads to Old Ideas in Beethoven's *Missa solemnis*', *The Musical Quarterly*, 56/4 (1970), pp. 665–701, at pp. 675–80; Theodor Göllner, '"Et incarnatus est" in Beethovens *Missa Solemnis*', *Annuario musical*, 43 (1988), pp. 189–99; David Wyn Jones, 'The Stylus a cappella Masses of the Viennese Classical

(a)

(b)

Example 9.3 Declamation of 'descendit', choral parts: (a) Mass in C, Credo, bars 102–110; (b) *Missa solemnis*, Credo, bars 98–100

Beethoven's engagement with the resonances of single words that pricked his curiosity also led to some subtle cross-referencing in the final composition. One notable instance is the word 'iterum' in the clause 'Et iterum venturus est cum gloria'. Feßler's German text had translated it very simply, 'von wannen' ('from whence'). Turning to Scheller's dictionary for further thoughts, Beethoven found, in addition to the prosodic markings, the definition 'wiederum; zum zweiten male' ('anew; for the second time') and duly made a note of it. Translated in this way, the fundamental Christian tenet of the Second Coming is much clearer. Beethoven's score subtly points this out: 'iterum' is heard in D flat major (bar 215), the same key used earlier in the mass for the clause 'miserere nobis' ('have mercy upon us', a prayer addressed to the Son of God) in the Gloria (bars 274–277) and for 'Qui propter nos homines et propter nostram salutem' ('Who for us men and for our salvation came down from heaven', the first coming of Christ) in the Credo (bars 90–96).[28]

One of the best-known instances of Beethoven's original attitude to the setting of the mass text is the 'Et vitam venturi' fugue at the conclusion of the Credo – the portion of the mass that particularly confounded Josef Karl Bernard in his report for the *Allgemeine musikalische Zeitung* quoted at the beginning of this essay. Beethoven does, indeed, follow custom by setting the words 'et vitam venturi' as a lengthy fugue, but its musical character and manner are unique. As Bernard noted, the listener would have expected a 'fiery magnificent fugue' that, following passages of contrasting intensity, moved towards unequivocal affirmation, the approach that Beethoven himself had used in the Mass in C. In complete contrast the fugue in the *Missa solemnis* begins with utmost restraint, a gentle motif in a series of minims that turns into a melismatic arc only on the word 'seculi'.[29] From this near stasis Beethoven gradually unfolds music of ever increasing presence, including a learned diminution of the main theme in a *fortissimo* dynamic (bar 379 onwards). But the expectation of an irresistibly radiant conclusion is completed thwarted. The final nine bars move from *piano* to *pianissimo*, avoid an affirmative cadence and dissolve any lingering thematic identity to nothing: 'as if floating in distant ethereal starry heights', to quote Paul Bekker.[30]

Exactly what prompted this highly individual setting has eluded traditional commentary. It is clear that Beethoven did not subscribe to the conventional wisdom of a joyously fulfilling afterlife, but is more interested in the 'otherness' of this condition, in its immateriality; he had encountered this image in the *Bhagavad Gita* some years previously, making a note of it in his Tagebuch: 'Blessed is he who has supressed all passions.'[31] This is

---

[28] For the Gloria see Birgit Lodes, '"When I Try, Now and Then, to Give Musical Form to My Turbulent Feelings . . .": The Human and the Divine in the Gloria of Beethoven's *Missa solemnis*', *Beethoven Forum 6* (Lincoln and London, 1998), pp. 143–79, at pp. 170–1; Lodes, *Das Gloria in Beethovens Missa solemnis*, pp. 155–8.

[29] The fact that this very individual shape to the thematic line was Beethoven's final, rather than initial thought is a clear indication that he kept his notes on the text close to hand.

[30] Paul Bekker, *Beethoven* (Stuttgart and Berlin, 1922), p. 394.

[31] Solomon, 'Beethoven's Tagebuch', p. 245 (translation amended).

strikingly consonant with the musical atmosphere at the beginning and at the end of the Credo, an atmosphere that puzzled Beethoven's contemporaries.[32] The composer had defied convention in order to capture in music the idea of an otherworldly disembodied eternal life. Scheller's dictionary, too, played a part in the formation of this outlook. As noted earlier, Beethoven tried to unlock the meaning of the text 'Et vitam venturi saeculi. Amen' using a variety of approaches. For the word 'vita' he did not confine his reading to the obvious definitions of 'life', 'vitality' or the like – the basic understanding that informed the composition of fugues at the end of the Credo – but moved on to 'Seele oder Schatten in der Unterwelt' ('soul or shadows in the underworld') and the reference to Virgil's *Aeneid*, 'tenues sine corpore vitae' ('the semblance of life without a body'). This led to a wholly different area of association: that of the disembodied life of the soul and of shadows, not quite those of Virgil's *Aeneid* admittedly, but after death nevertheless: an existence devoid of earthly materiality. In Scheller's dictionary, Beethoven had stumbled on a nuance of meaning that he then used to characterize his composition, a creative link that is supported by an annotation in the musical sketches: 'et vitam venturi seculi verklärt/und künftige Leben' ('et vitam venturi seculi transfigured/and future life').[33]

Missa solemnis and Late Style

Numerous curiosities in the *Missa solemnis* puzzled Beethoven's contemporaries and continue to do so today. This compositional individuality, I would argue, is largely due to the composer's fundamental decision to place the text at the very nerve centre of his compositional efforts; with no compromise. This approach embraces the sound of the text (in the sense of prosody and accents) as much as it refers to substantive elements, such as questions arising from various forms of translation as well as theological issues, and laid the foundations for a musical construction that is peculiarly and uniquely rich, so much so that it perplexed Adorno and many other commentators. Almost alone, Andreas Friesenhagen has encapsulated

---

[32] See the review of the first performance quoted at the beginning of this essay (p. 189). Both Franz Joseph Fröhlich and Ignaz Seyfried described the conclusion as 'original' ('originell'); Kunze, *Die Werke im Spiegel seiner Zeit*, pp. 440, 449.

[33] Wittgenstein sketchbook, fol. 12r, lines 1 and 2; Joseph Schmidt-Görg (ed.), *L. van Beethoven. Ein Skizzenbuch zu den Diabelli-Variationen und zur Missa solemnis, SV 154*, 2 vols., facsimile (Bonn, 1968) and transcription (Bonn, 1972), p. 23.

Beethoven's achievement: 'While [in Haydn and, particularly, Mozart] the desire to overcome the competing elements of a prosaic and formally cumbersome text through musical homogeneity is visible in the foreground, the relationship in Beethoven is exactly reversed: he uses precisely these textual features to craft a dramatic structure that is predicated on contrasts and developments.'[34] The goal, therefore, is a gesturally sculpted presentation of the meaning of the words, one that Beethoven himself had developed through a complex hermeneutic process. With this constant focus on the text and the associated avoidance of the routine Beethoven addresses a listener who is critical and sensitive. Two movements, the Kyrie and the Sanctus, have the performance marking 'Mit Andacht', 'With devotion', the very quality that Johann Michael Sailer had sought to instil in the reflective believer.[35] The question of formal relevance, of musical unity and focus that arises from this attitude was a challenging one, but it was not the starting point, rather the natural conclusion of a process that was led by the text. It was a self-imposed challenge that the composer readily accepted. For Beethoven, the experience of composing the mass also informed his development as a composer in general. Those instances of musical quietude followed by abrupt change that arose out of an unremitting focus on the text in the *Missa solemnis* have their equivalents in works without a text, notably the late string quartets, five masses without words one might say. Exposing that relationship[36] would seem to be central to a nuanced understanding of Beethoven's late style.

---

[34] Friesenhagen, *Die Messen Ludwig van Beethovens*, p. 307.

[35] On 'Andacht' in Sailer's writings, see Chong, *Beethoven's Catholicism*, pp. 289, 385–6.

[36] In Adorno's view the *Missa solemnis* did not exhibit the stylistic parameters of late Beethoven; Adorno, 'Verfremdetes Hauptwerk', p. 149; on that view see Nikolaus Urbanek, *Auf der Suche nach einer zeitgemäßen Musikästhetik. Adornos Philosophie der Musik und die Beethoven-Fragmente* (Bielefeld, 2010), pp. 226–7. On thematic similarities between the *Missa solemnis* and other works see William Kinderman, 'Beethoven's Symbol for the Deity in the *Missa solemnis* and the Ninth Symphony', *Nineteenth-Century Music*, 9 (1985/86), pp. 102–18; David Benjamin Levy, '"Ma però beschleunigend". Notation and Meaning in Ops. 133/134', *Beethoven Forum 14* (2007), pp. 129–49; Birgit Lodes, '"In der ungeheuern Weite". Beethoven und die Ahnung des Göttlichen in *Meeres Stille und Glückliche Fahrt, Missa solemnis* und Neunter Symphonie', *Beethoven und der Wiener Kongress (1814/15). Bericht über die vierte New Beethoven Research Conference Bonn, 10. bis 12. September 2014*, eds. Bernhard R. Appel, Joanna Cobb Biermann, William Kinderman and Julia Ronge (Bonn, 2016), pp. 139–64.

10 | Deafly Performing Beethoven's Last Three Piano Sonatas*

TOM BEGHIN

> Jetzt ist er freilich Jedem als ein unerschöpflicher Genius bekannt; man wird es gewohnt, sich in ihn hinein zu studieren und das blinkende Metall aus seinen Schachten sich zu eigen zu machen.
>
> [To be sure, now he is known to anyone as an inexhaustible genius; one becomes accustomed to studying one's way into him and to making one's own the glittering metal from his shafts.]
>
> Adolf Bernhard Marx, on Beethoven
> *Berliner allgemeine musikalische Zeitung* 1 (4 February 1824), p. 37

When I initially approached Chris Maene, eminent piano maker in Ruiselede, Belgium, with the request to make me an English piano, I was thinking of the copy of the 1798 Longman, Clementi, & Co. piano that he had already made, or if he felt up to it, a John Broadwood & Sons from the 1810s or 1820s. But Maene had a counterproposal: why not make *Beethoven*'s Broadwood? Once made, the suggestion was difficult to ignore. It would be hard not to copy an instrument that had been hand-picked in a prestigious London showroom on Great Pulteney Street by a committee of five highly ranked London musicians – Frederick Kalkbrenner, Ferdinand Ries, John Baptist Cramer, Jacques-Godefroi Ferrari and Charles Knyvett. Each had carved his signature on the wrest plank of the piano, embossing his name on an instrument that was poised to make history.

Leaving London in December 1817, the six-octave grand piano with the serial number 7362 made it to Vienna sometime towards the end of May 1818, following a long and arduous journey over sea and by land.[1] After some fine-tuning was done at the Streicher workshop, Beethoven put it to

* This essay is an expanded version of booklet notes that appeared with a CD recording by the author, *Inside the Hearing Machine, Beethoven's Piano Sonatas Opus 109, 110, and 111 on His Broadwood* (EPR-Classic, 2017). I would like to thank Ellie Nimeroski, Tilman Skworoneck and Robin Wallace for their feedback and help during the writing of this essay. I presented parts of it at the 83rd Annual Meeting of the American Musicological Society in Rochester, NY (November 2017).

[1] 'Ehrende Auszeichnung', *Wiener Zeitschrift für Kunst, Literatur, Theater und Mode* (23 January 1819), p. 79.

use immediately in the fourth movement of his 'Hammerklavier' sonata, Op. 106. There's fascinating evidence to this effect: the three first movements of Op. 106 are written for a six-octave Viennese piano, with range from FF to f^4. The fourth movement not only adjusts to the highest note c^4 of the new Broadwood, but also has the bass drop to the lowest note, CC; together these span the typical English six-octave range, one fourth lower than its Viennese counterpart.

Beethoven's Broadwood, on display now at the Hungarian National Museum in Budapest, is one of three extant Beethoven pianos, as they are often called. (Franz Liszt owned the piano last and bequeathed it to his home country.) The second Beethoven piano is the Graf that Beethoven received on loan in 1825; it is currently in the Beethoven-Haus in Bonn. The third is the Erard that Beethoven acquired in 1803; it is presently in the Oberösterreichisches Landesmuseum in Linz, where it ended up through Beethoven's brother Johann, who owned a pharmacy there. But once we adopt the label 'Beethoven piano', the emphasis unavoidably shifts from object to owner, from thing to idea, from artisanship to Art. Beethoven himself seems to have participated in this process of abstraction in his thank-you note to Thomas Broadwood, promising that he would keep the piano as an 'altar where I'll place the most beautiful offerings of my spirit to the divine Apollo'.[2] (One easily forgets, though, that Beethoven sent this note before he received the instrument and that this kind of lofty language would have been rhetorically entirely appropriate for expressions of gratitude.) More neutral, and preserving equal focus on donor and beneficiary, is the following inscription on the instrument's wrest plank: *Hoc Instrumentum donum Thomae Broadwood (Londini) propter ingenium illustrissimi Beethoven* ('This Instrument is a gift from Thomas Broadwood (from London) to honour the genius of the most illustrious Beethoven').

Beethoven is known to have proudly demonstrated the beauties of his English-made piano to continental visitors, but these would have been keen, first and foremost, to hear the notoriously reclusive Beethoven *play* (that is, improvise) on any piano. Liszt kept the instrument in his library long after Beethoven's passing; how much of Broadwood – whether father John or son Thomas – was still part of the memory, or to what extent had the piano become a (mere) reliquary of Beethoven's spirit? Conversely, the question deserves to be asked whether, back in 1818, during several months of awaiting the announced English piano, Beethoven really expected to *use* it – that is, not just to play on it or to keep it on display

---

[2] Letter of 3 February 1818. BG, vol. 4, p. 173.

as some honorary award, but to actively seek inspiration from this new artistic tool, different from the ones he had known before. So who (or what) was worthy of whom: piano maker, pianist–composer, well-crafted instrument, or Beethoven's genius?

Pandora's Box

With these questions, we open a Pandora's box of conceptions and assumptions that have long shaped Beethoven scholarship and popular wisdom – hopefully not beyond repair. We're familiar enough with the objections. Could Beethoven even hear his Broadwood? It is true that Beethoven was largely deaf when he received the instrument. By embracing his Broadwood, was Beethoven dreaming of the modern Steinway? It is true that English pianos may be seen as precursors of the modern piano, certainly more so than their Viennese counterparts. Did he even care what kind of piano he had at this point in his life, when he had all but perfected the art of sketching compositional ideas away from the piano? It is true that Beethoven was a champion of a new method of sketching and made a point of teaching it to his privileged student and patron, the Archduke Rudolph of Austria. Are not Beethoven's last three sonatas special testimony of the power of the work concept, by definition transferable onto any piano? It is true that the compositional idea of transformation or even transcendence is strongly present in each of the three sonatas, and arguably most in his last sonata, Op. 111. In light of these powerfully seductive teleological lines of reasoning, why even bother replicating Beethoven's Broadwood?

To make matters worse, there has been scepticism within the field of historically informed performance. In 1988, William Newman, in his influential book on Beethoven's piano music, dismissively referred to the Broadwood as 'an unsolicited gift' and in his liner note to a landmark 1996 recording of Beethoven's piano sonatas on period instruments, Malcolm Bilson (in reference to Newman's book) proclaimed it 'clear that Beethoven was never happy with it, and maintained a firm allegiance to the Viennese instruments he knew'.[3] In this recording (which included myself as one of seven players under the leadership of Bilson), English instruments remained notably absent. Instead, we performed anything from Op. 90 onward on six-and-a-half-octave Viennese pianos.

---

[3] William Newman, *Beethoven on Beethoven: Playing His Piano Music His Way* (New York, 1988), p. 52; Malcolm Bilson, introductory note (CD booklet, p. 34) to Bilson, Tom Beghin, David Breitman, Ursula Dütschler, Zvi Meniker, Bart van Oort and Andrew Willis, *Ludwig van Beethoven: The Complete Piano Sonatas on Period Instruments*, Claves Records (1997), CD 9707–10, 10 compact discs.

It is true – here we go again – that in his later years Beethoven's pianistic-composing instincts remained largely Viennese, and it is also true that at the time Newman wrote his book, the iconic status of the Beethoven Broadwood had unjustly eclipsed the many Viennese-style pianos in Beethoven's life. Historically informed performance was only starting to discover the latter type of instruments. Long-standing ignorance of any historical pianos had led to the peculiar association of the big 'Hammerklavier' sonata, Op. 106, with 'the Beethoven Broadwood' as somehow representative of a more modern, forward-looking piano – but the irony is that only its last movement can be played on it because the first three movements include high notes that do not exist on the Broadwood keyboard. That assumption, intriguingly, lasted until only a few years ago. As I have established elsewhere, Op. 106 is not some grand six-and-half-octave piece, but one that actually combines two ranges – first Viennese, then English.[4] From the perspective of range, then, the Broadwood constituted a step *back* for Beethoven, and we can infer from various accounts that he regretted this aspect of the new instrument. (According to Anton Schindler, when Ignaz Moscheles asked Beethoven to use his Broadwood for a concert in 1823, Beethoven 'suspected Moscheles of some kind of financial speculation, since the piano had too short a keyboard to be of use to him'. Almost certainly, Beethoven projected his own frustration onto his younger colleague.)[5]

In spite of all possible objections, I ended up commissioning the instrument from Maene not *propter ingenium illustrissimi Beethoven* ('because of' or 'in honour of Beethoven's genius') but *ad intelligendum ingenium illustrissimi Beethoven* ('to study and understand the genius of the most illustrious Beethoven'). In his excellent revisionist work on Beethoven as pianist, Tilman Skowroneck has reminded us that starting with the fugue from Op. 106, Beethoven stayed within the six-octave range CC to c^4 for all his remaining piano works, including the Bagatelles written after the receipt of the Broadwood, Op. 119 (starting with No. 6) and Op. 126; the Diabelli Variations, Op. 120; and the three late piano sonatas, Op. 109, 110 and 111.[6] There are only two exceptions, two instances of notes that lie outside the range of the six-octave Broadwood: three high C♯s on the last page of Op. 109 and one high E♭ in the first movement of Op. 111. For the

---

[4] Tom Beghin, 'Beethoven's Hammerklavier Sonata, Opus 106: Legend, Difficulty, and the Gift of a Broadwood Piano', *Keyboard Perspectives*, 7 (2014), pp. 81–121.

[5] Anton Schindler, *Beethoven as I Knew Him*, ed. Donald W. MacArdle, trans. Constance S. Jolly (Mineola, NY, 1996), p. 372.

[6] Tilman Skowroneck, 'A Brit in Vienna: Beethoven's Broadwood Piano', *Keyboard Perspectives*, 5 (2012), pp. 41–82.

latter note, however, already in the autograph – that is, the original manuscript – Beethoven specifies an alternative version, or *ossia*; it is a remarkable reflex betraying his own private reality. The high C♯ in Op. 109 requires more explanation, but just acknowledging this note and finding the solution to play it spectacularly increases the relevance of the Broadwood for this sonata. (I discuss the note below.)

So if having the Broadwood was good enough for Beethoven while he was composing his late piano works, ought we not try to play them on it as well? And – dare I take the next step – listen to them in this way too? With this essay, along with a new recording of the three last piano sonatas on the Maene/Broadwood replica, I set out to refute all of the assumptions offered above.[7] Let us spell them out again, along with the refutations. Beethoven did not hear well – but he went to great lengths having a *Gehörmaschine* (hearing machine) built to go on top of the Broadwood. Beethoven was a man with a disability – but something in the Broadwood (its touch, its power, its energy) must have compensated for it. Beethoven went on long walks with a notebook in his pocket – yet he made sure to arrange for the best possible piano at whichever summer residence he moved to, so he clearly needed tangible input from the instrument too. Beethoven had little time for dreaming of some future piano: he was too busy keeping his beloved Broadwood in reasonable shape, and he called on Viennese builders such as Wilhelm Leschen, André Stein and Conrad Graf to help him do so. The idea of transcendence in the last three piano sonatas becomes all the stronger when anchored in Beethoven's concrete inter-actions with his instrument. These interactions, finally, are by no means limited to just hearing, but reflect a multi-sensorial experience that includes feeling and seeing – not at all untypical for a 'deafly hearing' person, as Robin Wallace has argued so eloquently.[8]

Beethoven at His Broadwood

In Johann Nepomuk Hoechle's drawing of Beethoven's living room, made shortly after the composer's death, we see the Broadwood in use – with music stand still open and candles half-burnt (see Figure 10.1). Beethoven's other piano, the Graf, had just been returned to its manufacturer and

---

[7] Tom Beghin, *Inside the Hearing Machine: Beethoven on His Broadwood–Piano Sonatas Opus 109, 110, and 111* (EPR Classic, 2017).

[8] Robin Wallace, *Hearing Beethoven: A Story of Musical Loss and Discovery* (Chicago, 2018).

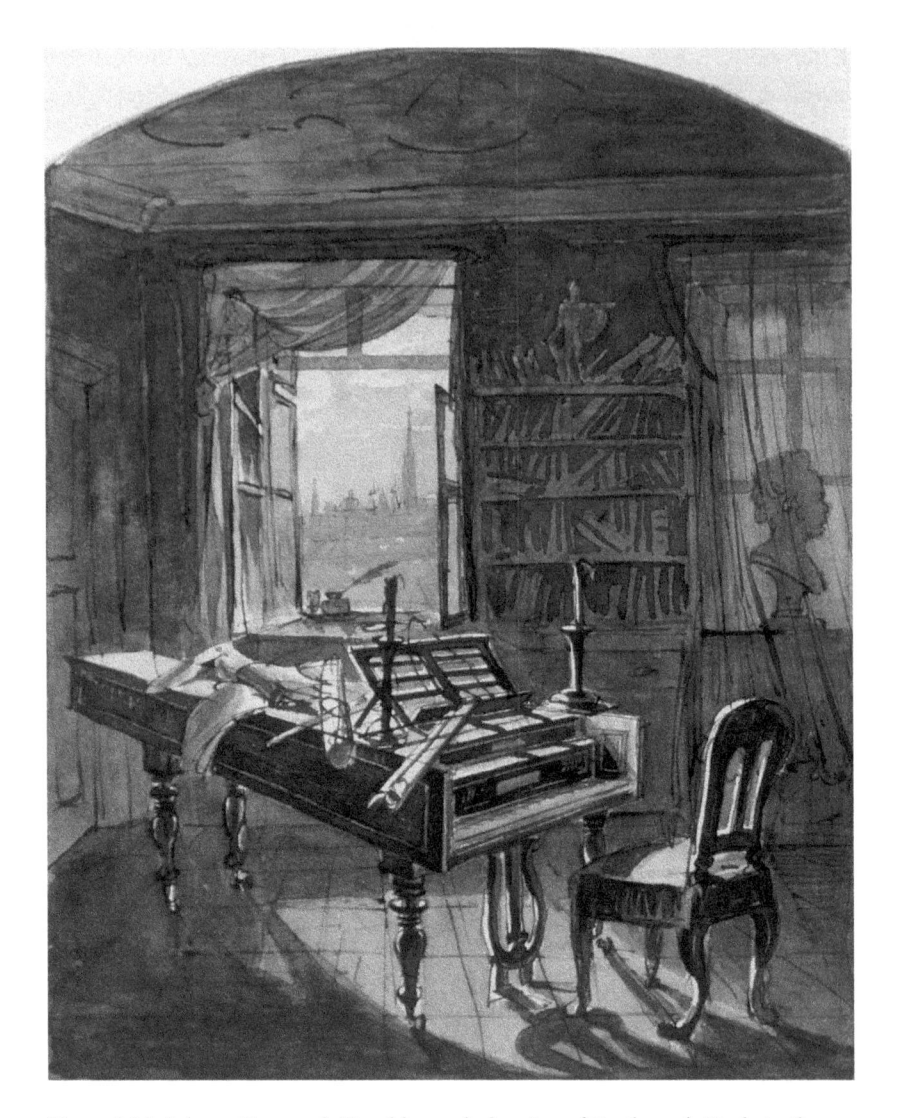

Figure 10.1 Johann Nepomuk Hoechle, wash drawing of *Beethoven's Study in the Schwarzspanierhaus*, 1827
Reproduced by permission of Wien Museum, Vienna

owner. Gerhard von Breuning, who lived just around the corner and as a young teenager visited Beethoven often, remembered that the two pianos had been 'set curve to curve', with the Broadwood the other way around: Beethoven would have had its keyboard at the window, the perfect well-lit spot for improvising, while the Graf may at this time (1825–27) have served as Beethoven's composition instrument, its keyboard closer to the adjacent 'composition room', or study, outside the frame to the right.

(The title of the drawing is misleading: the room depicted was in fact Beethoven's combined living room and bedroom.) Of the two instruments, the Graf was outfitted with a hearing machine. Breuning remembers, 'Above its keyboard and action was a sort of trumpet, like a prompter's box (*Souffleurkasten*), made in the shape of a bent sound board of thin wood; the idea was to concentrate the sound waves of the instrument in the ears of the player.'[9]

Hoechle's drawing would bring us the closest to restoring a reality of Beethoven at his Broadwood, were it not for one detail – one 'addition of the artist's', as Breuning clarifies.[10] As if making up for the empty chair, Hoechle positions a fictitious Beethoven bust behind the closed curtain on the right windowsill. It faces away from inkpot and pen, which Hoechle himself may have carefully placed on the left windowsill, to fit the composition he had in mind. The right window, furthermore, is drawn incomplete: there is no hint of the skyline of Vienna, which the left window vividly opens up to; while the room is clearly demarcated on the left by a door and wall, the right-hand side suggests no end. Beethoven's spirit, Hoechle's composition suggests, leaves behind all earthly things and confidently looks toward a future when also those manuscript rolls still chaotically scattered on the piano lid will be revered as true masterworks.

We turn around Beethoven's bust to face his piano again – but it is 'I', a well-hearing pianist, who takes the seat (or 'Beethoven Stuhl'). Like Beethoven, I also adopt my newly built replica as a tool for artistic (re-)creation. Beethoven had no choice, but I, instead of either ignoring or sublimating the issue, acknowledge his hearing disability as a component of his art – as something that influenced his craft of composing, not just conceptually but also empirically. Finally, even Beethoven's evocation of Apollo as the god of music may be deflated: gracing the top of the bookcase that Hoechle drew between the two windows stands an elegant, full-figure statuette of Apollo Belvedere. Beethoven's promise to Thomas Broadwood to treat his piano as an 'altar to Apollo', then, may have sprung from a practical consideration: Beethoven anticipated making room for the new instrument in front of the bookcase and the statuette overlooking it.

But the piano alone does not tell the full story. In 1827, Beethoven may have benefited from Graf's hearing contraption, but back in 1820–22,

---

[9] Gerhard von Breuning, *Memories of Beethoven from the House of the Black-Robed Spaniards*, ed. Maynard Solomon (Cambridge, 1992), p. 63, translation of *Aus dem Schwarzspanierhause: Erinnerungen an L. van Beethoven aus meiner Jugendzeit* (Vienna, 1874).

[10] Breuning, *Memories*, p. 66.

when he wrote his last three sonatas, the talk was all about the construction of a similar hearing aid, the first of its kind, for his Broadwood. We turn to it now as a crucial piece of the puzzle.

The Hearing Machine

The story of Beethoven's 'hearing machine' (*Gehörmaschine*), built to go on top of his piano, is usually told backwards, from the perspective of selected witness accounts in the last few years of Beethoven's life. These typically focus on the old master's playing (mostly whether or not he could be convinced to do so, and if yes, on finding glimpses of genius) or on his utter inability to hear (always assessed from the perspective of a pitying, well-hearing visitor). No wonder the fifty-plus-year-old Beethoven would have felt self-conscious.[11] It is telling, in this respect, that Friedrich Wieck, father of Clara Schumann, relates gaining access to Beethoven through André Stein, who introduced Wieck as someone especially experienced 'in hearing aids and hearing machines' – that is, not just as a colleague-musician, but as someone capable of relating to Beethoven's physical condition. 'Otherwise, in Stein's experience, [Beethoven] would not have received me,' Wieck explains. And he got his reward: 'For more than an hour long [Beethoven] fantasized, after he had connected his hearing machine (*seine Gehörmaschine*) and placed it on the soundboard of his piano; this piano had been given to him by the city of London; it was rather beaten up and had a strong, puffy tone.'[12]

It is not clear what exactly Beethoven placed on the piano: the machine that Stein had made in 1820, some unknown connector between the piano's soundboard and Beethoven's ears (whether or not in conjunction with the larger machine and whether or not involving ear trumpets), or some new contraption altogether. Another uncertainty concerns the date of Wieck's visit: the newest scholarship dates it in 1823, three years earlier than Wieck remembered at an advanced age.[13]

Unambiguously referring to Stein's original machine, however, is a witness account by the portrait painter August von Klöber, who visited

[11] For a compelling analysis of these visitors' stories, see K. M. Knittel, 'Pilgrimages to Beethoven: Reminiscences by His Contemporaries', *Music & Letters*, 84/1 (2003), pp. 19–54.

[12] Friedrich Kerst, *Die Erinnerungen an Beethoven*, vol. 2 (Stuttgart, 1913), p. 159.

[13] Klaus Martin Kopitz and Rainer Cadenbach (eds.), *Beethoven aus der Sicht seiner Zeitgenossen in Tagebüchern, Briefen, Gedichten und Erinnerungen*, vol. 2 (Munich, 2009), p. 1094.

Beethoven at his summer residence in Mödling most probably in late September 1820.[14] The machine, barely two weeks old at the time of Klöber's visit, would have been shiny and impressive. In this scene, Beethoven's nephew Karl was practising 'on the piano, which had been a present from England and which was outfitted with a big metal cupola (*Blechkuppel*)'. Posing for his portrait, Beethoven sat with his back to the piano. 'The instrument stood approximately four to five steps behind him and in spite of his deafness Beethoven corrected each of the boy's mistakes, made him repeat the one or the other passage etc.'[15] Granted, this is an anecdote – a witness account with no bearing whatsoever on the formal performance of a Beethoven sonata – but still, two observations seem relevant: the Broadwood-*cum*-cupola had become a fixed entity so that fifteen-year-old Karl had no choice but to practise in what must have been rather aggressive acoustic circumstances; second, the machine seems to have been effective: even without visual clues, Beethoven was capable of distinguishing between correct and incorrect sounds.

Building the Machine

The building process (what, who, when, how and at what cost) may be most vividly reconstructed from Beethoven's 1820 conversation books. (A complete compilation of communications about the hearing machine makes for a surprisingly good read and may be found in the Appendix to this essay; source references may be found there as well.) Countless discussions take place, having to do mainly with the choice of material (wood or metal) and shape (early on, Stein launches the winning idea of an 'arch'). Beethoven clearly has a preference for wood. (What about metal causes him to be sceptical?) But when Stein finds a tinsmith 'who's skilled and inexpensive', the opinion becomes unanimous: 'The gentlemen all agree that metal is better than wood', as Beethoven's personal assistant Franz Oliva summarizes for the ever-doubting Beethoven. From the outset, Stein has proactively volunteered his services, but Beethoven appears doubtful about that too, at some point even contemplating switching to Graf. The ever-diplomatic Oliva again talks Beethoven out of his indecision, arguing that 'Stein knows you better and seems more technically

---

[14] Wallace (*Hearing Beethoven*, pp. 250–1, n. 79) has corrected this date from earlier scholarship.
[15] 'Miscellen', *Allgemeine musikalische Zeitung, Neue Folge*, 2 (4 May 1864), p. 325.

skilled' and reminding Beethoven of the current momentum, 'One shouldn't allow this fire to go out.'

Measurements are made at Beethoven's house. Once the final production has started, Beethoven must temporarily part with the Broadwood – something he's been dreading all along. The piano is transported to Stein's workshop, while Beethoven moves to Mödling for the summer, possibly with a rental piano from Stein. Oliva meanwhile keeps moving the project toward the finish line, navigating between Beethoven's impatience and unavoidable delays at Stein's. But all looks good: 'Stein doesn't doubt that [with additional ear trumpets, to be customized onto the new machine] you will hear [even] the softest [of sounds].' Also Joseph Czerny (friend and piano teacher of Beethoven's nephew Karl) has tried out Stein's hearing machine and assures its efficiency – from a well-hearing person's perspective, that is. On 7 September 1820 the Broadwood and the completed machine make it back to Beethoven's house, five and a half months after Stein initially broached the idea. New ear trumpets, to be modelled after the ones Beethoven already has from Johann Nepomuk Mälzel, will follow. (There is no evidence that these new ear trumpets ever arrived.)[16]

During the months before our recording in July 2016 I shared this wealth of material with a growing team of collaborators (a piano builder, an acoustician, a master artisan, a record producer) and received additional advice from friends and colleagues. As we experimented – with cardboard, with wood, with zinc foil – parallels with the activities back in 1820 quickly became palpable. We also made a prototype in wire, and like those of our historical counterparts, our attempts had varying degrees of success. Through trial and error, we ended up making three versions of a hearing machine. The ultimate goal, however, was to create what we started calling a flexible backward-projecting lid.[17]

In my wish to make our efforts also artistically rewarding for a well-hearing person, I kept insisting on my expectation of a grand piano that would behave acoustically like some giant clavichord, with a lid that projects sound backwards toward the player. In my mind this was to be an improved version of a clavichord, on which the soundboard is located to the right-hand side of the player with strings running sideways, both constructional features heavily favouring one's right ear. A backward-

---

[16] Robin Wallace, personal communication, 22 June 2017.

[17] Collaborators included Thomas Wulfrank (acoustical engineer), Chris Maene (keyboard builder), Marc Loncke (organ builder), Robin Wallace (musicologist), Martha de Francisco (Tonmeister) and Steven Maes (recording engineer).

projecting Broadwood, again in my thinking, would yield a stereo image between bass and treble, the piano's collected strings now neatly perpendicular to the player, nicely divided over the whole soundboard. I hypothesized that the resulting clarity in sound, to be experienced binaurally, would be akin to Beethoven's focused listening through his respective ear trumpets. I also wanted us to construct something that would include the listener in this acoustic experience. The backward projection would have to focalize the sound (which was the priority for Beethoven), but also diffuse it (softening the blow on the player's ears and opening up a soundscape that becomes attractive for the listeners seated behind the player).

One side effect of using the hearing machine – and a potentially important component in the story – is that with any keyboard-oriented amplification device, the Broadwood would sound more like one of its Viennese counterparts. Outfitted with harsher hammerheads, Viennese pianos were designed to articulate better, while the priority for English instruments, which used a softer kind of leather for their hammer coverings, was to sing, at the expense of a clear attack. The conventional lid helps restore definition in those long and full English piano sounds, but these are projected sideways, away from the player: it is no coincidence that the modern concert setup of the piano, with the lid opened toward the audience, originated exactly in late eighteenth-century English concert practice. By contrast, when one opens a Viennese piano, either by lifting one side of the lid or by taking the lid off completely, it loses some of its direct, articulatory power in favour of more resonance and spaciousness. Outfitting Beethoven's Broadwood with a hearing device, then, would have 'Viennicized' his English instrument to some degree, lending it more directness and articulatory power.

We find support for our vision of Beethoven's Broadwood as a giant clavichord in a remarkably accurate report published in a Viennese cultural journal of 1819. The journalist, who may well have interviewed Beethoven in preparation for his piece, compares the touch of Beethoven's Broadwood 'to that of a good clavichord: all modifications of a single tone may be produced without the need of a special register'.[18] The comment is unusual, but it makes sense if it did indeed come from Beethoven, whose earliest pianistic memories had been formed when he practised the clavichord extensively during his childhood in Bonn. Anyone used to Viennese *prell*-actions (as Beethoven was) would be impressed by the larger key-dip

---

[18] 'Ehrende Auszeichnung', p. 78.

of the English instrument, which in combination with the English *stoss-action* generates what I like to describe as a spongy feel – similar to the sensation of pressing a clavichord key. (In a clavichord, however, the sponginess is created by direct contact with the struck string, and not by what is called after-touch in an English piano action.) The illusion, then, of direct tactile contact with his piano strings, raising for Beethoven associations with the instrument of his youth, may have helped Beethoven compensate for his hearing loss – however, not through sound, but through touch, the latter being the dominant sensation on a soft-sounding clavichord also for a well-hearing player.

The Last Three Sonatas

How relevant was the existence of a hearing machine for Beethoven's composition of his last three sonatas? To be sure, Beethoven tried the machine for the first time only after his sonata Op. 109 had been largely thought out and sketched. It is possible that he made revisions before sending the completed sonata to his publisher, Schlesinger in Berlin, by January or February 1821. The first sonata to have been fully conceived under the amplification device was Op. 110; its finished autograph is dated 25 December 1821, more than a year after the arrival of the machine.[19] The final sonata, Op. 111, was finished by February 1822; on 9 April of that year, Beethoven announced that he had sent a new fair copy of the second movement.[20] But Beethoven's first response to his amplified piano may well be encapsulated elsewhere. His Bagatelle in C major, Op. 119 No. 7, written exactly around the time of the hearing machine's arrival, is a quirky fifty-seven-second piece with an ear-deafening climax, perfect for testing the dynamic extremes of the arched, metal contraption.[21]

Figure 10.2 shows three acoustical setups, which I started applying to my performances of each of the sonatas: (a) the Broadwood's regular lid for Op. 109 (here opened for the purpose of recording, though in Beethoven's room it would have been kept closed); (b) the horn-like hearing machine for Op. 110; and (c) our interpretation of a 'flexible backwards-projecting

---

[19] For most of the year, Beethoven had suffered from jaundice, causing delay in delivering the three sonatas to Schlesinger.

[20] BTW, vol. 1, pp. 697–9, pp. 703–6, pp. 710–12.

[21] For a comparative 360-degree video performance of this bagatelle in three different acoustical circumstances, see www.insidethehearingmachine.com/360/ (accessed 16 July 2018).

(a)

(b)

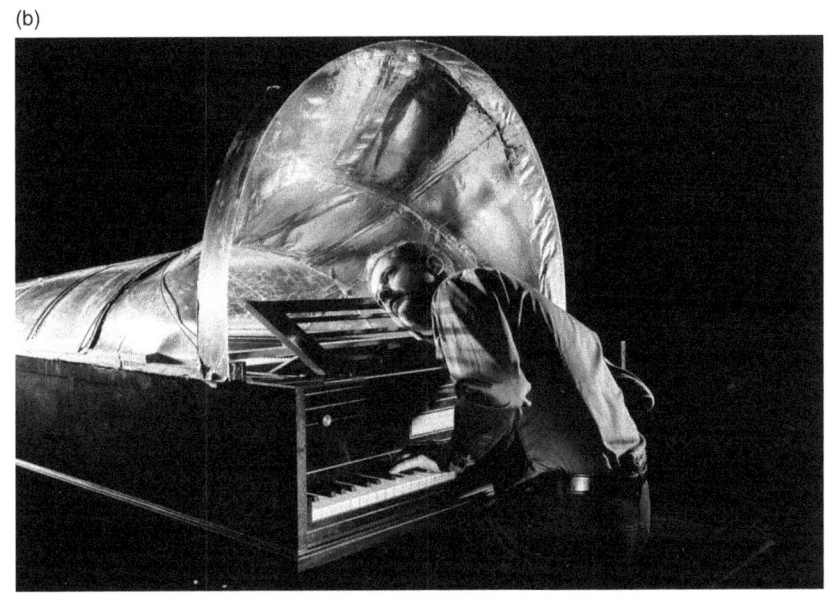

Figure 10.2 Three acoustical setups for recording Beethoven's last three sonatas: (a) regular lid of the Broadwood; (b) horn-shaped hearing machine; (c) flexible backwards-projecting lid

Photos by Steven Maes and Pieter Peeters

(c)

Figure 10.2 (*cont.*)

lid' for Op. 111. Granted, there is artistic assumption in these choices: Op. 109, as the poetic opener of a trilogy, benefits from a less conscious projection of sound (at least, from the perspective of the performer, who starts the sonata by 'casually' improvising); Op. 110, as the most directly 'speaking' of the three (think not only of the recitatives in the third movement but also the cantabile of the first movement and the scherzo based on a folk tune) would exactly be in need of more sonic force and focus; from its side, it would be hard to insist that Op. 111, with its ever-blossoming *Arietta*, remain contained in any acoustical enclosure. Still, in this narrative of a trilogy of sonatas, each doing something distinctly different with sound, granting these various lids or machines a Latourian kind of mediating agency between instrument and interpreting performer makes sense, especially if we accept Beethoven's disability as central to his compositional *modus operandi*. Empathizing with his deafness – as performer, listener and critic – opens up possibilities for a new kind of analytical discourse where 'hearing' yields to multi-sensorial ways of experiencing Beethoven's late piano music, including 'feeling' and 'seeing'.  The following descriptions of that multi-sensorial experience are attempts to engage in such a discourse: ideally, they're to be read in conjunction with six video clips (demonstrations at the piano), accessible through the website InsideTheHearingMachine.com.

Sonata Op. 109: Video Clips 1 and 2

There is one note in Op. 109 that exceeds the six-octave range of Beethoven's Broadwood: a high C♯ that recurs three times as part of the last variation, at the end of the third movement, just before the final return of the unadorned *cantabile* theme.[22] Figure 10.3 shows the third of them. After having been avoided for so long, this highest note of the whole sonata (played by my right pinkie) soars triumphantly over a long sustained trill (played by the lower fingers of my right hand) and wild scalar flourishes that criss-cross the middle part of the keyboard (played by my full left hand). The C♯ is itself part of a note-by-note reminder of the theme that has been transposed up by two octaves. It functions as a major-second appoggiatura, gorgeously stretching the reach of the melodic line. But there is no key for it on the Broadwood. What to do? Leave out the note? Replace it?

Figure 10.3 Beethoven, Piano Sonata in E Major, Op. 109, third movement, bars 180 to end, first edition
Berlin: Schlesinger, 1821

---

[22] See also my essay, 'The C-natural That Wants to Be a C-sharp: Visions and Realities of Beethoven's Broadwood', in *Artistic Research in Music: Discipline and Resistance*, ed. Jonathan Impett (Leuven, 2017), pp. 43–87.

Nowhere else in the sonata does Beethoven write a high C♮, leaving open at least the option of retuning the high C as a C♯. I stress option over obligation, because Beethoven was known to have retorted to a well-meaning colleague, 'they all like to tune it, but they shall not touch it' ('it' in reference to his new Broadwood and 'they' to his Viennese piano builder friends),[23] and visitors had heard him playing on the instrument despite its wretched tuning, so it seems fair to assume that the issue of an accurate single pitch would not have been important at all. The note in question, furthermore, is part of the highest of registers, which would have been all but impossible for him to hear.

For Beethoven, then, the discrepancy between imagined and actual, realized sound could easily be lived with. But also for a well-hearing person, there is something intensely powerful about playing a sharp on a key that is supposed to be a natural. It is as if at that very moment one succeeds, by sheer force of will, in embodying those highest piano strings (all three of them, for one key) and making them behave like one's vocal cords, stretching what physically still feels like a minor second (one's fifth finger gliding to the next key below) to a major-second appoggiatura (creating a full tone or the equivalent of an additional key in between). The pianist, finding this sublime voice, self-identifies with the piano in such a way as to transcend technological reality. (An association with the human voice is entirely warranted: in the autograph of the sonata Beethoven had called the theme *Gesang* or 'song', but had changed this indication to *gesangvoll*, 'singingly', by the first publication.)

At the same time, Beethoven would have found comfort in the option of scordatura: to take the tuning hammer and raise the pitch of a single note on the keyboard without making another pitch unavailable in its stead. The sonata, in other words, remains executable in its entirety on the kind of keyboard that Beethoven had. Beethoven may have been the only pianist–composer with a magnificent Broadwood in Vienna – a unique circumstance that must have flattered his ego – but the context is still one of a composer at his keyboard, the latter serving as a tool or interface for his ideas. Writing the C♯ is not a story of vision or sheer imagination: Beethoven's 'C♮ that wants to be a C♯' may tweak materiality, but it does so in an utterly clever and concrete way.

Variation 4 of the third movement of Op. 109 explores the sensation of vibration to an extreme: the feeling of vibrating parts – of the instrument's

---

[23] Elliott Forbes (rev. and ed.), *Thayer's Life of Beethoven*, rev. ed. (Princeton, 1967), p. 695.

case, its keys and its pedal lyre through the pianist's fingers, feet and entire body. I became especially aware of this as I practised the sonata alternately on the Broadwood and on an 1808 Viennese Nannette Streicher on the hardwood-floor stage at the Orpheus Institute in Ghent, and felt a noticeably more constant vibration in the Broadwood. From an organological perspective, this makes sense, since the outer frame of an English instrument is structurally anchored to its soundboard, whereas the outer case of a Viennese piano encloses yet another inner frame, making the transfer of vibration from inside to outside indirect only.

Because of their precise action and articulatory focus, Viennese pianos call for a clear differentiation between dissonance and consonance – the former to be played louder, the latter softer (as a resolution of the former). But at the outset of the fourth variation, gorgeous pairs of appoggiatura and resolution elide with one another, almost to the point of the one negating the harmonic function of the other. This is a rather drastic shift in harmonic thinking, and Beethoven's explorations must have been based on touch rather than sound: every tone or key on an English-action piano requires an individual finger stroke, while a Viennese-action piano allows for the second of a slurred two-note pair to be hung onto the previous one, requiring only a gentle, caressing stroke of the resolving finger. Without physical clarity of good (or strong) versus bad (or weak), the duality easily reverses to bad versus good. What starts mattering more, then, is the sine wave of the oscillation itself: the up and down of it (or, as the case may be, the down and up). In this variation, Beethoven taps into the accumulating energy of a relentless play of back-and-forth vibration, first cautiously and softly, then with ever-increasing vigour and obsession.

Measurements carried out by acoustical engineer Thomas Wulfrank established that Beethoven's Broadwood is indeed consistently 'vibrationally louder' than a Viennese piano (an 1823 Graf) for a significant three to five decibels.[24] This result reflects what the pianist feels through fingers or hands at the keyboard. Measurements taken on the floor, reflective of the sensations felt through the pianist's feet and legs, are even more significant: the wooden floor vibrated up to ten decibels more under the Broadwood than under the Graf the equivalent of ten times more vibrational energy. No wonder the Broadwood appealed to Beethoven.

---

[24] See Thomas Wulfrank, 'The Acoustics of Beethoven's Hearing Machine', CD booklet, Beghin, *Inside the Hearing Machine*, pp. 72–4.

Sonata Op. 110: Video Clips 3, 4 and 5

While in Op. 109 Beethoven searches for his pianist's singing voice – its vibrations excited either by piano strings or the pianist's inner vocal cords – at the beginning of Op. 110 Beethoven does exactly what visitors reported him doing when demonstrating the beautiful tone of the Broadwood: he plays a single four-voice chord, with the third on top.[25] He lingers on it: he listens. It is a celebration: hearing or listening becomes an essential *topos* of this sonata. When in the fourth bar, I pause on a dominant-seventh chord, the trill under the fermata allows me the freedom and time to lean forward into the machine and analyse its inner workings, the clashing sounds of my trill reflecting erratically against all possible surfaces and finding their way toward my probing ears.

But here I must pause for self-criticism. Granted, the described choreography of putting my head into the machine has a precedent: in 1824, a few years into the machine's existence, Stein asked Beethoven, 'You do hear better, don't you, when you bring your head under this machine?', presumably in response to Beethoven's scepticism. But my curiosity to find out whether Stein's machine 'works', let alone the suggestion of Beethoven's behaviour as he composes the first bars of his Op. 110, may be just as naïve as Stein's well-meaning question. Of course, Beethoven would have loved to answer, yes, but how could he, after shreds of hope had been dashed time and time again for most of his adult life? 'Disablist hearing', defined by Joseph Straus as 'the ways that people whose bodily, psychological, or cognitive abilities are different from the prevailing norm might make sense of music',[26] may well also have been what Beethoven had largely got used to: how was he at the age of fifty-four to tell the difference between deaf and 'normal' hearing? This question has especially been on my mind as I submitted myself several times, with live audiences as my silent witness, to performing Op. 110 with earplugs. Drawn into my inner body (an experience intensified by not seeing the audience behind my back), I became all the more conscious of the optics of the hearing machine in front of me (see Figure 10.4): a large dark cave that I explore with my eyes both for its depth and its width. After that fermata with the trill (where 'bringing in my head' no longer made much of a difference),

---

[25] 'It has such a beautiful tone,' Beethoven is quoted as saying about his Broadwood, as he turned to Ludwig Rellstab, playing a C-major triad in the right hand but mistakenly grabbing a B in the bass. Ludwig Rellstab, *Aus meinem Leben*, vol. 2 (Berlin, 1861), p. 255.

[26] Joseph N. Straus, *Extraordinary Measures: Disability in Music* (Oxford, 2011), p. 150.

Figure 10.4 Sitting in front of the hearing machine
Photo by Pieter Peeters

I found myself scanning the machine's outside rim, the same that may have inspired Beethoven to come up with slurred melody lines (bars 5–9) and feather-light arpeggios (bars 12–16), drawing half-circles all the way up and down the keyboard, looping within the largest half-circle of all: the gigantic arc that looms over my keyboard. For a pianist with 'normal' ears, playing these arpeggios is a daunting task: fingers are made to navigate from one black key to another, with no other choice than to use one's thumb on the staccato-marked quaver downbeats, which often come out louder than we'd expect. Playing with earplugs, however, any self-imposed pressure to make notes equally soft and audible diminished significantly; or to put this differently, all the more conscious of sonic vibrations in my inner body and oblivious of any absolute level of sound outside my body, I happily lived in the illusion that I did indeed play *piano* and *leggiermente*. Rather than feeling hindered by those deep English keys (strikingly incompatible with lightness), I actually enjoyed their sponginess as my hand swayed confidently from the one thumb-staccato to the next, every turn of my hand adding yet another waving gesture between keyboard (under me) and horn (over me). Without earplugs, I had found myself all too self-consciously tiptoeing my way around the keyboard, keen not to disappoint Beethoven and to uphold the *leggiermente* effect that I thought Beethoven intended. Now, on the contrary, I felt room for more – even for much more. When at the recapitulation I combine the cantabile opening melody with those arpeggios (bars 56 ff.), I aim for both sound and gesture to fill the entire acoustical space in front of me, using my hands no longer as delicate little pencils but rather as thick brushes that paint extroverted waving lines (at the beginning of the recapitulation Beethoven indeed removes the piano mark that he had prescribed at the outset of the sonata), without experiencing any sense of exaggeration, but through my nerves fully absorbing the tactile thickness of the English instrument.

The third movement's fugal theme (C and A♭, the pitches of the sonata's opening third, now inverted, marking the beginning and end of a series of fourths and thirds) subjects itself to the same inflection of a single slur, now extended from two to nine notes. In what feels like a recapitulation (starting in bar 174), the final section combines the fugal subject with figurations that gradually take on the form of arpeggiations, ever more reminiscent of those in the first movement as we head to final tonal closure on an extended A♭ pedal in the bass (bar 200 to the end). Even when wearing earplugs, leaving my head in the machine is no longer an option: accumulating their way to a climax, the vibrations simply become too strong – whether felt or heard. I straighten my back and lean backward, and as I play one final grand arpeggio – from the highest C (also the highest of the keyboard) all the way down and up again to A♭, together the beginning and end of one grand arc, one major third apart – I feel at one with the instrument in front of me, conscious of the powerful impact this 'deafening' climax must have left on my audience. (From every performance I also remember the shock when a few seconds later the audience's clapping sounds start reaching me from behind, invading the cocoon of space I had created around myself.)

Mostly, by allowing earplugs to create a division between inner- and outer-body sensation, I became aware of two distinct dimensions in Beethoven's Op. 110: a *lateral* dimension – captured by all those up-and-down moving gestures along the keyboard, both left and right of my body – and a *deep* dimension – things that ought to happen in front of me, from where the action in the piano takes place, behind the music stand. But I must exaggerate their shape so as to bring these 'things' nearer to me. The *messa di voce* on the trill in bar 4 is a good example: I want to feel part of the oscillating vibration; the *sforzando* on the highest note at the end of a surging *crescendo* in bar 11 is another: so typically for Beethoven, it comes at the far end of a long phrase, as if making it to this point has required a true effort to break through that inner-body aural veil and to connect with

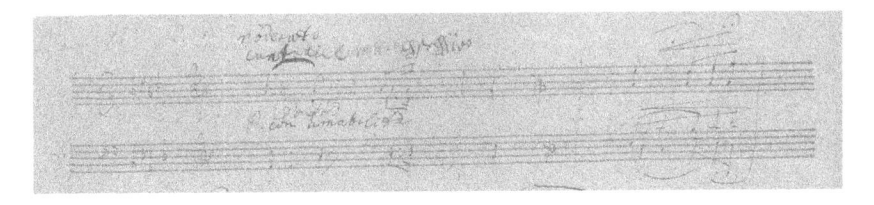

Figure 10.5 Beethoven, Piano Sonata in A flat Major, Op. 110, 1st movement, bars 1–3, autograph
Reproduced by permission of Figaro-Verlag, Laaber

strings whose vibrations hit the soundboard at least one full metre in front of me. But nowhere do acoustics and optics combine more evocatively than in the third movement, where the hearing machine provides the appropriately gothic setting for a dramatic recitativo-like voice (swelling in and out between one and three strings in bar 5) emerging from within a deep and ever narrower cave.

The most intriguing clue to Beethoven's visual awareness of his intimate surroundings may be a little scribble of his own. Figure 10.5 reproduces the opening bars of Beethoven's manuscript: note the thickly drawn two-note slur at the outset, as the very first articulated little idea of the piece. Are we looking at a miniature version of the hearing machine's outer rim, somehow centrally occupying Beethoven's probing mind?

Robin Wallace has made me aware of the significance of a peculiar series of single G major chords in that same third movement, ten of them, ever louder (see Example 10.1). They reflect, perhaps, the kind of hearing exercise Beethoven may have submitted himself to as he sat down at his piano. The third of the triad initially on top, just like in the opening of the sonata, the chords grow louder, an effect that in his earlier years Beethoven would have underlined by *poco a poco due e alora tre corde* (gradually two and then three strings), but here to be played with one string only (*una corda*) throughout. With every new blow of the chord we concentrate more on the sound of single vibrating strings, without interference from any other possibly out-of-tune unisons. That the chords are to be struck on syncopating offbeats is significant too: not only is the pianist discouraged from arpeggiating them (which would have been a normal reflex for downbeats on a Viennese piano), but it's listening rather than playing that is provoked as the sole activity on every new downbeat: after every new blow we lean our head more closely toward the strings.

As the exercise intensifies, the attention shifts to also hearing the specific quality of a consonant chord: in a well-tempered tuning (like the Vallotti/

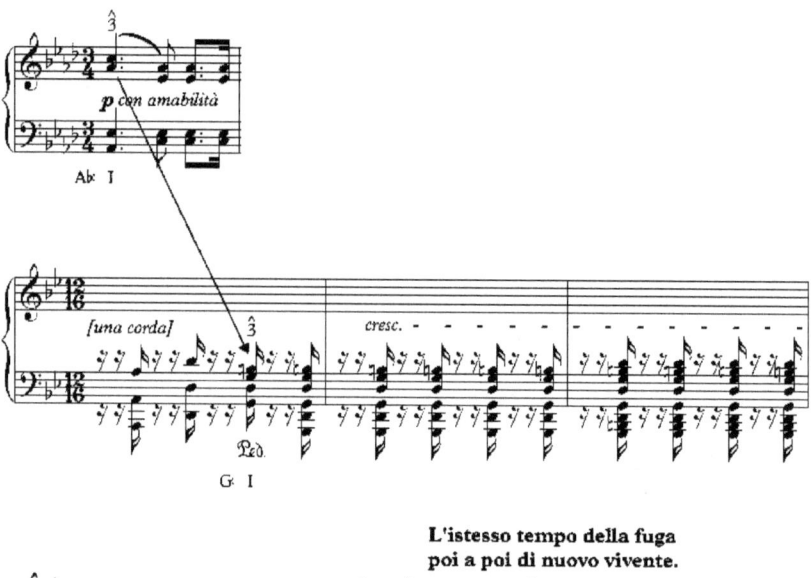

Example 10.1 Piano Sonata in A flat Major, Op. 110: (a) first movement, bar 1; (b) third movement, bars 132–140

Young that I use), a G major chord is noticeably calmer than the A♭ tonality of the overall sonata. We know that Beethoven, again in his earlier years, was a big defender of key characteristics and loved a good debate on the subject with his good friend Friedrich August Kanne.[27] He may have delighted in hearing different affects again, encapsulated here in a simple chromatic drop from A♭ to G. Even with this biographical association of nostalgia for earlier, more fortunate times, the suggested scenario is that of an actual experience – the composer–pianist in front of his new hearing machine, intensely listening.

Sonata Op. 111: Video Clip 6

Of the three sonatas, Op. 111 best encapsulates our vision of a flexible backward-projecting lid. The dark and hollow hearing machine is still a

[27] Schindler, *Beethoven as I Knew Him*, pp. 368–9.

fitting décor for the first movement's *Sturm und Drang* in C minor, but once C major takes over (at the end of the first movement and then throughout the second), we break out from any claustrophobia we might have felt inside the hearing machine. (Heinrich Schenker, at this point in his analysis, speaks of 'a world in which light no longer meets any resistance'.)[28] We still sit in front of the piano, but we straighten our back and allow sound or vibration to engulf us, oblivious of exactly how these have reflected against the lid or wall. From a multi-sensory perspective, Op. 111 in many ways acts as a synthesis of the two previous sonatas. Beethoven no longer compensates: all senses – visual, tactile and aural – come together in a single holistic experience that takes up its own space.

From Op. 109, as William Kinderman has observed, Op. 111 borrows the principle of rhythmic diminution: systematically shifting from larger to smaller note values within the same speed.[29] But while in Op. 109 this technique is restricted to the third movement's last variation (transforming only the theme of the *Gesang*), it is omnipresent in the second movement of Op. 111 (turning transformation into a reigning principle, systematically increasing the number of notes per beat from one variation to the next). Diminution means ever faster vibration, and the ultimate step would have to be the trill, as the fastest oscillation possible between two notes. In Op. 111, the trill makes its appearance at first disruptively and without preparation or context (in bar 105), but at its second entry (in bar 160) oscillation becomes the essence of the musical message. Diminution has stopped being a process; time yields to timelessness.

With the third movement of Op. 110, the *Arietta* theme shares a remarkable series of G major chords. There are seven of them, firmly placed between the two hands, their succession interrupted only by a root-position tonic and subdominant chord, which, if anything, end up emphasizing G major even more. As in Op. 110 these identical chords are grouped under one large crescendo. In Op. 110 the tonality of G major had been attractive, but foreign and isolated. Upgraded to the status of dominant harmony and in a regular *tre corde* context, G major now instils an irresistible, and, as time goes on, tranformative aura throughout a long C major movement.

When I perform the *Arietta* movement with the flexible backward-projecting lid, there is always one point where I imagine Beethoven putting away his ear trumpets once and for all (if indeed he had been using them in

---

[28] Heinrich Schenker, *Beethoven: Die letzten Sonaten – Sonate C moll Op. 111*, ed. Oswald Jonas (Vienna, 1971), p. 46.

[29] William Kinderman, *Beethoven* (Oxford, 2009), pp. 245, 253.

conjunction with the hearing machine) and becoming one with the sounds-cape in front of him. This point occurs when the *Arietta* returns in its original form as the movement's fifth and final variation (bar 130). The whole preceding passage (which sank one step lower, from C major to B♭ major) was a fantasy-like cadenza, in which I threw snippets of sound – trills and syncopated fragments of the theme – against the reflective lids above my strings. For one last time, each of my hands explored the extremes of the keyboard (bars 114–119), their distance from one another causing a stereo-phonic divide in my brain that felt unbearably self-conscious: imagining the painful pressure of the ear trumpets' metal edges in my ears, like Beethoven I just wanted to put them aside for good. No longer restrained by a stiff body negotiating machine-like extensions, both hands find one another just below the centre of the keyboard on a striking pre-cadential harmony (bar 129). The ensuing cadence metamorphoses into the opening theme, which makes its glorious re-entry. A single wave of sound has now been set in motion, unstoppable and growing in momentum.

Undergoing these events, we are also in complete control. As we adjust the movement of our fingers to that of our keys, hoppers and hammers, we settle into that ideal rhythmic pulse, all note values together, large and small, saturating every subdivision of the bar in perfect triple metre. As we keep increasing our sound (it is still not clear who or what is in charge: the pianist or the piano), our strings radiate overtones that together sculpt a perfect tonal balance of outer calmness and internal energy, the triple divisions within the beat taking over the role of 'beats', now in a harmonic-acoustical sense, in a C major well-tempered tuning. Fingers, hands, arms – the entire body finds perfect synchronicity with the English piano; all together create a state of transcendent bliss or perfect balance between sound, touch, body and instrument.

Op. 111, then, shows a before and after. The first movement initially re-connects with the rambunctiousness of Beethoven's fugue from Op. 106 (when he first received the piano); now the *Arietta* goes far beyond what Op. 109 and Op. 110 have achieved in terms of poetic sensitivity. At the very end of the sonata (bars 175 onwards), we revisit a little remnant of the *Arietta* theme: a three-note call on a tonic harmony that blends with its echoes across dominant harmonies – freely vibrating, almost evaporating in the upper echelons of the piano. Casually tagged on at the end of a long movement, these echoing calls act as its large-scale structural resolution. They're a farewell of some sort, but to what of whom? To time and space? Having effectively achieved closure, we are jolted back into having to accept them. A farewell to sound? But as the sound ebbs away, one would swear there is still some left, the English instrument's after-ring prolonging the after.

A farewell to the piano? But Beethoven was still to write the most magnificent of his Op. 120 Diabelli Variations (the last of which mirrors this *Arietta* in many ways) and all of his Op. 126 Bagatelles. A farewell to life? But Beethoven wrote Op. 111 exactly in a period of physical and mental recovery.

Conclusion

And so we have come full circle. The simplified assumptions about late Beethoven with which we took issue at the outset of this essay have morphed into complex paradoxes steeped in Beethoven's life and work. We can embrace them, or like the bust in Hoechle's drawing, we can turn the other way.

When Beethoven died, his childhood friend and lawyer Stephan von Breuning insisted on supervising the sale of Beethoven's estate. As related by his son Gerhard, he bought several items himself, such as 'the little black box and the yellow one, which we had so often handed to Beethoven in his bed', 'the writing desk that stood in the ante-chamber' and 'a stand from the bedroom'.[30] But when it came to the piano, the sixty-nine-year-old Gerhard sounds almost apologetic: 'The Broadwood piano, which was put up for sale, was not purchased by my father because it went up only to C and did not meet the demands of the modern, that is Beethoven, era.' Not only is it telling that Gerhard felt compelled to mention the piano at all, but his rationalization for his father's not purchasing it – which he presumably heard directly from his father – sounds unconvincing exactly in that so-called Beethoven era, when anything that had once belonged to Beethoven (especially his piano!) would have been fetishized. But Gerhard conflates *modern* with *Beethoven*. Like Beethoven, Gerhard's father had belonged to an older generation, one that had grown up in a different century, with a different outlook on life and art: why purchase a ten-year-old piano that his late friend had so often complained about?

We live in different times yet again. Limited range and all, a new replica of Beethoven's Broadwood gives us the tools to reconnect with Beethoven's concrete ambitions and tangible frustrations. And a reconstruction of his hearing machine creates a new context in which to enjoy his last three sonatas as masterful examples of embodied artistic expression. It is this reality, and not some ideology shaped in the 'modern Beethoven era', that is truly Beethovenian. The statuette of Apollo, I like to think, would have nodded its head in approval.

---

[30] Breuning, *Memories*, p. 113.

Appendix 10.1 | Building the Stein/Broadwood Hearing Machine: A First-Hand Report from Beethoven's Conversation Books

COMPILED AND TRANSLATED BY TOM BEGHIN

From February 1818 onward, Beethoven's visitors and household members started communicating with him mostly through conversation books, notebooks that Beethoven kept especially for this purpose. The conversation partner typically wrote something down and Beethoven would respond orally. We find first-hand conversations about the Stein/Broadwood hearing machine from 19 March 1820 (when André Stein proposed what it would be) to 7 September 1820 (when the completed machine was delivered). It is possible that Stein referred to the same machine years later, in 1824. The dates are based on timelines established by the editors of Beethoven's conversation books. On a few occasions I've taken the liberty of removing qualifiers like 'probably' or 'almost certainly'.

19 March 1820   During pre- and post-lunch conversations, Matthäus Andreas ('André') Stein (piano maker and brother of Nannette Streicher) offers ideas as to how to make the Broadwood piano more audible to Beethoven.

We want to make it closed in the front and insert two horns, directed towards your ears | ~~it won't be of much good in sheet metal~~ | ~~it's possible, just~~ because it costs too much and you can't make it stand well, we'd like to try first in wood | this sheet of paper proves that we don't need brass | but I believe that brass has more of an effect on the ears | that was the case already with Mälzel's machine [i.e., ear trumpet] | tomorrow I'll do a try-out at my house | . . . [after lunch:] we have a new idea; I hope it will be good | an arch. it extends all the way to the back of the piano | no tone can escape from the top nor from the sides, this arch will be of very thin soundboard wood | and it has the big advantage that the piano is completely open and yet the tone cannot escape | if I make this for you, then you'd have to send me your piano, I would | only if | I'll make a test in cardboard | Because if I'd make it from wood, I'd need your piano | because the form of my instruments doesn't fit | if it works in wood, it also works in cardboard

6 or 7 April 1820   Stein reports on his attempt, which hasn't been successful.

It won't work the way we had discussed. | The tone remains too much in the back | just allow me some time, I will make a few more tests.

19 April 1820   Franz Oliva (bank clerk and personal assistant to Beethoven) is ready for action: no more talking.

I'm of the opinion that one shouldn't talk any longer but just start, to move things forward | There's no difference in price for wood; – but Mr. Stein believes that sheet metal is better than wood, if only because of the bendability of sheet metal, since the machine has to be round and this curve is hard to produce with wood | Stein knows an artisan who's skilled and inexpensive[;] he's the one he wants to talk to | Sunday at 11:00 he wants to visit you with this artisan and discuss the particulars | if you wish, I can come too; – Stein cannot stay for lunch

22 and 23 April 1820   Sigmund Wolfsohn (physician and expert on surgical machines) recommends Graf over Stein.

I believe that Graf would be willing and would be more accommodating to you | he [Stein?] thinks he knows it all | consequently it becomes an act of grace to serve someone

Oliva disagrees, and thinks that Stein is the man for the job.

On the subject of the machine, you will hear tomorrow how expensive the metal machine will be; – if it's cheap and adequately manufactured, it would obviously be better than to spend double of the money for wood + metal | Is the machinist also coming tomorrow at 11:00? | Stein thinks that metal is better. | I think that you'd better off doing this project with Stein than with Graf | he knows you better and seems more technically skilled

Stein comes by. At some point, he takes off the lid of the Broadwood for inspection.

It'll be very good. The tinsmith is a very skilled man who himself has great desire to make something adequate and therefore he's also very cheap | if in metal it is so much stronger | there's another difficulty because the lid comes out too far in front | there's not enough room: the tone cannot escape sufficiently | if we make it so high then it's no longer strong. | there's no other way than to try it in metal. | ~~In wood we already have two~~ | ~~In wood we already have two, now we must~~ | ~~Do you have any pliers~~ | You must decide now whether it should be made of metal. | The tinsmith thinks that it will come to around 60 to 70 *f W:W:* [gulden, Viennese currency] | We now have to make a lid, but one of soft wood: that doesn't cost much.

>   Oliva weighs in, urging Beethoven to make a decision while arguing that there's positive momentum.

the gentlemen all agree that metal is better than wood; – what matters now is whether the expense wouldn't be too great; – please, decide then | Because otherwise the tone would be too locked up, | it's a newly invented kind of metal; – zinc-metal, it is called, which is the best for this machine, | the situation is that the pianoforte has to stay here [i.e., in Vienna] until the machine is ready, which would be at the latest by 10 May, or in 3 weeks; – as long as you're here it can stay in your house, but you couldn't take it to Mödling because of the many tests that are necessary | then it would go to Stein | Because the cavity is too great | but it will work now, | all three are serious about the project and one shouldn't allow this fire to go out | ... | Stein would like to come back tomorrow and the day after with a journeyman to take measurements for the frame on which the machine will be placed; – can he also enter the house in your absence, | ... | he is all fired up to execute this work, – he will certainly do anything possible; – | very deficient, | The best thing about him is that one can trust him – that he keeps his promise + that nobody else could take on this task

25 April 1820   Oliva reports on the progress and expresses high hopes that the machine will work even without cumbersome ear trumpets.

[Stein] told me a few things about his life and that of his father; – about your machine he said that as soon as the frame is ready, the tinsmith must make a prototype in wire from which one can finally see what may still be missing in the test. | I cannot doubt its best success after the experiences you've already been through | ~~now~~ even without the closer hearing machines [i.e., Beethoven's ear trumpets] it will have a good effect

1 May 1820   Josef Karl Bernard (editor of *Wiener Zeitung*) sends regards from Stein.

Best regards from *Herr* Stein [who asks] when you will move out to Mödling.

>   Beethoven is about to head out to Mödling, where he'll spend the summer. He'll leave on 12 May 1820. He makes a note to inquire about a rental piano because the Broadwood needs to stay behind in Vienna.

Oliva should ask Stein how much an instrument costs from him.

Between 8 and 12 June 1820   Oliva has an update.

I was with Stein yesterday, as well as with the tinsmith where your machine is being made, in 6 to 7 days everything will be ready | well, he's never at home | the wife said to me yesterday that they're working hard on it

A day or two later   Oliva reports clear progress.

Next to [the café where you can buy a bottle of wine] is a tinsmith – the one who makes your hearing machine | . . . | your machine has made it to Stein today already

Between 12 and   Oliva tells Beethoven that Stein needs an ear
19 June 1820   trumpet prototype; the end is in sight.

There will be ear trumpets in cardboard: they're already being constructed; – The lid will be completely closed | he'd like you to pass by to try out the ear trumpets, by the middle of next week | it is made in the weakest sheet metal | you have an ear trumpet of Mälzel[;] Stein would like to have it, he will probably come to Mödling tomorrow | he's coming with a few people | if he doesn't come tomorrow, then he requests that you'd send the ear trumpet by carriage | by the end of next week everything is finished | Stein doesn't doubt that with the ear trumpets you will hear [even] the softest [of sounds]

Early August 1820   Joseph Czerny (pianist, not related to Carl)
    has seen and tried the machine.

Stein has made you a very efficient hearing machine.

Late August 1820   Oliva starts wrapping up business.

You should tell Stein today that the machinist wants to come tomorrow as well, otherwise nobody will be there . . . | by Thursday or Friday you will get the piano, and everything else | by Saturday, noon, at the latest | Stein wants to give the small ear trumpet some more thought | he has appreciated your opinion | he will have such a separate ear trumpet made as well | *f* 190- convention coins [*Conventionsmünze*] | it's far for you | to take it away | it costs *f* 55- | he doesn't want to accept anything other than the [total amount on the] bill | it's rare that a craftsman makes the estimate higher than the actual work costs | you may want to give the man the pleasure of saying that you're satisfied | . . . Stein has a room in the spa of Mödling + he often comes there, he says he's been to your place often + has never found you | Why don't you come on Tuesday | then you don't go | if he sees that you haven't come for a week, he'll change his ways | he apparently praised you very much.

4 September 1820   Oliva anticipates the delivery of the piano.

Surely, you will get the piano any day now.

Tuesday,   Oliva forces the matter. The Broadwood with the
5 September 1820   hearing machine arrived (almost certainly) at
                                       Beethoven's summer home in Mödling on Thursday,
                                       7 September 1820.

Friday [September 8] is a holiday | They'll surely come on Saturday then | ... if I go alone, then I'll go tomorrow, so you'll have the piano on Thursday

Thursday,   Beethoven makes a note, possibly in the presence of
7 September 1820   Stein. Oliva inquires whether the piano has arrived.

(Beethoven:) A case for the hearing machine
(Stein:) The other machines [i.e., ear trumpets] you'll receive in a few days | they're not quite ready yet
(Oliva:) Has the piano come?

20 June   Possibly referring to his hearing machine (which by
(or before) 1824   1824 would have been almost four years old), Stein
                                       asks, perhaps countering a negative comment from
                                       Beethoven:

You do hear better, when you bring your head under this machine, don't you?

Source: BK, vol. 1, pp. 360, 362; vol. 2, pp. 41, 74, 81–5, 88, 105, 113, 140–1, 151, 192, 223, 226, 228, 239, 241, 244–5; vol. 6, p. 276.

Index of Beethoven's Works

General Index